THE
ARMORED FIST

THE
ARMORED FIST

THE 712TH TANK BATTALION IN THE
SECOND WORLD WAR

AARON ELSON

FONTHILL

Fonthill Media Limited
Fonthill Media LLC
www.fonthillmedia.com
office@fonthillmedia.com

First published in 2013

British Library Cataloguing in Publication Data:
A catalogue record for this book is available from the British Library

ISBN 978-1-78155-091-5

Typeset in Sabon 10.25/14 pt
Printed and bound in England

Connect with us

 facebook.com/fonthillmedia 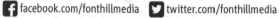 twitter.com/fonthillmedia

Contents

About the Author

In 1987, Aaron Elson attended a reunion of the tank battalion with which his father served in the Second World War. He was so moved by the stories the veterans shared among themselves, yet often did not tell to their families, that he returned two reunions later with a tape recorder. He has been recording the stories of America's Second World War veterans ever since. Elson has written five books of oral history and his work has been used as source material in more than two dozen books and several documentaries. These include *The Color of War* and *Patton 360*, both of which appeared on the History Channel. When he is not interviewing Second World War veterans, he works as a copy and layout editor at the *New Britain Herald* and *Bristol Press* and lives in New Britain, Connecticut, US.

Acknowledgments

This book would not have been possible without the encouragement of some of the best storytellers on earth, the veterans of the 712th Tank Battalion. I only wish that more of them were still around to receive some of the acclaim they so richly deserve. Thanks especially to Paul and Annie Wannemacher and Louis Gruntz Jr whose father was a veteran of B Company. My editor, Susan English, has kept my prose from wandering too far astray ever since I began collecting the stories of America's Second World War veterans. Thanks also to the folks, or should I say blokes, at Fonthill Media, Jay Slater, Alan Sutton, David Wightman and Julie for her input on the title. And to Mike Schroeder and my new city of New Britain, Connecticut, for providing me with the kind of supportive environment that made it possible for me to complete this work.

Introduction

The 90th 'Texas-Oklahoma' Infantry Division landed on Utah Beach on 6-8 June 1944. Although its symbol was a 'T' connected to an 'O' and its nickname was the 'Tough Ombres,' the division did not fare well in the bitter hedgerow fighting of its first month in combat.

The 712th Tank Battalion landed in Normandy on 28-29 June 1944. An independent battalion, its three line companies, one company of light tanks and assault gun platoon, were initially divided between the 90th and the 82nd Airborne Division. On 3 July, its first day in combat, the battalion lost nearly half of its sixty-seven tanks, either knocked out, tipped over, bogged down or with mechanical trouble. July saw the 90th Division suffer such heavy casualties in two battles, known as the Foret de Mont Castre and Seves Island, that, according to the late John Colby in *War From the Ground Up*, it was in danger of becoming a 'lost division' with its remaining troops assigned as replacements. After a brief stint with the 8th Infantry Division, the tanks of the 712th were assigned almost exclusively to the 90th, but at first the battle-hardened veterans wanted little to do with tanks as they drew fire from the enemy.

And then something happened. It might have been on Hill 122, the high point of the week-long fight for Mont Castre when on 10 July, a platoon of 712th tanks rescued a battalion of infantry that was surrounded by elite German paratroopers. It might have been because squads of infantry discovered that tanks came in handy when they were pinned down by machine gun fire. Whatever it was, the tankers and infantrymen began working together as a team. Although it would suffer the third highest rate of casualties in the European theatre of operations, the 90th Division, with its attached 712th Tank Battalion and 773rd Tank Destroyer Battalion, gained the respect of an enemy it fought from Normandy to Czechoslovakia, through Northern France, the Battle of the Bulge, the Siegfried Line and the heart of Germany. Shortly before the end of the war in Europe, the 11th Panzer Division asked if it could surrender to the 90th 'Armored' Division.

The Armored Fist: The 712th Tank Battalion in the Second World War is not so much about the 90th Division. There are many great books about the division and Colby's *War From the Ground Up* is considered by collectors to be among the finest unit histories ever written. You can find the titles of many individual memoirs, some of them posted in their entirety, at the official 90th Division website. This is a book about the 712th Tank Battalion, the unit with which my father served. It is not a comprehensive history of the battalion, nor is it a 'big picture' book. But I got to know and understand my father a lot better after he passed away by meeting the men he served with – even though most of them did not know him – than I did when he was alive. The experiences these veterans shared – the fear, courage, hunger, camaraderie, anger, reactions to man's inhumanity to man – are deeply individual and at the same time universal.

Preface
Joe Blow from Breeze

In 1938, Dale Albee, a skinny nineteen-year-old kid from Independence, Oregon, tried to join the Navy, but failed to pass the eye test. He therefore memorised the eye chart. The next day, he joined the Army. 'E-FP-TOZ, even the big E was fuzzy,' Albee, who became a sergeant in the horse cavalry and received two Purple Hearts and a battlefield commission with the 712th Tank Battalion, recalled decades later.

In 1942, Ed Forrest, a thirty-two-year-old rail-thin graduate of Clark University in Worcester, Massachusetts, applied for officers candidate school, but was rejected as he was colour blind. He returned to Stockbridge, Massachusetts, where he lived in the parish house of St Paul's Episcopal Church and had his friend Dave Braman help him memorise the test. He passed on the second attempt.

Clifford Merrill enlisted in the Army in 1936 to get away from an abusive father and the abject poverty in which his large family lived in Springfield, Maine. Army pay was not much, but he managed to send his mother enough money to buy a washing machine. Merrill graduated with the first armored officers candidate class at Fort Knox, Kentucky, where Col Tom Chamberlain, who later would be his commanding officer in the 10th Armored Division, was a member of the staff. 'I got caught shooting crap one night,' Merrill said when interviewed in 1992. 'We were making a lot of noise in the wooden barracks and the officer of the day made a big deal out of it. In the morning I had to report to the day room. There was a Colonel Calais, his left hand had three fingers cut off from a tank. He had his hand on the edge of the turret when the tank hit a tree and the hatch cover came down. He still had his thumb and his index finger and when he talked

11

to you he would point with the one finger. I had to report to three of them – Chamberlain, Calais and Colonel Morrill. Chamberlain was the first one to talk.

'"And what were you doing?" he said.

'"I was trying to make a hard ten," I said.

'"Did you make it?"

'"Yes, Sir."

'"Good."'

Merrill went on to become the first of several company commanders in A Company of the 712th Tank Battalion. His executive officer was Ellsworth Howard. Howard grew up in Louisville, Kentucky, and volunteered for the draft in 1941. After basic training at Fort Knox, he was assigned to the 5th Armored Division where he was sent to a motorcycle school. 'I hate motorcycles with a passion,' Howard said in the hospitality room during a reunion of the 712th. 'I struggled with that thing for thirteen weeks and unfortunately there was a colonel there who apparently took a liking to me because no matter what I did he thought it was a big joke and wouldn't let me go. I graduated and I thought, "I'll get out of this now." He had me reassigned to be an instructor in the motorcycle school. So one day, they put a notice on the bulletin board that they needed candidates for officers candidate school.'

Ed Stuever, a maintenance sergeant in the 712th, grew up in Breeze, Illinois. People kidded him about his Uncle Joe Blow from Breeze. But when he was eighty-eight and living in Chicago, Stuever returned to Breeze and helped a group of local history buffs find the site of the one-room schoolhouse where he received his education and where he learned the Song of Illinois. It was such a beautiful song he told the group's guide that if children performed it at their graduation – he pronounced it 'gradjy-ation' – all the elderly folks in the audience would '...jump up out of their wheelchairs in exuberance.'

Billy Wolfe was the fifth of seven children born to Hobert and Anna Wolfe in the hamlet of Edinburg, Virginia, on the north fork of the Shenandoah River. A sensitive, vibrant, fresh-faced kid of seventeen, he could hardly wait to be drafted after his older brother Hubert went into the service. Hubert Wolfe was in Europe with the 78th Infantry

Division when Billy was drafted early in 1945. Billy reported to Fort Meade, Maryland, for basic training and was sent to Fort Knox to be trained as a tanker. Army food agreed with him and he gained fifteen pounds at Fort Knox.

Bob Rossi, about 5 foot 6 inches and 110 lbs 'soaking wet,' grew up so poor in Jersey City that he and his brother John would play football using rolled-up newspapers. Reuben Goldstein of Dorchester, Massachusetts, was not much better off. He and his brother would stand on an overpass and throw rocks on the back of coal trucks as they left the rail yards and then gather up the coal that the rocks displaced. Tony D'Arpino, who would drive the tank in which Rossi was the loader, worked in a foundry in Whitman, Massachusetts, before the war, making eight dollars a week. His father worked in the same foundry. Tony did not say anything when he reported for the draft, and with two weeks to get his affairs in order, he stopped going to work. The foreman called his father aside and said, 'What's the matter? Is Tony shacking up?'

Jim Rothschadl and Jim Flowers spent two days and nights in no man's land. Flowers was wounded so seriously he would lose both of his legs and Rothschadl badly burned during the battle for Hill 122 in Normandy. They never saw each other after they were rescued. But Flowers suggested I interview Rothschadl and said he was an Indian living in Waubun, Minnesota. What kind of an Indian name is Rothschadl, I wondered? But I looked up Waubun and there it was, smack dab in the middle of the White Earth Indian reservation. It turns out that Rothschadl's father was a Czechoslovakian immigrant who dreamed of having his own farm. He was swindled into buying land at an inflated price from a company that in turn had swindled the land from the Indians with the help of an act of Congress. Between Jim's father and uncle, they owned 300 acres.

Quentin 'Pine Valley' Bynum was a tank driver in A Company. Bynum was a tall, husky young man with the rugged good looks of Li'l Abner and an almost superhuman strength. He was responsible for the battalion's first taste of combat, initiating the first of several pillow fights in the barracks at Fort Benning in 1943.

These are a few of the people you will meet in the pages of this book. Some will live. Some will die. Many will be wounded. At full strength, there were 765 men in the 712th Tank Battalion. With replacements, 1,165 men passed through its ranks. Some, like my father, 2nd Lt Maurice Elson, a replacement, were there for a cup of coffee and a couple of Purple Hearts. Others, like Dan Diel, a sharecropper's son from Kansas, and Jule Braatz, the sergeant whose platoon my father was assigned to lead, were together for as long as five years, from their days in the horse cavalry in California to their time as occupation troops in Amberg, Germany.

Heimboldshausen

As dawn broke on Easter Sunday, 1 April 1945, nineteen-year-old tank driver Dick Bengoechea of Boise, Idaho, stood guard outside his M4A3 Sherman tank in a village in Germany whose name he could not remember fifty years later. An enemy soldier emerged from the woods with his hands laced over his head. 'Kamerad! Kamerad!' The German prisoner who spoke fairly good English told Bengoechea that an '88' – a weapon universally feared by tankers – was located in a nearby clearing and that it had the intersection Bengoechea was guarding zeroed in.

As the day wore on, the thought weighed heavily on Bengoechea's mind that all the time he stood guard, a simple decision to fire that 88 at a preset target would have turned him into one of the countless bodies his tank had rolled past and, on occasion, over. Just a couple of days before, his tank stopped in the rain beside a hastily-made burial ground where the earth was washed away and the bodies of several German soldiers were partially exposed. Rigor mortis had set in and one of them, Bengoechea recalled, had his arm stretched up in the air. One of the members of his platoon, Budd Squires, fired a burst from his Thompson submachine gun into the makeshift grave. Just then, a jeep appeared and the company executive officer, Lt Edward L. Forrest, scolded Squires for wasting ammunition. 'And Forrest had just returned from a firing demonstration. Talk about wasting ammunition,' Bengoechea said with a laugh as he recounted the incident at a reunion of the 712th Tank Battalion. Later that day as Bengoechea went to shift gears, his knees began to tremble. Soon they shook uncontrollably. In retrospect, he said, that might have been a premonition.

Two days later, the battalion's A Company, of which Bengoechea was a member, was approaching the village of Heimboldshausen, Germany, on the west bank of the Werra River. There was a firefight on the outskirts of town. Soon, the German fighters, including die-hard SS troops, faded from the town. The tanks and infantry followed in pursuit and the service personnel moved in for the night. Ed Forrest, the executive officer, selected a three-story house with a concrete foundation near a small railroad depot and set up his headquarters in the basement. Two tanks that needed repairs – one of them Bengoechea's – were parked outside. A petrol truck was parked nearby. Its driver was Pfc Joseph Fetsch of Baltimore. Fetsch was scheduled to drive a truckload of ammunition to the front, but at the last minute switched assignments with Harry Moody of Asheville, North Carolina. The parked truck held 300 jerry cans, each filled with five gallons of fuel. Fetsch was proud of the way he stacked the cans on the truck, which was only meant to carry 250 cans. On the front of the truck there was a ring-mounted .50-calibre machine gun.

By 6 p.m., the support personnel of A Company – thirty-two maintenance, kitchen and supply people, including the crews of the disabled tanks – were beginning to settle in for the evening. Ervin Ulrich, a German-born cook who grew up in Wyoming, was preparing a rare hot meal for the tankers, some of whom only a few days before had their first bath in six weeks. A hot meal. A bath. The end of the war in the European Theatre of Operations was definitely in sight. Three thousand miles away in Stockbridge, Massachusetts, the Rev. Edmund Randolph Laine, an Episcopalian minister who raised Ed Forrest from the time he was fourteen, was already preparing his sermon for VE Day.

Several railroad cars were parked on a siding at the depot in Heimboldshausen, but no one had inspected them. One boxcar, it would later be learned, contained linens and clothing that the people of the village hoped to liberate just as soon as the 'Amis' – as the American troops were called, even by enemy soldiers – departed. Another car was filled with bags of black powder intended for use in artillery. There were several empty ore cars for hauling potash from a nearby mine. And there were two gasoline tanker cars which, although empty, were filled with fumes. On the other side of the railroad tracks was a large open field. Off in the distance was an oval-shaped copse of woods on a hill created by slag from the mine. Bengoechea stood on the running board of the fuel truck with a can of oil in his right hand, trying to free up the .50-calibre machine gun that had failed to swivel the day before as it was rusted in place. Suddenly, his buddy Fred Hostler, who was standing nearby, pointed his .45 calibre pistol in the air and began firing. Then someone shouted, 'Plane!'

2

Boots and Saddles

The highlight of the 1988 reunion of the 712th Tank Battalion was the dedication of the battalion's monument in the Memorial Garden behind the Patton Museum at Fort Knox. Engraved on two panels were the names of ninety-eight men killed in action – two more have since been added, due to record keeping oversights – while a third panel lists the battalion's decorations: eight Croixs de Guerre, two Distinguished Service Crosses (actually, three battalion members received the DSC, the nation's second-highest military honour), one Legion of Honor, fifty-six Silver Stars, 362 Bronze Stars, 498 Purple Hearts, fourteen battlefield commissions and three Presidential Unit Citations.

In his speech at the dedication, the battalion's third and final commander, Colonel Vlad Kaye – who changed his name after the war from Vladimir Kedrovsky – remarked that the 712th was 'the best tank battalion in the Army.'

Capt Jim Cary, a retired journalist, recalled thinking, 'Aww, come on, Vlad. But you know,' he said in the hospitality room during one of the battalion's annual Florida mini-reunions, 'after a while, over the years, I've almost begun to believe it. If it wasn't the best, it was sure one of the best. There were a lot of professional soldiers in the 712th,' he added, 'who had come right out of the horse cavalry.'

In February 1941, a troop train with 500 recruits from the Chicago area pulled into a whistle stop called Seeley, California. It was the middle of winter when they left the Midwest and they were wearing wool uniforms when they arrived in one of the hottest spots in the country. The recruits – who volunteered for the draft, expecting to put in their one year and return to civilian life, but were kept in 'for the duration' following the Japanese attack on Pearl Harbor – were not exactly drawn from the ranks of the equestrian elite. Many of them grew up in the city, like Andy Schiffler or Hilding Freeberg, who said the only place he ever saw a horse before arriving at Camp Seeley was in front of a milk wagon when he stumbled home from a bar at 4 a.m. Some of the recruits were afraid of the horses. 'They even used to cry,' Freeberg said. But not all of them were city slickers. Bob 'Big Andy' Anderson of Prophetstown, Illinois; Pine Valley Bynum; Dess Tibbitts of Orland, California; and Percy Bowers were farm boys.

'I never took basic training because I got in there and they put a sign on the bulletin board. Who wants to join the stable gang?' Anderson said when interviewed in 1992. 'I was a farmer before I went in. I really wanted to be in the coast artillery. When they asked me at Fort Sheridan what branch of service you'd like, I told them the coast artillery and I ended up in the horse cavalry. I was in the stable gang for a couple of weeks and they wanted to know who wanted to be a horseshoer. And a boy from Chetak, Wisconsin, by the name of Percy Bowers and myself signed up for horseshoeing. Instead of going to school we just picked it up right there. Then there was a flip of a coin to see who was to be the first horseshoer and who would be the second horseshoer. It didn't make any difference because we both made shoes, but he was the first horseshoer and I was the second. We got a rating in those days of what we called first-third. That was one stripe down and four turned up. And we were getting paid more than what a buck sergeant was. We went in at eighteen dollars a month, but after we got our rating we were getting thirty-eight dollars a month, where a sergeant was only getting thirty-six a month. Then when I came home for my granddad's funeral in October of '41, "Man, look at what a rating he has!" Hell, I'm nothing but a Pfc.'

Jim Cary, who grew up in Douglas, Arizona, was assigned to the 11th Cavalry as a young reserve officer. Many of the officers were from West Point and most of the sergeants were regular Army. The training was rigorous and disciplined. There was a Sergeant Roberts, some of the men who arrived from Chicago recalled, who could stand on the stoop of the barracks and reach down and touch the ground without bending his knees. The West Pointers '...had this tradition,' Cary recalled, 'that if you fell off your horse and didn't get dirt on the pommel of your saddle' – in other words, if the horse did not go all the way over – 'then you had to buy drinks for every officer in the damn 11th Horse Cavalry.' (Cary noted that he fell off his horse a number of times, but said he had sense enough to rub some dirt on the pommel.)

The enlisted men had similar, if less expensive, rituals. 'They'd say, "Today we're gonna ride one and lead two,"' said Bob Hagerty, who grew up in Cincinnati. Hagerty took his basic training at Fort Riley, Kansas, and was sent to the 11th Cavalry in 1942. 'Here you are sitting on that horse trying to keep your position, trying to handle the reins correctly with one hand, then with your free hand you have two ropes connected to two more horses. The first horse wants to go in one direction, the two others horses want to go in another direction. And the old-time cavalrymen would look down on a guy who let any horse go loose.'

In his scrapbook, Andy Schiffler had an article that appeared in the *Chicago Tribune* on 30 May 1941. Under a headline proclaiming 'Chicagoans Train in Desert,' the correspondent wrote:

> El Centro, Calif. – Here, under the broiling sun of America's hottest spot, the men of the 11th Cavalry, many of them Chicagoans, are preparing for extensive maneuvers along the border. For weeks on end, the sun pours down from a cloudless sky at Camp Seeley at the gateway to California's great Imperial Valley. It is the lowest Army camp in the world, 50 feet below sea level, and is only 12 miles from the Mexican border. Any sort of work is impossible during the midday heat and the Army day begins at 4:30 in the morning. Work is over by 11:30 and the afternoon is devoted to swimming, parades and the time-honored Spanish custom of a siesta.

'That's a lot of bunk!' Schiffler interjected as I read the article into my tape recorder. 'We had plenty of work!'

> On a recent day it was 110 in the shade of the post exchange and 140 degrees on the rifle range by the river where the sun quickly made rifle

barrels too hot to touch,' the article continued. 'Camp officers, however, say that the men are gaining stamina, 'an ability to take it,' and that now with their 13 weeks' basic training completed, they'll be able to go through maneuvers without discomfort.

There was little question in the 11th Cavalry about which was more important, the horse or the trooper. 'When you came in from the field you had to wash the horse's eyes, nostrils and dock,' said Dale Albee. 'Now when you wipe out a dock, that means you take a sponge and you run your arm just about that far up under there and you wash out his little doodoo.'

'You had to do that?' I asked.

'Sure. See, down in the desert and riding in the cavalry, you collect so much dust and dirt. Back in their sheath, this dust would get damp and it'd form little balls. Now if that wasn't cleaned out, the horse would get an infection because it would rub it raw. So this was one of the things you had to do periodically. You got your little bucket and soap, went up in there and cleaned it out. And every day, when you groomed your horse, the drill was wipe out eyes, nostrils and dock. You wiped their eyes out, you wiped out their nostrils and you went around and wiped their little butt.'

The troopers learned to jump with their horses, took part in cavalry charges and played games which were training exercises. 'So many of us, with what little we earned, the only time you smoked hard-rolled cigarettes was in town,' Albee said. 'The rest of the time we smoked Bull Durham. And one of the things we did when the recruits got real good at their training was to ride at a gallop and roll a cigarette out of Bull Durham. Some of them came in looking like matchsticks and some of them maybe only had three or four grains of tobacco, but we'd let them count as long as they had some tobacco in there. Some of them just never did make it. Another thing, after we knew they had their balance, was to have them twist around in the saddle, Indian style, to drop over and you twist one leg and come underneath and then ride and lean over the pommel. And you'd play Indian with one another, go riding by and bang-bang, you're dead, like that.'

Art Horn, one of the recruits from the Chicago area, sent his girlfriend, Margaret, a photo of a horse nuzzling up to him. On the back he wrote, 'Out here, this is the only loving I get.' Horn was on a different horse one day during an exercise in which the rider went in a figure eight carrying a long pistol and firing at targets at each turn. 'We had the mounted pistol course and you had seven targets because your .45 holds seven bullets,' said Albee who was Horn's sergeant at the time. 'I think the first four were to the right, then you had the left rear, the right rear and the left front. You went in with your horse at a canter and you went around this course and came around. Halfway through, you took the clip out, you had another clip, reloaded, and went around and finished the course. Horn had this one horse. We didn't know it, but he wasn't supposed to have been out there because he was noted for shying, and we didn't want him out there with the recruits. This is the reason we had the .45 mounted with .22 calibre bullets so that the noise wouldn't bother them. We told them it was for the horses, but actually it was so the recruits would get used to that heavy .45 firing without it coming back at them. Horn started out and he leaned forward as you're supposed to do, and what you do, you jab. It's just like you point your finger and you jab at the target and fire. And he reached forward and fired, the horse shied and threw Horn out of the saddle. When he hit the ground, Horn accidentally fired his pistol. The bullet went straight up through a leather halter and into the horse's mouth from underneath.'

Art Horn: 'Each one of us would make these figure eights, run the figure eight, and this horse that I had, as long as I fired away from him he was fine. When I went around the other way to fire crossover, the gun got too close to his ear and he bucked and threw me on the ground. And when I landed on my back, my elbow hit the ground and I still had my hand on the pistol. The bullet went straight up, because they always said when you're on the firing range, when you're not firing, always hold it straight up. If I had held it off to the side I might have hit one of the men that were standing around. So I did that. The horse stopped and I got up. I noticed that there was a little blood coming down from his throat. But I also noticed on the halter there was a double leather thong that was underneath there. The bullet went through that and I then found out later that the bullet only entered into the horse's mouth. When they got to the vet they were able to take it out and it healed up and he was back in the saddle again.'

'If it had been a .45, it would have gone right on up through the top of his head and it would have killed the horse,' Albee said, 'and $160 would have galloped across Horn's payroll. It was his error because he should have controlled the horse.'

3

Colonel Whitside

According to a lovingly written obituary by his daughter, Lieutenant Colonel Samuel Whitside Miller 'commanded the 712th Tank Battalion with the 10th Armored Division, one of General George S. Patton's spearhead units into Germany,' and he 'delighted members each year at the Founder's Day dinner' of the West Point Society of San Diego 'with stories of his Army experiences.' While I am sure Colonel Whitside, as he was known in the 712th, had some memorable tales to tell at those Founder's Day dinners, he never saw a day of combat with the battalion. A 1929 graduate of West Point, the colonel had an impressive pedigree. His grandfather was Brigadier General Samuel Marmaduke Whitside, who as a major accepted the surrender of the Sioux chief Big Foot at what would later be known as the Massacre at Wounded Knee. And his father was Lieutenant Colonel Archie Miller, who as a lieutenant in 1909, earned the Medal of Honor during the Philippine Moro uprising. Whitside Miller, however, 'was an inadequate, obsessive compulsive neurotic, replete with facial tics and picking at his fingernails,' one of the battalion's two medical officers, Captain Jack Reiff, wrote in a series of notes that he made during and after the war. Reiff compared Whitside to Humphrey Bogart's Captain Queeg in *The Caine Mutiny*.

Stan Freeman, a sergeant in Headquarters Company, was more succinct. Colonel Whitside 'was absolutely crazy,' he said. 'We had a problem one night in England with night compass reading. He told me to go over to the finish point and said, "When the first man comes in and tells you that the first unit is coming in, come and wake me up." The first unit was recon and they came in and told me they were ten or fifteen minutes from the finish line. So I went over to the barracks and woke Whitside up. And he chewed my ass out for waking him up! One day I got a telephone call and someone at group wanted to talk to Colonel Miller. So I got up, took off for the officers' quarters, saluted and said, "Sir, you are wanted on the telephone." And I stood there getting my ass handed to me for interrupting his supper. Then he came to the phone and whoever was on it had hung up and I got another chewing out. The first time I ran into him was in California. We had a weekend pass to go to San Diego. One of the favorite drinking and meeting spots in San Diego was a dance hall that had seven entrances. And when you went in any entrance you ran right into a bar. We were drinking at this bar and he walked in and gave us a lecture on drinking. Then he sat down and ordered a drink.'

Colonel Whitside committed his most egregious offence in England when he ordered his executive officer, Major Baxter Davis, to double-time in view of several enlisted men as he did not respond to a command quickly enough. He also told Captain Forrest Dixon, the battalion's maintenance officer, to put blackout lights on the tanks. Dixon said Miller misinterpreted a directive that called for blackout lights on all GPW, or general purpose wheeled vehicles, such as jeeps and trucks. Tanks and halftracks were considered ordnance vehicles rather than general purpose. The colonel in charge of ordnance told Dixon the tanks did not need blackout lights. 'So we had a night exercise and here he sees the tanks,' Dixon recalled.

'"Captain Dixon! Captain Dixon! I told you to put blackout drive lights on those tanks. You haven't done it!"

'I said, "Sir, it can't be done."

'"But you do it!"

'I went back to the ordnance colonel and he said, "Captain, you can't do that."

'I said, "I got the order from my colonel."

'He said, "If you think you're in trouble with your colonel for not putting them on, try putting them on and you'll find out you're in bigger trouble."

'Two weeks later we had another night exercise. And here come the tanks. Then he saw the tanks still had no blackout drive lights and he was really on a high pitch.

'"Captain Dixon!"

'"Yes, Sir?"

'"You don't have blackout drive lights on those tanks."

'I said, "It can't be done, Sir."

'"But I gave you a direct order. I don't have anybody that will obey me. I'm charging you. When we get back to camp, you and Major Davis are gonna be court-martialed."

'When we got back, I went down to the ordnance headquarters. I got in to see the colonel and told him what happened.

'"You can't be serious," he said.

'The colonel sent his warrant officer with me up to General Middleton's headquarters. We didn't see General Middleton, but we did talk with his G-1. He said, "You know, I wouldn't pay any attention to what you're telling me if yesterday we didn't get a petition signed by a bunch of men of the 712th Tank Battalion telling us that they had a crazy colonel."'

On 6 June while the invasion of Normandy was underway, the men of the 712th who were still in England were introduced to their new commanding officer, Lieutenant Colonel George B. Randolph. Colonel Randolph, forty years old, was a reserve officer from Birmingham, Alabama, where he taught high school mathematics. He would become as loved by his men as Colonel Whitside was despised.

Stan Freeman recalled the first time he saw Colonel Randolph. It was dinnertime and as always there was a lengthy chow line. A group of officers arrived and went to the head of the line. Colonel Randolph followed them. Walter 'Red' Rose, a jeep driver, described what happened next. 'Colonel Randolph was sitting on a truck fender and two or three GIs were waiting for the mess hall to open up. They said, "Hey, right over there's our new commander." So I leaned over and saw this old man. He didn't look to me like an officer. He was sitting there for a few minutes. We'd waited there for an hour before the meal. Just about the time they got the meal ready, here come the officers. They didn't have to stand in line. They just went in and grabbed what they wanted. Randolph let two or three of them get their food. He then jumped up off that truck bed. He said, "Whoa! There will not be one officer to eat until he sees that every one of his men is fed and that's the way it's gonna be from now on." I knew Dixon and the other officers had gotten Colonel Whitside thrown out and I said, "Oh boy, your ass is gone too!" But he came on and made a good enough colonel, didn't he? The officers all went over and sat with him and the enlisted personnel ate first, then the officers ate.'

'And I'll tell you, that man earned one thousand points that day,' said Freeman.

The battalion's executive officer, Major Baxter Davis, was also replaced so as to avoid any speculation that he might have orchestrated the campaign against Colonel Whitside in an effort to get his job. Davis' replacement, Major Ira Hawk, was killed on 3 July 1944, the battalion's first day in combat. Because he was with the battalion for such a short time, none of the many veterans I have interviewed could recall exactly how Major Hawk was killed or tell me anything about him.

4

Nine Ways to Sunday

The 712th Tank Battalion landed on Utah Beach on 28-29 June 1944, three weeks after D-Day. The men spent the next three days absorbing the sights and sounds of war: the signs that read 'Achtung! Meinen'; GIs in foxholes; wrecked gliders; marching prisoners; myriad explosions and whistles and muffled thuds like distant thunder. 'This is it, dear Mother,' Morse Johnson, a sergeant from Cincinnati, wrote in a letter. 'We are all ready. We've got the equipment, the ability and the spirit.' All three would be put to the test on 3 July when the battalion's tanks were split between supporting the 82nd Airborne Division and the 90th 'Texas-Oklahoma' Infantry Division in a sweeping offensive in the Haye du Puits sector of Normandy. Preceding the assault, a thunderous artillery barrage began at 5.30 a.m. and lasted fifteen minutes. Veterans of the 712th Tank Battalion recalled that it was like the Fourth of July a day early.

Before they went overseas, Phil Schromm turned to his buddy from the horse cavalry, Dess Tibbitts, and said he was going to be the first man in the battalion to be killed. 'Quit talking like that,' Tibbitts said. 'Back in the cavalry, I played a dirty trick on Phil,' Tibbitts recalled when interviewed at his home in Orland, California. 'We both took our training in Fort Riley and on our way out to Camp Lockett we said, "Now, we're not gonna get in the stable gang." There was an old sergeant. He said, "If you get in the stable gang, you've got it made. You eat ahead of everybody, you get everything you want and you don't have to stand duties." So when we were walking down there that morning I said, "Phil, remember now, we're not gonna get into the stable gang." First thing, one of the officers said, "Does anybody want to join the stable gang?" And my hand shot up!'

Tibbitts was a genuine cowboy before the war. He competed in rodeos afterwards and even at the age of seventy-six sported a lump on his arm the size of an orange from a mishap while roping a calf. He loved the horse cavalry and became a tank driver when the outfit was mechanised. Schromm, from San Mateo, California, would have made a good tank driver. He was 5 foot 6 inches, stocky and played on the 10th Armored Division football team at Fort Benning. However, he did not want to go into combat inside a tank. When the 712th was broken out of the 10th Armored Division as an independent battalion, Schromm received a transfer to its Headquarters Company.

Shortly after noon on 3 July 1944, Schromm was leading a patrol when mortars began dropping in. If he was not the first member of the battalion killed, he was among the first. 'He had a direct hit with a mortar,' said Fred Steers, a corporal in the reconnaissance platoon who was not with Schromm when he was killed but heard about it later that day. Steers was talking with a paratrooper from the 82nd Airborne Division who had jumped into Normandy on D-Day. 'I said to him, "You lucky sonofagun. You've been here three weeks."' After his first day in combat, Steers did not expect to live to see the sun go down.

Jule Braatz, a sergeant in A Company, was standing in the turret of the fourth M4A3 Sherman in his platoon as it clambered down a narrow Normandy road. There were hedgerows on either side and it was raining lightly. Braatz was from Wausau, Wisconsin. He liked to ski and hoped to be assigned to the 10th Mountain Division. Instead, he was sent to the horse cavalry in Fort Riley, Kansas. Although he did not grow up around horses, Braatz was a natural horseman and had a way even with the remounts that made them respond to his commands. Remounts were wild horses which had been ridden at least once so they could be considered broken, but they often needed a lot more breaking. Braatz rose quickly through the ranks, skipping private first class to become a corporal and then a sergeant, much to the chagrin of the regular Army cavalrymen at Camp Lockett, some of whom were in the service fifteen years and had not made private first class.

That morning in Normandy, Braatz was about to acquire a reputation few sergeants cherish: a reputation for losing lieutenants. Suddenly, the radio crackled to life. Cpl John Pellettiere, the gunner in the lead tank, was shouting that Lieutenant Tarr was hit. (My father, who joined the battalion in late July, always said he replaced the first lieutenant to be killed. That lieutenant, I learned at the 1987 reunion, was George Tarr.) Capt. Clifford Merrill, the original A Company commander, and Lt Ellsworth Howard, his executive officer, recalled the train ride from Fort Jackson, South Carolina, to the port of embarkation at Camp Myles Standish, outside of Boston. Tarr's wife, Dorothy, had recently given birth to a son and Tarr was fidgety on the train, so Merrill and Howard conspired to keep him distracted. Howard told Tarr to take a head count. 'Go count noses,' is the way Merrill recalled the request. Tarr replied that he had done so only a short while ago. 'Yes,' Howard said, 'but the battalion was going into combat and you never know when one of these soldiers might get a notion to jump off the train.'

Tarr was looking for the company from the 82nd Airborne Division his tanks were to support. He ordered his driver to stop and climbed down from the tank to consult with an officer of the engineers. As he hoisted himself back onto the tank, he apparently thought of something else and dismounted to confer with the officer. As he was climbing back up, a mortar or artillery shell struck the side of the tank, followed by a second shell that landed nearby. As the platoon sergeant, Braatz left his own crew and took Tarr's place in the lead tank. But now, instead of five tanks, he had only two: the No. 3 tank was bogged down in the mud and the fourth and fifth tanks could not navigate around it. For Braatz's first fire mission, a captain of the 82nd Airborne pointed to a farmhouse from which his men were taking fire and asked him to shell it. The captain assured him the road was cleared of mines. The tanks began moving towards the house and Braatz shouted to Pellettiere, 'Fire when you're ready.' A moment later, the tank shuddered and Braatz heard a noise that sounded like the back blast from the 75-mm cannon. He could not understand why his gunner and loader were trying to push him up through the turret. The tank had run over a mine. When the crew reached the safety of a ditch, Braatz saw that his assistant driver was missing.

'Where's Levengood?' he asked.

'He came out the escape hatch,' the tank's driver, Percy Bowers, replied.

However, Russell Levengood of Pottstown, Pennsylvania, did not go through the escape hatch on the floor of the tank. The explosion ripped the hatch cover from the ridge that secured it and blasted it upwards with such force that Levengood was skinned alive. Braatz found his remains when he returned to inspect the tank. The commander of the second tank, 'took his tank and turned around and ran down that goddamn road as fast as he could go,' Braatz said when interviewed at his home in Beaver Dam, Wisconsin. 'I suppose he was scared. And here I am, these guys are chewing my ass out they want tanks,' he said of the company from the 82nd Airborne Division that had been promised the support of a platoon of five tanks and now Braatz had none. The No. 3 tank was bogged down, Nos. 4 and 5 could not get around it, the platoon leader (George Tarr) was dead, the lead tank struck a mine and the No. 2 tank retreated.

As Braatz saw it, and this is one of the reasons he would receive the battalion's first battlefield commission, there was only one thing left to do. He went on foot in pursuit of the second tank commanded by Ray Anderson and when he found it parked by the side of a road, Braatz took command and returned with it to the front. Soon, Sgt Joe Gaffron, commander of the No. 3 tank, arrived after it had freed itself from mud. 'So, now I've got two tanks,' Braatz said. 'We're going through an open field and I can see pockmarks and I don't know what the hell they are. Finally, we realize we've run into some outfit that are shooting armor-piercing shells at us and we're out in this open field. So we get back out of there. That was the end of the first day. After the first day, I didn't think we'd last much longer.'

After several years of attending battalion reunions and hearing the story many times, I figured I knew all there was to know about how George Tarr was killed. This meant a lot to me because of the personal connection: he was the officer my father replaced. Unlike other incidents where individual accounts by eyewitnesses, participants and secondary sources differed wildly, all the stories I heard about Tarr's death were virtually the same: he got off the tank to ask directions, was getting back on, climbed off again and was getting back on when he was killed. One day I would learn there may have been a detail that altered the story dramatically.

In 1995, I interviewed Joe Bernardino in Rochester, New York. Bernardino was in A Company, but never attended a reunion. He felt slighted as his company commander, Captain Merrill, fired him as his jeep driver and sentenced him as an assistant driver in a tank. Bernardino was wounded at the Falaise Gap in August and after recovering was assigned to a different tank battalion. The way Bernardino recalled it, Merrill asked him to drive him to the front and ordered Bernardino to wait for him. Bernardino said he waited more than an hour when two paratroopers approached and told him he had to leave the area. He replied that he had to wait for his captain. The paratroopers said a counterattack was coming through and ordered him to leave. Merrill arrived at company headquarters by foot and the next morning Bernardino was a 'bog' or bow gunner/assistant driver.

At some point that first day, Bernardino said Merrill asked him to take him to see the body of a battalion officer who had been decapitated. Bernardino recalled the officer as being a Lieutenant Bell. When they arrived at the site where the dead officer lay, Merrill remarked, according to Bernardino, 'I always said George would lose his head.' Clifford Merrill was one of the most courageous officers in the 712th Tank Battalion, but he had an Arnold Schwarzenegger-type sense of humour. When he was wounded ten days later, Merrill handed his Thompson submachine gun to Sgt Morse Johnson and said 'Take it into Berlin,' a statement Johnson confirmed when interviewed in 1992.

There was a Lieutenant Harry Bell of Philadelphia in the battalion, but he came in as a replacement and survived the war. When Bernardino used the name George, I asked if he might have meant George Tarr and not Lieutenant Bell. On reflection, Bernardino agreed that it was George Tarr. Joe Bernardino, Cliff Merrill, Ellsworth Howard, Jule

Braatz, Jim Flowers are all deceased now, but while they were alive I asked Merrill, Flowers and Braatz if Lieutenant Tarr was decapitated. None of them recalled that as having been the case.

Like many of the veterans of my father's tank battalion, Orval Williams was hard of hearing. 'I'm an old country boy. Come off the farm and didn't have sense enough to stuff cotton in my ears. Nobody else did. We'd go out on that machine gun range at Fort Benning, a 50-gun emplacement about every 12 feet apart and pop them things all day long,' he said when interviewed in Macalester, Okla, in 1994.

'And then in them tanks, was you ever in one?'

'No,' I said reluctantly, although several years later at the Americans in Wartime Museum in Nokesville, Virginia, I did get the chance to look into the interior of a Sherman tank and was amazed at how cramped the quarters appeared.

'The machine gun don't bother you much. But the backlash from that big gun. *Boom!* And when that big brass shell kicks out and that metal and all the banging in there, I've got 60 per cent loss in my left ear and 40 in my right.'

And to think, some of the men in the 712th went through eleven months of combat. For Williams, the war ended on the battalion's first day in action. Williams was a loader in B Company. His tank commander was Sgt Dan Diel of Topeka, Kansas, and the assistant driver was Pfc Zygmund Kaminski of Pittsburgh. His gunner was Cpl George Vernetti and his driver was T-4 John Mitchell. Diel and Williams never saw each other after 3 July 1944. Their versions of what happened that morning differ on a number of points. According to Williams, the tank came around a bend and he heard an explosion. 'Someone took a shot at us!' he exclaimed. He recalled pressing his forehead into the rubber lining of the periscope and stared down the barrel of the gun on a German tank about a hundred yards away. According to Diel, his tank was stationary and it was the German tank that came around a corner. However, Williams states that the breech block was empty and Diel called for an armor-piercing shell. According to Diel, there was a high-explosive shell in the breech and he called for Williams to remove it and load an armor-piercing shell.

Diel said if he ordered Vernetti to fire the high-explosive shell, it would not have penetrated the German tank, but it might have thrown off the aim of its gunner. That was not the textbook thing to do and this was Diel's first day in combat.

The next shot from the German tank knocked Williams off his seat and mangled his left hand. As the crew bailed out, he looked down at Mitchell with whom he had become close friends during more than a year of training. Mitchell was husky, about 6 feet and 220 lbs. The top half of his head was missing. A second blast rocked the tank and flames shot up through the turret. Vernetti, Diel and Kaminski got out of the tank without serious injury, but once on the ground Vernetti was hit in the foot and Diel in the leg by machine gun fire. Williams pulled himself out of the tank with his good arm and dropped to the ground. The German tank took three more shots and blew the turret off the tank. It did not burn, but the ammunition inside began to explode.

Cleo Coleman of Phelps, Kentucky, was the loader in a B Company tank that passed Diel's tank a few minutes later. The Germans were being pushed back, but a jeep to the right of Coleman's tank took a direct hit and burst into flames. Coleman's tank commander, Sgt Leslie Vink of Grand Haven, Michigan, ordered his gunner to fire at an ammunition dump off to the left. Coleman recalled looking through his periscope and seeing Germans scurrying around carrying boxes. An 88 fired on Coleman's tank from the right and just missed the bow. Vink shouted for his driver, T-4 Fred Bieber of Reading, Pennsylvania, to reverse the tank into woodland nearby. As the tank backed up, it sank into mud and got stuck. Vink ordered the crew to abandon the tank. Coleman was the last man out. As he emerged from the turret, his helmet fell off. Cpl Louis Gruntz of New Orleans, the gunner, left his gun in the tank.

'He sees that I have no helmet on, so he says, "You go back and get your helmet and pick my gun up." He then grabs my gun out of my hand,' Coleman recalled. 'And there I was with no gun and no helmet. No way I'm going back.' Coleman and Bieber became separated from the crew and were crawling through a ditch when a machine gun opened up on them.

'The ditch was on a hill,' Coleman said. 'On the other side, there were infantry boys digging in. So I walked up, no helmet, no gun and one of the boys says, "You're in bad shape. One of our boys is laying over there. Go and get his. He doesn't need them anymore."

'I said, "No way!" I was scared.

"I'll get it for you," he replied and got that carbine rifle. The boy that was dead had a death grip on the carbine. He pulled it out of his hands. The helmet was laying to his side. There was blood all over the helmet and on the gun. I took some leaves and wiped it off the best I could, put the helmet on my head and got down. And Bieber said, "Let's go this way." I followed him and there were halftracks and tanks and everything else of the enemy's burning as we went by.'

As they made their way to the rear, Coleman said, 'We ran into a new outfit that had just moved in. They wanted to know how it was up there.

'"Boy," I said. "It's rough. It is bad."'

When I attended my first reunion of the 712th Tank Battalion at Niagara Falls in 1987, I entered the hospitality room while one of the veterans was in the middle of telling a story. I stood transfixed while he finished telling it, not knowing how it began and later asked him to repeat it from the start. It was one of the stories that hooked me on oral history. That veteran was Wayne Hissong who drove an ammunition truck in Service Company. The story was about how he and a buddy entered the service together and both wound up in the 712th. They were in different companies and his friend was killed on their first day in action. When I entered in mid-story, he was describing all the things he did to avoid facing his friend's mother in the small town of Argos, Indiana, where she owned a dry goods store. He used the phrase 'Nine ways to Sunday' to describe his stalling tactics, until his father finally said to him, 'Son, we've got to go see her.' And so he did. That buddy was John Mitchell, Orval Williams' tank driver.

Tony D'Arpino, practical joker and assistant driver of Lt Charles Lombardi's tank in C Company's third platoon, felt his stomach tighten as the Shermans in the staging area started their engines. He thought a wisecrack was in order. The drill at Fort Benning was for the assistant driver to stand behind the tank with a fire extinguisher while the driver started the engine as flames would sometimes shoot out the rear. As he looked around the field at the four other tanks in his platoon, D'Arpino could see that this practice already was dispensed with. D'Arpino pulled the fire extinguisher from its clamp and shouted, 'Hey Lieutenant!' His voice was almost drowned out by the roar of his and the other tanks. 'Do you want me to get behind the tank?'

'Do I what?'

D'Arpino held the fire extinguisher up for Lombardi to see.

'Forget all that shit!' D'Arpino recalled.

Sgt William Schmidt of C Company's second platoon was the first tank commander in his company to be killed. According to other members of the platoon, he was riding with more of his upper body exposed than was necessary – the way many tank commanders rode when not in a combat situation – when he was shot by a sniper. The second platoon was commanded by Lt Henry DuVal of Mount Vernon, New York, and the first platoon by Lt Jim Flowers of Dallas. In the afternoon, the two platoons joined up with GIs from the 90th Infantry Division and attacked a strong point in the German lines. The C Company commander, Capt. James Cary, was trailing the tanks in a halftrack. One of DuVal's tanks shot up a machine gun nest in a ditch and the Germans pulled back, leaving several wounded among their dead. A wounded GI was on the ground nearby and was crying out for help. Some of the original 712th tankers recall with a touch of irony a lecture Captain Cary delivered on how to avoid booby traps. The wounded infantryman was on the far side of a gate in a hedgerow. Cary vaulted the gate setting off a booby trap. The blast knocked him flat and the brunt of the explosion went over his back. For a few moments he was dazed. When his senses returned, he pulled up his shirt and saw that he was skinned in a few places. He was lucky: his trench coat got the worst of the blast and was shredded. He returned to his halftrack. Later, he watched another firefight and felt good as his tanks helped the infantry progress into a village. Later, he began to have difficulty walking.

The next morning, Cary could barely walk and felt as if liquid was running down his back. He went to an aid station where he was told he had a penetration wound in his left thigh as well as several cuts across his back, one of them pretty deep. 'You'll have to go back to the rear,' he recalled an enlisted man at the aid station saying. 'They can't handle that thigh wound here.'

'I can't go back,' Cary replied. 'I have a company to run.' He limped out of the aid station.

The enlisted man caught up to Cary. He had a doctor and an officer in tow. The doctor told Cary, 'You'll have to go back. That has to be taken care of. You could lose that leg if they don't get that slug out.' He assured Cary it would only take a few days and he could then return to his outfit. Cary asked if he could call Colonel Randolph and the officer said he could. He tried for four hours but failed to get through. It would be four months before he returned to the battalion.

When Dale Albee looked at the snapshots of Sgt Harold Heckler in his photo album, he called Heckler 'Old Sad Eyes.' Heckler is smiling in the photos, one of which shows him bare-chested, mugging for the camera beside a tank with the name 'Backbreaker' stencilled on its hull. However, there is indeed a kind of sadness in his eyes. The picture was taken at Fort Benning. D Company comprised three platoons of light tanks. These were 17.5 tons instead of 33 tons and had a crew of four instead of five. They were armed with a 37-mm cannon that the company's personnel likened to a 'peashooter' when compared with the armament on German tanks. The light tanks, however, were much faster and were used primarily for reconnaissance. Heckler came from Chicago while the other three members of his crew – Stanley Jezuit, Joe Ezerskis and Arthur Roselle – were all from Detroit. Heckler returned from a briefing in Normandy with his platoon's first assignment and the crew began piling into the tank. One of the men lost his footing as he jumped into the turret and his foot hit the solenoid that fired the coaxial machine gun. A burst of three .30-calibre bullets struck Heckler in the groin. He was rushed to an aid station where he later died. I first learned of the death of Harold Heckler from Andy Schiffler who refused to name the soldier who was killed by friendly fire, possibly as his family may have believed him to have been killed in action. After interviewing Schiffler, I drove to another part of Chicago to interview Hilding Freeberg, another D Company veteran. Freeberg asked if Schiffler had told me about Harold Heckler. In later interviews, Dale Albee and Lt Lex Obrient also described Heckler's death as did Caesar Tucci in an earlier interview, although I did not realise that until Heckler's great-niece, Melissa Heckler, contacted me and asked if I could tell her anything about her uncle.

As best I can remember, and most of the transcripts of my interviews bear this out, the veterans recalled Heckler as having been killed on the battalion's first day in combat. Yet in the company's after-action reports, it is not until the entry for 15 July, twelve days after that first day of combat, that an entry reads 'Sgt. Harold J. Heckler was accidentally killed while preparing to return to the battalion assembly area.' I can only venture a guess, but it is possible he was evacuated to an aid station and it was not until then that the company learned of his death.

Art Hary, an ammunition carrier in Headquarters Company, was wounded by shrapnel as he walked in formation along a road. Hary had been a tank driver until the Tennessee Manoeuvres in 1943, during which he drove the way his father taught him: hugging the right-hand side of the road. In a car on an open highway, this should not be much of an issue; however, in thirty-three tons of steel on a narrow mountain pass, it could give a tank commander a heart attack. After the tank came perilously close to falling over a steep embankment, Sgt John Young shouted, 'Hary, stop the tank! Androkovich, drive the tank!' Thus, Michael Androkovich, of Needham, Massachusetts, became a tank driver and Hary an ammunition carrier. (When Hary recovered from the wound he received in Normandy, he was reassigned to the 357th Regiment of the 90th Infantry Division during the Battle of the Bulge. He was wounded again less than an hour after reporting to the front.)

The three assault guns in the Headquarters Company platoon were 105-mm cannons mounted on a tank chassis. The assault guns were intended to protect the battalion's headquarters, but were more often used as an extra line platoon. On 3 July, the assault guns were assigned to Company I of the 359th Infantry Regiment. In the afternoon, under cover of a smokescreen that was to be laid down by the Navy, they were to attack the village of Pont Auny. A battleship fired two smoke shells into the area, but the smoke quickly dissipated and the attack was made in broad daylight. Androkovich drove the lead assault gun between two hedgerows and into an apple orchard. Cpl Eddie Ritz was the gunner and Young the tank commander. Lt Sam Adair, the platoon leader, was along for the ride. A camouflaged Mark IV panzer in a corner of the orchard allowed the lead assault gun to pass and fired on the second. The armor-piercing shell penetrated the front of the second assault gun and went out the back. A second shot sent flames shooting out the top.

In the lead assault gun, Young rotated the turret and Ritz fired a high-explosive shell that was in the chamber. He watched as it flew harmlessly over the German tank. The gun of the Mark IV was now pointing at Young's tank and it fired, striking the assault gun in the track. Ritz lowered the 105-mm cannon as far as it would go and fired another round. It struck the German tank just below the cannon with a shower of sparks. The tank did not catch fire, but the crew bailed out through an escape hatch and melted into the brush. Bob Atnip of Clementsville, Kentucky, was the loader in the third assault gun. When the second assault gun was hit, he saw the tank commander, Sgt M. P. Shelton, pulling the gunner, Cpl Herman Hall, by the shoulders through the turret hatch. Then the second shell hit and the tank burst into flames. The assistant driver, Olen Rowell of Decatur, Mississippi, got out through the belly hatch and threw himself into a ditch. The driver, Philip Morgan of Arden, North Carolina, though badly burned, climbed out through the driver's hatch and made his way to a farmhouse that had just been abandoned by the Germans. The retreat was so fresh that Atnip had to confirm that Morgan was an American when GIs brought him out in shock and with his eyes swollen shut. As his tanker's helmet was different from the kind the infantrymen wore, they thought he was a German. The assault gun's loader, Pfc Richard Howell of Arcadia, Louisiana, burned to death inside the tank.

Young's assault gun could not move due to its broken track. Adair did not want to risk having it fall into enemy hands with a full load of ammunition and asked Ritz to stay with him and sent the remaining crew to the rear. He traversed the gun in the direction of the German lines, and with the lieutenant loading and the gunner firing, they used up most of the remaining 105-mm shells. When they were down to the last few rounds, Adair missed a beat in the rhythmic loading and firing, the cannon's recoil smashing his shoulder. Before retreating to the rear, Androkovich and Ritz went over to check out the German tank. The body of its gunner was inside. 'Look at this!' Ritz said. A round was in the cannon's chamber and the breech was closed. A split second more and their tank would have met the same fate as the second assault gun.

There were other casualties in the 712th that first day in combat. These are only the ones I have been able to chronicle by interviewing battalion veterans more than forty-five years after the war and by studying a handful of documents. B Company lost seven men that day including the crew of a tank. A Headquarters Company halftrack took a direct hit and Major Ira Hawk, the battalion's new executive officer, was killed. The motor sergeant, Earl Swanson, was also badly wounded and did not return.

On his first day in action, Jule Braatz lost his lieutenant. His tank ran over a mine. His assistant driver was killed. A tank in his platoon bogged down and came under fire by armor-piercing shells in the middle of an open field. If anyone told him he would survive eleven months in combat and the only thing that would take him off the front would be a severe case of diarrhoea, he would have told them they were nuts. On the evening of 3 July, Capt. Forrest Dixon, the battalion's maintenance officer, shared a cup of coffee with Colonel Randolph. Roughly half of the battalion's sixty-seven tanks were out of commission – some knocked out by enemy fire or mines, but most bogged down, tipped over or having suffered mechanical failure.

'I don't think we're going to last very long,' Dixon said.

'On the contrary,' said the officer who had taught mathematics at two high schools in Montgomery, Alabama. 'We lost half our tanks today. If we lose half of the remaining tanks tomorrow and half of those that are left the day after that, we should be good for several days.'

In 311 days of combat, the 712th Tank Battalion would compile, according to Dixon and Ed Stuever, the Service Company maintenance sergeant, one of the best records for maintenance in the European Theatre of Operations.

5

Peanut Butter and Crackers

Reuben Goldstein, twenty-four years old, of Dorchester, Massachusetts, commanded the fifth tank in the third platoon of A Company. Charles Fowler, the platoon sergeant, commanded the No. 4 tank. The two tanks were supporting troops of the 82nd Airborne Division on 5 July when Goldstein's tank was struck in the track by a round from an anti-tank gun. Although his tank was immobile, his gunner, Charles Bahrke, managed to take out the German weapon with a high-explosive round. There was not much time to admire his gunner's accuracy as a shell from another German field piece exploded nearby. Goldstein thought Fowler's tank might be able to get a shot at it, but saw that the tank, which should have been in front of his, was quite a distance behind. So he ran back to Fowler's tank. Finding it 'buttoned up,' he pounded on the outside of the tank with the handle of his .45. Still, there was no response.

While he was pounding on the side of the tank and hollering for the crew to open up, a shell from the anti-tank gun slammed into the far side of the adjacent hedgerow. The force of the explosion lifted Goldstein off the ground. Though dazed, he got up and resumed pounding on the outside of the tank. A second shell struck the far side of the hedgerow. The concussion lifted Goldstein in the air where he landed on the ground heavily. This time he was unable to stand. His head felt like a balloon that kept getting bigger and bigger until he was sure it would burst. A minute passed, then two. He got onto his hands and knees and crawled into bushes at the base of the hedgerow. He had a can of rations in one of his pockets and took it out. He had several crackers and peanut butter. Goldstein ate the peanut butter and crackers, and the throbbing in his head subsided. He stood up and returned to his tank.

A short while later, a pair of infantry officers came up to the immobilised tank. One of them was a one-star general, the other was his aide. The general's star was smudged with dirt to obscure it from snipers. The general asked Goldstein what had transpired and made some notes. He then asked if Goldstein had anything to drink. Goldstein retrieved his canteen, but had replaced the tepid water with cider. The general took a swig and said, 'That's not bad.' He passed the canteen to his aide and both left the scene.

Charles Fowler was an excellent garrison soldier, disciplined, tough on his men, with a muscular physique. Going out of their way to point out that they were not passing judgement, some men in the platoon said he was not cut out for combat. A short time later, he took his tank out of action because a tree limb jammed the gun's traversing mechanism, but later admitted he had put the limb there. He was relieved of his position and sent to the rear. He was not the first member of the battalion to crack under the strain of combat and he would not be the last.

Goldstein and Bahrke were awarded Silver Stars for their role in preventing a counterattack.

6

Hill 122

The first platoon of C Company, led by James Franklin Flowers, a thirty-year-old lieutenant from Texas, was lucky during its first week of combat, if you can call not having anyone killed and only one man seriously injured lucky. That all was about to change in what would become a turning point in the battalion's history.

The late *60 Minutes* commentator Andy Rooney, then a young war correspondent, wrote in his memoir *My War* that while Hill 122 carried a nondescript name, to anyone who was there, its very mention conjured the same imagery and horrors associated with Iwo Jima. There were at least two Hill 122s – so named for their height in metres above sea level – in Normandy and both saw intense fighting. I cannot say for sure to which hill Rooney was referring, but no one who was in the 90th Infantry Division would dispute the assertion that he meant their Hill 122. At reunions and in phone calls, letters and e-mails, veterans often attempt to reconstruct certain battles or incidents. The events on Hill 122 on 10 July, having fuelled all manner of speculation, were one such incident. Jim Rothschadl's daughter Judy – one of nine children he and his wife Elizabeth had after the war – once told me her father was conflicted between thanking Flowers for saving his life and cursing him for almost getting him killed in the first place. Ray Griffin, who took over the first platoon after Flowers was wounded, often wondered why the makeup of the platoon on 10 July differed markedly from that of 9 July and why Sgt James Bailey, who was not even in the platoon, was among the nine crew members who were killed. Flowers believed for many years – mistakenly, my research has led me to conclude – that one of the five tanks in his platoon feigned engine trouble and that had it been there for the battle things might have turned out differently.

Flowers' crew included his gunner, Jim Rothschadl of Waubun, Minnesota; loader Edward 'Mother' Dzienis of Fitchburg, Massachusetts; driver Horace Gary of Stuarts Draft, Virginia; and assistant driver Gerald Kiballa of Olyphant, Pennsylvania. The second tank was commanded by Sgt Judd Wiley, a southern Californian. Wiley's gunner was Harold Gentle, a Philadelphian; his loader was Eugene Tannler, from Scranton, Pennsylvania; the assistant driver was Laverne Patton from northern California and the driver was Paul Farrell of Haverhill, Massachusetts. The third tank was commanded by Sgt William Montoya, a Mexican-American from California. Montoya's gunner was Donald Knapp of Springfield, Massachusetts; his driver was Frank Perry of New London, Connecticut; the assistant driver was Wes Harrell of Ada, Oklahoma (whom Knapp dubbed 'Corporal Wac' as he wore blousy uniform trousers with pockets that could get caught if he had to evacuate the tank in a hurry); the loader was Ray Vuksick of Galveston, Texas.

Sgt Abraham I. Taylor commanded the No. 4 tank. His gunner was Louis Gerrard of Philadelphia; the loader was Earl Holman of Duncan, Oklahoma; the driver was Henry 'Milwaukee Hank' Lochowicz; and the assistant driver was G. B. Kennedy of Jackson, Mississippi. The No. 5 tank was commanded by Sgt Kenneth Titman of Norfolk, Nebraska (nicknamed as 'Goosy' for his tendency to jump when surprised); the driver was Clarence Morrison of Portage, Indiana; the assistant driver was Michael Vona of East Providence, Rhode Island; the gunner was Kenneth Cohron of Stuarts Draft, Virginia; and the loader was Steven Wojtilla of Unionville, Connecticut.

This was the makeup of the first platoon on 9 July. On the following day, the crews of Flowers, Titman and Montoya's tanks were intact. Wiley was evacuated due to an injury and Abe Taylor, the platoon sergeant who commanded the No. 4 tank, took his place in the second tank. Lt Harlo J. 'Jack' Sheppard took Taylor's place in the fourth tank and Sergeant Bailey of Christine, Kentucky, replaced Lochowicz as its driver. Sheppard, of Tampa, Florida, was the battalion motor officer when Captain Cary was injured by a booby trap. He became the C Company commander, a position he would hold for the next eleven months. Sgt James 'Jake' Driskill, a mechanic from Claude, Texas, became the C Company motor sergeant on 3 July when Earl Swanson was wounded.

On the morning of 10 July, Montoya's tank, which was up against a hedgerow, would not go into reverse and the platoon left without it. Driskill repaired Montoya's tank by tapping a transmission rod back into place, but it was too late for the tank to join the platoon, so Driskill said he would drive it to the rear. Later that day, a small convoy arrived in the first platoon area. Driskill was driving Montoya's tank, but Montoya and his crew were not with it. The tank was on its way to the rear when, according to Sheppard, it was stopped by an infantry colonel who said a battalion of infantry – the 2nd Battalion of the 358th Regiment – was trapped and needed support. When the convoy arrived, it comprised Sergeant Driskill with the tank; Lieutenant (and later Captain) Sheppard; Sergeant Bailey, who was driving Sheppard's jeep; and Sgt Harry Speier, the company cook, who was along to prepare a hot meal. There were now four tanks and four crews, but there were only three tank commanders. Sergeant Judd Wiley had been evacuated the day before after a hatch cover slammed down on his hand while his tank was backing over a hedgerow. Sheppard said he would command one of the tanks. Flowers set off on foot to scout the area and told the commanders where to meet him.

While he was gone, Jim Rothschadl, who was under his tank eating bread and marmalade that he scooped from a can the cook brought him, heard a commotion near one of the other tanks. Its driver, Hank Lochowicz, was refusing to drive. Bailey resolved the issue by saying, 'I'll drive it.' Lochowicz went back to the rear with Sergeants Speier and Driskill. Going up Hill 122, the platoon broke through the German defences and reached the 2nd Battalion unscathed. Flowers and the battalion commander, Col Jacob Bealke of Sullivan, Missouri, came up with a plan for Company K – well below its full strength of about 150 men – to follow the tanks down the steep slope of the hill, open a path and the remainder of the battalion would follow. It was already getting late in the day. The tanks began their descent. Rothschadl burned out the barrel of his coaxial .30 calibre machine gun and could see the bullets falling harmlessly in front of the tank. At the bottom of the hill there was a blacktop road. Most of K Company, which suffered 80 per cent casualties in the assault, dug in on the side of the road. Flowers crossed the road in his tank and kept going as did the three other tanks.

Sheppard's tank bogged down and he watched the other tanks disappear over a hedgerow. The three mobile tanks crossed a second field and were approaching another hedgerow when a shell caromed off the turret of Flowers' tank. Rothschadl had his head pressed against the periscope and the impact knocked out two of his teeth. He fired a high-explosive 75-mm shell at a hazy area that might have been caused by heat from the anti-tank gun. Moments later, another shell struck the tank. This one did not bounce off.

At about the same time, all three of the tanks that crossed the field were hit and on fire. Michael Vona, the loader in Titman's tank, saw his buddy Abe Taylor come flying out of the tank. According to Sheppard, Taylor's body would be found in a ditch when the area was retaken. None of the other crew members in Taylor's tank – who originally were Wiley's crew – made it out of the tank. 'When my tank got hit,' Titman said when I interviewed him in 1993, 'we were coming into this open field. Three tanks were together. When we got in there, the German 88s got us. They hit my tank and it exploded and I hollered, "Abandon tank!" The tank was on fire. I looked around and I saw all these tanks running, one tank ran in front of me and hit the tank on the left and both exploded. That's what I saw. I jumped out of the turret and hit the back deck. Blood was coming out of the top of my combat boot and I knew I was hit.'

Titman knew that Cohron, his gunner, was dead; the shell struck him directly and chunks of his flesh were spattered on Titman's helmet. When he was on the ground, Titman looked up and saw the loader, Wojtilla, evacuating the turret and 'was on fire when he hit the ground.' Wojtilla was among those listed as killed in action. Morrison, the driver, and Vona, escaped through the hatch in the bottom of the tank. Vona saw a hand grenade come flying over a hedgerow. It exploded and the concussion knocked him senseless. Then, a German soldier jumped over the hedgerow and the two fought hand to hand. The German jammed a Luger pistol against Vona's head and pulled the trigger. The gun was empty. Someone else shot the German – Vona thought it may have been a medic, but it might have been Flowers. Flowers never would go into detail about what took place other than to shake his head affirmatively and mutter 'm-hmm' when asked if there was hand to hand combat. However, in a statement he wrote from his hospital bed a year later after he was recommended by the 90th Division for the Medal of Honor – he was awarded the Distinguished Service Cross – he said that he shot a German soldier who was strangling an infantryman. I never put two and two together, but it is possible Vona was the GI he thought was an infantryman.

Morrison, the driver, recalled his tank as having been hit twice. The tank shuddered when the first shell struck and he caught a piece of shrapnel near one of his eyes. He remembered Titman calling to abandon tank and was on the ground when the second shell struck, causing flames to shoot '75 to 80' feet in the air. He made it to the foxhole where Vona found him and was wounded in the arm and leg. Morrison passed out and when he came to he was in an aid tent. He remembered returning to the States on the *Queen Mary* on the same trip as Bob Hope who had been entertaining the troops.

Back in the marsh, Sheppard stood in the turret and looked around. Suddenly, a shell struck the tank a few feet from his head. Gerrard, the gunner, was wounded and would lose an eye. Sheppard gave the order to abandon tank. He told the crew to stay with Gerrard and said he would go back for help. On the way back, he felt his jaw flopping up and down and discovered that shrapnel had knocked out one of his teeth. A medic was with the remaining crewmen when the Germans attacked. Holman picked up a Tommy gun. Gerrard recalled the medic urging him not to fire as they were outnumbered and would be massacred. Holman, when I interviewed him by telephone years after speaking with most of the other survivors, said the gun jammed. I do not know what happened to Kennedy, the assistant driver, other than that he survived, but the medic told the others to play dead.

Holman recalled the Germans searching his pockets for cigarettes. Gerrard recalled feeling the Germans trying to pull a ring off his finger. The ring had the word 'Oran' engraved on it and was sent to him by his brother Jack who had been fighting in North Africa. On D-Day, while he was still in England, Gerrard had learned that another brother was killed in action. He thought the Germans would cut the finger off to get the ring, but they did not. As they dragged him a short distance and propped him up against a hill, he expected to be shot. He thought about his mother receiving a telegram stating that another of her sons had been killed. 'That's the only thing I can thank the Germans for,' he said when I interviewed him in 1992. 'That they didn't kill me.' They did, however, kill Sergeant Bailey. He may not have succeeded in playing dead or he may have had a Luger or a German dagger in his possession which would have been a death sentence.

After the enemy soldier was shot, Vona heard moaning coming from a nearby foxhole and saw that it was Morrison whose eyes were swollen shut. He dragged the German who was alive but in shock and pulled the German's body over him due to the shooting. Vona went through the German's pockets looking for anything he could use as a weapon. He found a bayonet and gave it to Morrison. He then heard someone sobbing nearby. Vona crawled over and saw that it was Dzienis who earned the nickname 'Mother' at Fort Benning. When the men from the Boston area went into town together, most would be looking to buy beer and have a good time. Dzienis did not drink or smoke and would look to buy linens and so on to send home to his mother. Titman and Dzienis were wounded and captured. Titman would be taken to Rennes where a schoolhouse was converted to a hospital and he would be liberated about a month later when the Allies captured the city. (It is likely Dzienis was taken there as well, but I never made contact with him while he was alive.) Vona passed out. When he came to, he was on a stretcher carried by four Germans. He assumed he was captured. It was the Germans who were prisoners of war and Vona was being taken to a ship bound for England.

For Flowers and Rothschadl, the ordeal was just beginning. The armor-piercing shell that penetrated Flowers' tank tore off his right forefoot and set the tank on fire. A tendon in Rothschadl's ankle was cut. As he tried to climb out, he fell back into the turret basket. Flowers reached down and lifted him to the point where Rothschadl could grab the outside of the turret and hoist himself the rest of the way. Flowers slung his Thompson submachine gun over his shoulder and went to climb out of the turret which is when he would recall, 'I found out that I didn't have anything to climb with.' He managed to grab the outside of the turret ring and, with flames shooting up around him, hoist himself out and drop to the ground. Both Flowers and Rothschadl were burned, Flowers most seriously on his hands and Rothschadl on his face.

The other crew members – Dzienis, Horace Gary and Gerald Kiballa – made it out of the tank. Dzienis would be captured, Gary remained with Flowers and Rothschadl and helped the pair get over to the far side of the hedgerow, away from the burning tanks. Kiballa was killed in the ensuing skirmish. Flowers gave the five morphine syrettes that were taped inside his helmet liner to Gary who administered a shot to Flowers, Rothschadl and a wounded infantryman. Flowers recalled that he then ordered Gary, who wanted to stay with them, to go back and send help. By now, it was getting dark. Sometime during the night, a German patrol passed by. The last man in the patrol was a medic. He stopped and checked the tourniquet Flowers tied around his leg and bandaged the lieutenant's burned fingers. Flowers asked for water, but the medic had none. Rothschadl's face had swollen so that he could only see if he pulled the skin down below one of his eyes. Nevertheless, he saw the German medic take out a canteen and hold it upside down. Rothschadl, too, was thirsty. (Note that they were not captured by the enemy. Their only explanation for not being taken prisoner or being finished off was that they were in such bad shape that they were left for dead or at least posed no threat.)

Early the next morning, Flowers heard movement on the other side of the hedgerow. He thought it must be the aid men Gary was sending back and he called out to them, but there was no response. He picked up a Tommy gun and two magazines that were on the ground. He then rolled over to the hedgerow and crawled to the top.

He saw several German soldiers walking away towards the American lines. He felt rage and emptied both magazines at the Germans who quickly disappeared. The tanks were still smouldering. He returned to Rothschadl and the infantryman who was wounded in both of his legs at the foot of the hedgerow.

Later that morning, a German platoon came into the field on Flowers' side of the hedgerow and dug in. They did not bother the three wounded Americans. 'They had already finished digging in when our own artillery opened fire on this field,' Flowers wrote from his hospital bed a year later. 'The German artillery is good, but ours is much better. Countless numbers of shells fell in that area. At times, I was deafened by the explosions and covered with dirt... A shell landed between the infantryman and me, which hit both of us. One shell fragment hit my left leg, knocking it off about seven inches below the knee. Other pieces of fragments hit me in both legs above the knees and in the back. I immediately tied my belt around my left leg as a tourniquet. The infantryman called to me that he had been hit. I crawled to him and saw blood spurting out of his right leg. Taking his belt, I used it as a tourniquet. I was unable to twist it tight enough. With his helping me turn the stick, I was able to stop the bleeding. I tore his clothes off as best I could to look for further wounds. He had been hit in several places on the right side. I had no first aid kit, therefore I was unable to do more for him except to bandage him with strips torn from his shirt and pants leg. When I had finished with him, he was apparently resting as well as could be expected. There was no excessive amount of blood lost. During the rest of that day, I maintained close watch on both our tourniquets. The artillery fired a few volleys every hour for the rest of the day. It was HELL!'

The barrage was not confined to the field on Flowers' side of the hedgerow. Louis Gerrard, still propped against the side of a hill, was caught in it. Dirt, cinders and stones were flying up and hitting him on the head. He clutched the hill and began crawling up it. He then heard someone say, 'Get the hell over here!' There were some GIs in a big slit trench and they pulled him in. When the artillery barrage was over, they put Gerrard on a stretcher and sent him on the back of a jeep to a field hospital on the beach. Titman and the Germans who captured him were also caught in the barrage and Titman was wounded again, this time in the chin.

Jim Rothschadl's father emigrated from Czechoslovakia to Yankton, South Dakota. His twin brother was supposed to come the following year, but did not. He was drafted into the Austro-Hungarian army and was killed near the end of the First World War. After working for three years to pay back the farmer who sponsored him, Rothschadl's father got a job in a cement factory and saved enough money to buy a house. One day, he was in a saloon with some fellow immigrants and found a brochure that was deliberately left on one of the tables. The brochure advertised virgin land for sale. The brochure did not state that the land for sale was on an Indian reservation. Nor did it state that the property – which was offered for $50 an acre – had been purchased from the Indians for between $2 and $5 an acre following passage of an act in Congress that allowed the Indians to sell some of the 800,000 acres on their reservation. The land company not only sold the property to immigrants like Rothschadl's father, but financed it at 14 per cent interest.

Rothschadl's father loved America with a passion. On the Fourth of July, he would say to his three sons, 'No work today. Today is the birthday of the United States of America.' Even though times were tough for the family in the Depression, he made sure that the boys got firecrackers and marshmallows and wieners to roast, and he put three little flags on the hood of his Model T. Rothschadl often thought of his father during the first few days of combat. When someone would say, 'Let's get the hell out of here, let's go AWOL,' Rothschadl would say to himself that he could never disappoint his father by doing a thing like that.

But as dawn broke on the morning of 12 July 1944 on Hill 122, Jim Rothschadl was feeling bad. He was thirstier than he had ever been, even on the gruelling 20-mile marches in Tiger Camp when the 712th Tank Battalion was still part of the 10th Armored Division. Back then, he had thought it was impossible for a man to have a more powerful thirst and he almost wished that someone would put him out of his misery. He now looked at the .45-calibre pistol he was holding and did not think about his father, the Model T Ford and the Fourth of July. He thought about taking his own life or what little was left of it. It was a request from Flowers that pulled him back from the edge. The lieutenant asked him for a cigarette. Rothschadl had cigarettes in his jacket pocket, but his burned hands were so swollen that he could not reach into the pocket to pull them out. He would have liked a cigarette himself. Flowers then asked him to go and look for help and said he was getting gangrene in his legs.

Jim Flowers was a stoic man and proud. He did not recall telling Rothschadl he was getting gangrene nor did he recall screaming in pain when the shell fragment tore off his left foot. He said that if that is the way Rothschadl remembered it, then that is what happened as far as Rothschadl was concerned. Rothschadl then crawled through a hole in the hedgerow and began feeling his way along, pulling down the skin below his left eye every few feet so he could see. Suddenly, he heard derisive laughter. He pulled the skin below the eye and saw a German machine gun crew. He thought, 'Go ahead, shoot me!' But the Germans did not shoot him. So, Rothschadl turned around and began crawling and pulling himself along in the other direction.

He did not know how far he went, but after a while he looked up and saw a face. It belonged to a GI. The infantryman's head must have been low to the ground, because it was level with Rothschadl's. Together they crawled through a large puddle and all Rothschadl could think about was how thirsty he was. In a few moments they joined other infantrymen. Rothschadl asked for some water. One of the GIs held out a canteen and another said, 'Only give him a little.' Too much water might have killed him, but the words made Rothschadl angry. He sipped the water and the GI pulled the canteen away. Rothschadl then told them his lieutenant was back behind the hedgerow and needed to be rescued.

'Sometime after noon of ... 12 July,' Flowers wrote in his account, 'the infantryman told me he was going to die. He said that our infantry would never attack through our field and find us. I knew that if he continued to feel that way he would surely die. I assured him that our men *would* find us and soon. I used every argument I could think of to persuade him to want to live. For a while I was successful. Later, he said that he was dying. I tried everything again. I begged him. I bullied him. I pleaded with him. But I failed. I was holding him in my arms, praying to God to not let him die when he took his last breath. I was heartbroken to lose him and I, too, wondered if our men would *ever* find us. Again, I asked Him, our creator, to send aid. No man can know the HELL of losing both feet and wondering if his men will find him in time to save his life until he experiences the things I did in that field.

'About an hour after the infantryman had died, I heard small arms fire near my position. I knew that it was our men making an attack. In a few minutes, our infantry came over the hedgerow chasing the German paratroopers. The first man I saw was Lieutenant Claude H. Lovett of the 357th Infantry. I called to him and he came to me. He gave me a canteen of water and left one man with me until a litter team came to evacuate Corporal Rothschadl and me. I knew then that we were safe again.'

Tony D'Arpino was a driver in the third platoon. He was seventy-two years old when I interviewed him at his home in Milton, Massachusetts, in 1992. He wore glasses and his hair was white. 'I can remember,' he said when the story of Hill 122 came up, 'we had a young kid in our crew...' He paused and repeated, '... young kid. We were all young kids. His name was Luigi Gramari. He came from Utica, New York. We had the honor to go back up Hill 122 after Flowers' platoon got knocked out. We were gonna go up there and take it, and Gramari threw a tirade. "All the goddamn first platoon just got killed and we're gonna go up there?" he said to Lieutenant Lombardi. There wasn't anything Lombardi could do about it. He was taking his orders from the infantry. It was getting dark and Gramari thought we were going to go right then and there, but we waited until the next morning. By then everything turned out pretty good.'

Dr William McConahey, in his book *Battalion Surgeon* written shortly after the war, remarked that of the hundreds of cases he treated in Normandy, three stood out in his mind. One of them, he wrote, 'concerned a young tank officer, a second lieutenant. When his tank had been knocked out by an 88 during the fighting for Hill 122, one of his feet had been virtually torn off. He had pulled himself out of his disabled tank and a passing aid man had stopped the bleeding and bandaged the wound. Then an enemy counterattack threw back the Americans so the wounded man lay in No Man's Land for two days. During the fighting back and forth, many shells fell near him and one large piece of steel shattered his other foot. The young fellow pulled off his belt and applied a tourniquet to the leg.

'Later, when one of my litter squads found and brought him in and I heard the story, I expected to see a moribund patient, but such was not the case. He was calm, cheerful and not in shock. In fact, he was in excellent general condition, although both feet hung in tatters and would have to be amputated. When I remarked to him that he was in surprisingly good condition, he smiled and said, "Well, Doc, I just had the will to live!"'

Jack Sheppard, his face bandaged, accompanied Lieutenant Lombardi's platoon to the base of Hill 122. He found Sergeant Taylor in a foxhole; he had been shot in the head. As for Taylor's crew, nothing remained but ashes in the tank. Someone found a ring among the ashes and wondered why it did not melt like the twisted metal around it. The ring was from Central High School in Scranton, Pennsylvania. Eugene Tannler, the tank's loader, was from Scranton. Lt James Gifford of Gloversville, New York, who had just been assigned to C Company as a replacement, was among the group that went to search for dog tags in Flowers' tanks.

'These guys had all been incinerated,' he said when interviewed in 1992, 'because these tanks were like a furnace. It was like getting into a furnace after something's been destroyed. I'd go where the tank driver was supposed to be sitting and I'd find a dog tag. I wouldn't even find the body. There was just one tank in particular that, one guy, a gunner, he was still sitting in the gunner's seat. There was nothing left of him but maybe his hips. The legs were gone. The body was gone. The head's gone. There was nothing there but a black crust. And when I was looking for the dog tags, I pushed this thing. I thought it was a piece of the machinery and a piece of it came off like a turkey. Like the skin on a turkey came off, this big black crust, and then I realised it was what was left of him.'

Charles Nuccio, another C Company veteran, remembered James Bailey as a likable mechanic with one little quirk: every time he took an engine apart and put it back together, there were a couple of parts left over. Maybe a nut, bolt or a couple of screws would be on the ground. But the engine would always work better than it did before. He also remembered that the only sign of Bailey the search party found was his helmet, which was identifiable as it was marked with his serial number. They never discovered Bailey's body or his dog tags, but inside the helmet they found pieces of his brain.

Judd Wiley could not recall who the sergeant was who visited him in the hospital in England some months later and told him about the battle on Hill 122. He only remembered that he cried all night. Eugene Tannler, his loader; Harold Gentle, his gunner; Paul Farrell, his driver; Laverne Patton, his assistant driver: 'I loved every one of those guys,' he said when I met him in Seal Beach, California, in 1994. 'Abe Taylor (the sergeant who took Wiley's place), all of them dead.'

The history of the 712th Tank Battalion is filled with stories of men who owed their lives to some curious twist of fate such as those who ducked inside a tank to hear what someone was saying a split second before a shell struck the spot where their head had been exposed. Most of them are thankful for such twists of fate. Wiley cursed the quirk of fate that spared his life. He not only wished he had died with his crew, but believed that if he had been there, he might have been able to do something to make things turn out differently. That he might have dissuaded Flowers from trying to push the Germans back one more hedgerow. He never saw Flowers after the war and blamed him for getting the platoon wiped out. Flowers said that if Wiley were there, it would not have made a damn bit of difference. But when you think about something every day for fifty years, it is not likely that anything is going to change your mind. Just as Wiley could not help thinking things might have been different if he had been there, Flowers always wondered if things might have turned out differently if Montoya's tank had been there.

When Flowers mentioned Montoya, he stressed the Spanish pronunciation 'Mon-thoya.' The first time D'Arpino saw Flowers at a reunion, sometime in the 1970s, he went over to the table at which Flowers was sitting and asked if he remembered him. Of course he did. Byrl Rudd, a lanky Oklahoma farmer who had been a tank commander in the second platoon, was also at the table. D'Arpino began going through the names he remembered, asking Flowers if he remembered them as well. Did he remember Farrell and Savio? Paul Savio was a tank driver who was killed on 7 July when Lieutenant Henry DuVal was wounded. Of course, Flowers remembered Savio and he remembered DuVal, the swarthy Frenchman from Washington, DC, who commanded the second platoon for all of four days in combat before the war ended for him. D'Arpino went through a few more names and then said, 'And do you remember Montoya?' The smile vanished from Flowers' face and the string of invectives that followed caught D'Arpino by surprise. He later asked Rudd about it and Rudd told him that Flowers always suspected Montoya may have feigned the engine trouble that kept him from taking part in the assault on Hill 122.

The problem was not with the engine, but with the transmission, according to Sergeant Donald Knapp who was the gunner in Montoya's tank that day. Frank Perry was the driver, Wes Harrell the assistant driver and Raymond Vuksick the loader. Although Montoya passed away before I was able to interview him, both Knapp and Harrell confirmed that there was a mechanical problem with the tank. Knap said that the four tanks were lined up at the base of a hedgerow on 9 July. He could not recall the precise order of events, but said Perry could not go forwards over the hedgerow and when he tried to back up, he could not get the tank into reverse. There was a brief exchange over the radio and the other three tanks took off. The next day, Knapp recalled he was sitting in the turret of a tank after they pulled back to reform the company and he never felt so down in his life. 'I've lost all my friends,' he wrote in a letter to his wife, Evelyn, in Springfield, Massachusetts. Jake Driskill lived in Claude, Texas, which would be a sleepy little town if it were not for the constant rattle of trucks whizzing by on Route 287 heading west toward Amarillo. It was Driskill who repaired the transmission rod on Montoya's tank and was driving it to the maintenance area when he was diverted by an infantry colonel.

Knapp was transferred to the second platoon as much to give him a fresh start as the platoon needed a tank commander and Sheppard felt he could do the job. Harrell came with him as his driver. Harrell did not have much experience driving, but then Knapp did not have much experience commanding a tank. Henry K Shute, who may have been the oldest man in the battalion, was his assistant driver. Montoya stayed with the first platoon under its new lieutenant, Ray Griffin. Lochowicz became Griffin's driver and acquitted himself well until September when he was wounded.

7

The Death of Shorty

There are nine names on the monument on the road to Perier that goes by Hill 122: Gerald Kiballa, Abraham I. Taylor, Paul Farrell, Laverne Patton, Stephen Wojtilla, James Bailey, Harold Gentle, Eugene Tannler and Kenneth Cohron. Kiballa was from the coal mining town of Olyphant in eastern Pennsylvania. His brother Myron told me that Gerry loved to play baseball, but one day when he was a teenager, he ran out into the street to catch a fly ball and was hit by a car. After the accident, he suffered from a trick knee that would sometimes lock up on him. He refused to let that keep him from serving in the tank. Jim Flowers spoke with Myron after the war and told him that Gerry did not die inside the tank, but was killed in the battle afterwards, which a letter written by Ed Dzienis, Flowers' loader, to Myron seems to have confirmed. Myron was wounded in Anzio and learned of his brother's death in a letter from his sister when he left hospital. He said that reading that letter made him feel like he was in *The Twilight Zone*. I can see now why he probably pressed Flowers as to whether Gerry got out of the tank.

Abe Taylor was the only child of Jewish immigrants who settled in Massachusetts. He became a sergeant in the horse cavalry. Jake Driskill, the motor sergeant, believed Taylor might have had a premonition of his death. Before the mission to Hill 122, Driskill recalled Taylor saying, 'So long, Dris.' Driskill spelled out the four letters, D-R-I-S, and said he responded by saying, 'I'll say goodbye but I'll see you,' to which Taylor replied, 'I feel like I'm going to get it sometime and this might be it.'

Paul Farrell often won a weekend pass for looking the best in uniform in the company according to Tony D'Arpino, the tank driver in the third platoon who, like Farrell, was from the Boston area. One day after my website was up for a couple of years, I got a phone call from Paul Farrell Jr who never knew his father. He had just returned from a visit to France where he toured the St Lo battlefield and found the story on my website after he returned. He did not know his father's name was on the monument or that his father was killed before the breakout from St Lo. I put him in touch with Tony D'Arpino, but I do not know if they ever spoke.

Eugene Tannler wrote home and mentioned that Sergeant Driskill chewed tobacco. When I interviewed Driskill, he recalled that Tannler's mother sent her son a package and in it was some Beech-Nut chewing tobacco for Driskill. Cliff Flora, a mechanic from Indiana, recalled a package from Tannler's mother that arrived the day her son was killed in the battle for Hill 122. It contained cookies. When I spoke with Flora at the 1996 battalion reunion in Pittsburgh, he recalled a brief discussion he and his colleagues had about what to do with the cookies. They finally passed them around and ate them. Flora recalled how badly he felt knowing the fellows were eating cookies from Tannler's mother who had yet to learn that her son had been killed.

Those are the nine men on the Hill 122 monument. There should be a tenth and that always bothered Ed Stuever, the Service Company sergeant. Marion 'Shorty' Kubeczko drove one of two tank recovery units that were sent to try and retrieve Flowers' tanks the day after the battle. Kubeczko's hatch cover was open and an artillery shell scored a direct hit, entering Kubeczko's body in the area of his shoulder, exiting through his abdomen and killing him instantly. Stuever was up in the turret only a few feet away. Although dazed, he managed to retrieve Shorty's body and then drove the recovery unit back to the rear. He kept the base of the shell that killed Shorty and planned to present it to Kubeczko's family until other mechanics convinced him that would be an awful thing to do. One of them heaved it into the countryside.

Before the recovery units were turned back, Forrest Dixon was sent to assess the damage to the tanks and had to crawl on his belly through a ditch with machine gun bullets flying over him. When he reached what most likely was Sheppard's tank and opened the hatch, there was a dead German inside. Jake Driskill saw the same dead German who had been using the tank as a pillbox and was picked off by a sniper. When he opened the turret hatch and the deceased enemy soldier seemed to be pointing at him, Driskill recalls saying 'Don't be looking at me. I didn't kill you.' When it was learned the Germans were using the knocked-out tank as a pillbox, Dixon was told to find an anti-tank unit and have them set the tank on fire. When he did, the officer was incredulous at being ordered to shoot at a US tank and insisted that Dixon sign an order to that effect.

8

Flipped Like Pancakes

'I was looking at a book called *Battalion Surgeon*,' Bob Hagerty, a lieutenant in A Company, said when I interviewed him at his home in Cincinnati in 1992. 'Boy, the infantry died in bunches, didn't they? Just imagine, if you're gonna try to take, let's say, that garage back there and the Germans have guns trained on that driveway, and the only way you're gonna get that garage is if you can absorb a hell of a lot of casualties and have enough left to take it. That's about what it amounts to. And some of your casualties would be gruesome, horrible kinds of wounds, disfiguring wounds. But that's what the infantry pays to take a given piece of territory. The tanker's got it easy, when you stop to think about it. You have all that armor around you. Every once in a while he gets hit by something that can pierce the armor, but it isn't often. The guy in the tank had a far different job than the guy out there on the ground. The doggone infantryman, if he lives through that assault, there's another one after that and another one.'

At the 1993 reunion of the 90th Infantry Division, I attended the annual luncheon of the 358th Infantry Regiment that concluded with an unusual ceremony. You almost have to have been there, in combat, which I never was, to fully appreciate the ceremony. Table by table, the hundred or so aging men in the room rose and paraded past the podium, pausing long enough to announce, 'My name is So and So. I was in Such and Such company. And I was wounded at Such and Such a place.' Almost all of them were wounded at one place or another. Occasionally, one of the veterans made a remark like, 'I don't know how they missed me,' and the room burst into laughter. Sometimes, the veteran would recite his serial number, which also drew laughter since the same veteran would probably have difficulty reciting his social security number or remembering what he had for breakfast that morning.

The men of the 90th Division were wounded in a lot of different places. They were wounded on the Cotentin peninsula, in La Haye du Puits and on Hill 122. They were wounded in Mayenne, Avranches, Le Mans and at the Falaise Gap. They were wounded at Mairy, Maizières lès Metz, Distroff, Pachten and Dillingen. They were wounded in Luxembourg, Belgium, France and Germany. And they were wounded on 'the Island.' The battle for Seves Island followed close on the heels of Hill 122 and between them the 90th Division suffered so many casualties it was at risk of becoming a 'lost division.' In other words of being broken up with its survivors used as replacements.

Arnold Brown was a twenty-four-year-old captain who joined the 90th Division as a replacement during the battle for Seves Island. The company to which he was assigned, G Company of the 358th Regiment, had lost all of its officers and half its men on Hill 122. Charles Bryan, a lieutenant who took over L Company of the 358th and eventually became a battalion commander, remarked in a privately published memoir that he believed he owed his survival of the war to the fact that he came in after the battles for Hill 122 and Seves Island, and that the men of the company he took over looked 'like zombies.' During the battle for Seves Island, a chaplain from the 90th Division and an officer from the German 5th Parachute Division arranged a three-hour truce so that the two sides could remove their casualties from the battlefield. Then, as Arnold Brown recalled, the two sides 'started making more casualties.'

In Periers, France, there is a monument to the 'Tough Ombres' of the 90th Infantry Division. It depicts four soldiers killed in or around Periers: Virgil Tangborn, a litter bearer who was killed on 14 June 1944 at Amfreville; Andrew Speese who died on 6 July at Beaucoudray; Richard Richtman who was killed on 26 July; and Tullio Micaloni who perished on 26 July when his tank struck either a concealed bomb or a land mine. His 37-ton Sherman tank was flipped in the air, its turret blown off, killing everyone inside. At the battalion's

1994 reunion in Fort Mitchell, Kentucky, I sat at a table with three veterans of B Company: Leslie Vink, a sergeant who received one of the battalion's fourteen battlefield commissions; Roy 'Rip' Bardo, who was a loader; and Cleo 'Deadeye' Coleman, a gunner who served at times in Vink's tank. I asked them about Sergeant Micaloni. 'He was in the first platoon and was ordered up to help take the crossing of the river,' Bardo said, 'and the tank was hit by a teller mine and demolished, killing all the five members of it. One infantry boy was in it. One of our boys was sick and couldn't go in and at least one infantry and three of our men, Krusel (Frank M. Krusel) and Micaloni and Milczakowski (Nicholas Milczakowski), those three were killed in the tank. Little Nick and Krusel was the driver, wasn't he?'

'I believe he was,' Vink said.

'Those three names still ring with me as being in the tank,' Bardo said, 'and I always thought two infantrymen...'

'Weren't they short of a crew?' Coleman replied. 'They drew names on that. I was told by one of the other boys, "You're lucky."'

'What do you mean?' I said.

'They drew names. They lacked one man to have enough to build a crew. They put names in a hat or whatever and drew this other boy, and I lucked out. Or I'd have been in it.'

'What happened with Mic's tank,' Vink said, 'was when they pulled down to the corner where he was going to get in position, just as he got at that position, unbeknown to us there was probably a 400-lbs charge of TNT, a bomb. It literally blew that tank apart, that's how big the charge was. It lifted the turret right off.'

'We saw the crater,' Coleman said. 'When the tank came down it was practically in a hole. It was that big a charge.'

Difficult as it may be to imagine 33 tons of steel being flipped like a pancake, it is not much easier to imagine the same thing happening to a 17-ton 'light' tank. Only a day after Micaloni's tank was destroyed, a D Company tank ran over a string of mines stacked two deep. Miraculously, two of the tank's four crew members survived.

At one of the battalion's Florida mini-reunions, Caesar Tucci gave me a copy of a D Company log. The log is more detailed than the general after-action reports and in two places individuals wrote up brief accounts of particular actions in which they were involved. One of them was written by Sgt Max 'Lucky' Lutcavish about the time his tank knocked out a Mark V Panzer with its 37-mm gun. I do not know of the author of the other, but it took place on 27 July.

'It was the 27th of July 1944,' the account begins. 'The sun was unusually hot and the roads unusually dusty. The blueness of the sky was clouded only from attack bombers levelling the town of Periers to a mass of dust and debris. Rolling billows of smoke arose from our right and the air was contaminated with the pungent odour of powder smoke and death. The five light tanks of the 3rd platoon were pulled into a field about 500 yards E. of Periers waiting to get into action. A barrage was falling and the infantry was moving up in between the shell bursts, but the main advance was held up due to some unknown resistance up ahead. Finally, the big picture was ready. Four Mark V tanks were reported holding up the advance of the Division. The mission – two of the Platoon's light tanks ... were to lead three medium tanks mounting a platoon of infantry towards the enemy tanks, and then act as flank protection with the possibility of getting in a few hooking blows while the mediums attempted to knock out the Mark Vs. The mission was far from a tasteful one as the enemy had the advantage of concealment, exactly what was ahead was unknown, and the roads had not been swept for mines. There was a feeling of a suicide mission ahead.

'The terrain opened up, displaying larger fields and small, rolling hills. At least it gave one a good feeling to be leaving the dogged hedgerow country behind. That had been Hell too. The road led through woods and a curve was ahead. Curves were always good places to lay mines, and somehow there was a feeling that this curve was "it." The leading tank commander, S/Sgt Charles L. Reynolds, told his driver to slow down to a creep – here, a parenthetical remark is made with an arrow directing it to be inserted before the beginning of the current sentence – (They had to go onwards. Before they started they were told to go regardless of what was ahead.) Slowly and tensely, the lead tank edged its way carefully around the curve and then it happened. There was a loud bang – the author crossed out the word "bang" and wrote "explosion" – a dense cloud of black smoke and flying particles, and the strong odour of cordite. When the smoke had cleared, the twisted and torn wreckage of what had once been a tank could be seen upside down on the road. There was a hole across the road 3 feet deep, 5 feet wide. Approximately 9 Teller mines had been set off, stacked three deep.'

Eugene Sand of Syracuse, Nebraska, was one of the mechanics sent to clear the road. 'D Company one time had a light tank, this was in Periers,' Sand said when I spoke with him at the battalion's 1995 reunion in Louisville. 'We went through the town and there was kind of a main road went on through, and a light tank from D Company took one of the side roads. It was just a dirt road. The Germans had put a row of mines across the road and they stacked them two or three deep, and then they covered it all over. And D Company came along with a light tank. They had a couple of infantry boys following behind the tank. When it hit those land mines, that light tank flipped completely over and bounced on top of the turret, right on top of those infantry guys and that was kind of a gruesome mess. They were smashed flat. If 17 tons of steel lands on top of you, you're smashed. We weren't positive whether there were two or three guys there. But we scraped up the remains and wrapped them up in a raincoat and put a rifle in the ground there for the grave details to come along and pick them up. The driver and the assistant driver in that tank were still in there when we moved it. The blast went through the bottom of the tank and took all the flesh off of their legs. Just their GI shoes were still on their feet, but the flesh was off of their legs from the blast. We could see them, but we didn't take them out.'

The tank commander, Sergeant Reynolds, and the gunner, Corporal Bill Holt, both of whom were in the turret when the tank ran over the mines, survived. One of them, Holt, was at the Louisville reunion. Holt was born in Illinois and was twenty-seven when he was drafted in 1942. He was eighty-one at the Louisville reunion. I had no idea he was one of the two survivors of that tank when I asked how he was wounded. 'The tank was blown up by mines. Jenkins and Cerullo were killed. Sergeant Reynolds and myself lived through it. When the tank ran over the mines, I just felt a jar on the tank, and when I woke up I was upside down. I guess the tank was upside down. The infantrymen who were killed were riding on the tank. I got out through the front of the tank. I was helped out. I wound up in the hospital. I just had a bunch of cuts and bruises and splinters of steel. That happened in July and I came back in November.'

'Here was this village with a high wall on it,' Ed Stuever, whose recovery team was sent to remove the tank, recalled. 'A big tank broke through the wall and then a D Company tank went down the road with five infantry guys on it. One of them had a Browning automatic weapon, a BAR, a big heavy thing. And these five guys are riding on the back end of that tank. And I'd say a quarter of a mile from town down the road, there's a big tree over here on this side, then over here was a patch of young evergreens, big ones, and there were Germans hidden in there. So this light tank went down there and when it hit the mines they flipped it like a pancake, and it chewed up those guys that were on the back end of it. My guys, they couldn't pick up these pieces of body, they were vomiting. And I said, "Let's get some canvas over them and roll them up in there." I had the stomach for that because I was born and raised on a farm. We butchered pigs. But my guts were boiling, too. It was drastic. I picked up a piece of flesh, an earlobe, a guy's nose and mouth. We got the bodies on the truck and got it out of there. We turned the tank over and turned it around with the recovery unit and started to go out and I said, "Hold it! Hold it! Let's thank the Lord."'

'"Why?"'

'"We're still here. Look over there. There's two mines that didn't go off. And we're working all around this.

'I said, "How come you guys didn't step on that thing?" Jiminy, they hugged me.'

9

The Second Lieutenant

Sgt Jule Braatz did not know it, but when his platoon leader, Lt George Tarr, was killed on the battalion's first day in combat, Braatz was about to develop a reputation for losing lieutenants. The second one he lost was a little different than the others: he was my father. At age thirty-four, 2nd Lt Maurice Elson was one of the older men in the battalion when he was assigned as a replacement during the lull between the battle for Hill 122 and the attack on Seves Island. I do not know much about his life before the war. The youngest of four children, he was born in a Polish village called Rypin and came to America when he was four years old. He had a girlfriend before the war, but my mother allegedly stole him away from her when he came home.

He was supposedly very good at playing chess as was his father before him, but when I took up the game as a child I could rarely get him to play it with me and eventually lost interest. Once, when I asked about his youth, he said that in his twenties he wanted to see the world. So he signed onto a steamship that went to South America and all he saw was the inside of the engine room. Now he was going into combat and all he could see was the inside of a tank. When I was a kid, he would say the first time he got wounded was because he wanted to see what a battle looked like, so he stuck his head up.

The way Braatz told it was a little different. My father was the replacement for Lieutenant Tarr. According to the company reports, Lieutenant Elson was wounded on 28 July, so he probably arrived only a few days before. Braatz said at the 1987 reunion that my father told him his training was with the infantry and he knew little about tanks. His only experience with tanks was at a demonstration and it probably showed up on his MOS, the military classification system. Braatz had been running the platoon and my father told him to continue doing so until he felt more knowledgeable. Braatz offered to show him around the tank and explained to be careful getting off as the turret was two stories high. He said my dad jumped off and twisted his ankle. The platoon was ordered to move out while he was at the aid station.

The rest of the story, Braatz said, was 'hearsay' as it was told to him by Quentin 'Pine Valley' Bynum who was later killed. Bynum, a driver, told Braatz a lieutenant hitched a ride in his tank, hoping to catch up with his platoon. The lieutenant rode in the 'bog' or assistant driver/bow gunner's seat. The platoon was held up and the lieutenant wanted to get out of the tank. He might have been anxious to see what was going on as he told his children or he might have felt compelled to continue on foot in search of his platoon. Bynum told him not to get out of the tank, but my father did not listen. I always had an image of him being struck by a bullet, but the likelihood is he was hit by shrapnel from a mortar or artillery shell. This was on 28 July. A similar situation almost six months later would cost Bynum his life as well as that of a relatively new lieutenant who ordered his crew to abandon tank after it was struck by a high-explosive rather than an armor-piercing shell.

10

A Cow in a Tree

'My first taste of combat,' Ray Griffin wrote in a collection of stories he compiled for his grandchildren, 'began with an operation which later came to be rated as one of the more spectacular actions of the war.' Griffin edited the battalion newsletter I wrote to in 1987 and passed my letter on to Sam MacFarland who invited me to attend that year's reunion. I met Ray there but never thought to sit and talk with him. I missed the 1988 reunion, at which the battalion's monument was dedicated, and he died the following year. In 1992, Ray's widow, Frances, gave me a copy of his collection of stories.

The operation was 'a terrific aerial bombardment of the German lines on the St Lo-Periers road,' Griffin wrote. 'I very vividly recall watching wave after wave of bombers fly over as I was sitting on the top of my tank. The first planes over the German lines received some "ack-ack." Several of the four-engine bombers were hit. I remember counting the parachutes that opened up after one of the big planes went out of control and started falling to the ground. Any attempt to describe what 2,000-plus planes looks like is a hopeless undertaking. The first thing that attracts one's attention is the roar of the many motors... It was an awe-inspiring sight. The big planes do not appear to be moving very fast. The fact that they hold rigidly to their formations gives one the impression of seeing some giant machine in operation.'

Jim Gifford: 'The sky was lit up with bombers, big bombers. As far as you could see in any direction there were these little airplanes up there, wingtip to wingtip, formation after formation, out of sight, going in all directions. And these big 'ack-ack' explosions way up there were hitting them and the planes would come down like streamers on

New Year's Eve. They were catching hell, but they were just droning along. You could hear that roar all day long, into the night, as the planes were going over. Then we started to move out.'

The 712th Tank Battalion was moving quickly now and on 1 August would become part of Patton's famed 3rd Army. Tony D'Arpino, then an assistant tank driver in C Company's third platoon, was saving the cigarettes he received with his rations for a trip to Paris, which had not yet been liberated but about which tankers fantasised. On 28 July, however, D'Arpino lost all his cigarettes along with much of his hearing when his tank ran over a mine. Moments before, Jim Gifford, riding in a jeep, saw the carcass of a sheep wedged in the scraggly branches of a tree. There was only one way the sheep could have got there. He radioed Lieutenant Lombardi whose tank was about to go through the gate in a hedgerow and told him the area was mined. D'Arpino recalled Lombardi ordering everyone to open their hatches. If they were closed, the concussion from the mine the tank set off would have likely killed everyone in the tank.

The driver, Cardis Sawyer of Cherokee, Texas, lost his hearing and never returned to the battalion. D'Arpino lost his hearing too, but not so much that he could not hear Sawyer screaming inside the aid station. So he did an about-face and went back to the tank. Lombardi told him to take over as driver and D'Arpino said that might not be a good idea as Lombardi might tell him to retreat and he would keep going forwards. D'Arpino became the driver and would remain in that position for the next nine months until, with the end of the war in sight, he was promoted to tank commander. On his first assignment, he managed to get his tank bogged down in a manure pile.

A few days after the St Lo bombing, Griffin wrote in his collection of stories, the Germans 'decided they would have to cut the narrow corridor north of Avranches to prevent the Allies from breaking out of Normandy. Our turn to move through this corridor came during the night. Sometime after we had moved out, the Krauts ... mounted a bombing attack ... Company C was fortunate that the attack hit just a short distance ahead of us.'

Dess Tibbitts, a driver in A Company, was a short distance ahead. 'You never was scared till you got somebody shooting at you in them airplanes,' Tibbitts said in 1995. 'You just think you've been scared. When we went out of the hedgerows, they always said, "Give lots of interval between the tanks." We were bumper to bumper. And Germans lit that sky up and took their sweet time bombing us. They went up and down that column strafing and bombing. Guys would shut their tanks off and some of the boys jumped out and ran away from their tanks, but I stayed with mine and we didn't get hit, luckily. Boy, that was a bad one.'

Sgt Walter 'Red' Rose of Service Company saw the planes and did not think a jeep parked near an ammunition truck would offer much protection, so he ran away from the column. As he bolted through the backyard of a farmhouse in darkness, he ran into a clothesline. Even though the clothesline drew blood from his forehead, he declined the offer of a Purple Heart. The next morning, when the battalion moved out, Griffin wrote, 'someplace along the day's route I saw the carcass of a cow hanging up 20 feet or so in a tree. I have never been able to figure out how the critter got up there. I have talked to others who also saw it. So it wasn't a bad dream.'

The battalion was still together as it moved toward Mayenne, so it is quite likely that out of all the cows in Normandy and trees in France, George Bussell, a driver in A Company's third platoon, witnessed the same cow. 'There was a small cliff, just not too high,' he said when I interviewed him at his home in Indianapolis in 1993, 'with trees on top. And we're going along there, driving tanks and looking around. And way up in this one tree, I mean waaay up there, there's a cow. And he was hanging by his neck right in the fork. It was like somebody put him there. He got blown up there and when he come down his head got wedged in the fork of the tree and that's what's holding him. I said, "Man oh man, look at that!"'

Task Force Weaver

'General Weaver got up on the body of a pickup truck and Colonel Randolph got up there with him,' Red Rose recalled at one of the battalion's reunions. 'There was a couple of us soldiers gathered around. And General Weaver said, "We were coming down this road, spearheading, and he and I were leading the column, when we ran into a roadblock. I hit the ditch on one side and he hit the ditch on the other." Then he said, "And there we both lay. The column had stopped. In a few minutes, Randolph says, "General, how do we expect our men to advance if we're lying here in the ditch?" He said Randolph had an old submachine gun and he started shooting that, and he said, "I jumped up out of there. I can't let this colonel show me up. And the Germans broke and run." And he pinned the Distinguished Service Cross on Colonel Randolph. I seen it pinned on him. It might have been a Silver Star.'

During the breakout from Normandy, the battalion was assigned to Task Force Weaver, named after Brig. Gen. William 'Wild Bill' Weaver, a 1912 graduate of West Point who received a Distinguished Service Cross as a major in the First World War and would earn another in the Second World War. Task Force Weaver was an armored outfit '...that was going to break out of Normandy,' Gifford said, 'and that's what we did. We went through Caen to St Lo and we headed out of St Lo toward Mayenne. As we approached, we'd stop for the night and then start out in the morning.

'There were incidents happening every day. We got to a town, I don't remember its name. We pulled into an apple orchard and they had dropped gasoline off. How they got it there I don't know. They probably dropped it off of planes or gliders during the night. We were pulled into that point to replenish our gasoline. So we had spread our tanks around, and they told us to dig a foxhole. I said, "What are we going to do with a foxhole?" We're moving all the time. But they told us we'll be here all night. So we dug foxholes. The next morning we're putting more gas in the tanks and getting replenished, and suddenly I see these airplanes going over. I was counting them. I counted 38 Messerschmitt 109s. First I saw the cross. I hollered to the guys, "Geez, look at the French crosses." They looked like the Cross of Lorraine way up in the air. Then we watched them go out of sight. What we didn't know was that they were looking for us and they found us. The next thing I know, the planes are firing, bullets are flying all through everything and we all ran for our foxhole. And when I dove in the foxhole, geez, there were two guys under me.'

I first met Jim Gifford in September of 1992 at the reunion in Harrisburg, Pennsylvania. That November, I spoke with him at length in the office of his used-car dealership in Yonkers, New York. The battalion's after-action reports note that on 4 August 1944, Company C was 'strafed by three of a flight of thirty-seven enemy planes' while in bivouac at Grand Chemin.

'In the meantime,' Gifford said, 'one of our sergeants, who was a tank driver, had gone into a tavern across the street. The people had left and there was liquor in the bar. So he went in there and he got himself a few drinks, and there were two or three infantry guys in there with him and they were drinking. They got drunk and the next thing a shot went off. And some guy told me and I ran over. The sergeant was in there and was arguing with this infantry guy over some stupid thing and he had his Tommy gun. He was waving his Tommy gun around and the goddamn thing went off. It went underneath the guy's chin and blew off the top of his head. There were bare log rafters and the top of the guy's head was stuck right up in the rafter. I'll never forget it, it was a horror. I grabbed the sergeant and he's drunk. What are you gonna do with a drunk?

'So I told a couple of guys, "Take him over and put him in that potato cellar," because I didn't know how long we were gonna be there. "Put him in that potato cellar until he sobers up. We'll have to figure out what to do with him." In the meantime, one of the infantry guys was pissed off at him and I said, "We'll straighten it out later, we've got enough troubles here without this." That afternoon we got orders to wind up the tanks. We've got to get out of here and they're sending more stuff after us. So I sent two guys over to the potato cellar and I said, "Get the sergeant out of there, we need him as a driver." As drunk as he was, we threw him in the tank and he drove his tank. Then we continued into a town called Mayenne.' Gifford said the sergeant was later killed in action, but the name he supplied did not match up with anyone on the battalion's monument at Fort Knox. According to the battalion roster, the person with that name survived the war and was living on the West Coast. I never attempted to contact him.

Somewhere between Mayenne and Le Mans, Griffin wrote in his memoir, 'as we were entering another fair-sized town, an excited call came to me from the doughboys† of the I&R platoon to come up to an intersection in the main part of town. 'Milwaukee' Lochowitz, in good Hollywood style, slid our tank around the corner where the doughboys were waiting. They pointed to some Kraut vehicles hastily moving out of town. After (Bob) Gladson fired his first round, I heard glass breaking and crashing all around us. At about the same time there was a terrific roar right beside my tank. To say that I was scared and bewildered would have been putting it mildly. What had happened was that our first round of 75-mm high explosive had created a vacuum strong enough to suck out the windows bordering the typically narrow French streets. I suppose the buildings were two or three stories high. In many cases, the owner of the business had his living quarters over his shop. I don't know how far down the street this vacuum sucked out the windows, but I do know that there was a lot of glass lying around when it was all over.

'The roar that I had heard turned out to be from Sgt Carl Pernoja's

---

† Doughboys was a First World War term, and I imagine it meant green back then. I've had people tell me 'Doughboys is the wrong term,' but that's what these fellows used, only it was interchangeable with GI. By this point the 90th Division members were pretty seasoned.

tank. He had pulled his tank alongside mine at the intersection and started firing. The muzzle blast of a tank gun fired right beside one's ear is very strong. Pernoja's crew as best that I can remember were: Carl Pernoja, Painesville, Ohio; F. L. Eaves, New Ellenton, South Carolina; Claude Taggart, Columbus, Indiana; James Wall, Louisville, Kentucky; and Everett Bays, Evans, Colorado. Later in the day, while we were sitting off the road a short distance waiting for something or other, I saw a motorcycle and a truck approaching from the general direction of Le Mans. Gladson hit the truck with his first round and it burst into flames. The truck had been loaded with oil drums. It wasn't long until we really had an impromptu Fourth of July celebration. Every now and then an oil drum would explode and go flying 50 feet or so up in the air. I can't say as to what happened to the motorcyclist or the truck driver. I must have been watching the fireworks too closely.

'Major (Ed) Hamilton called a halt to the day's march late in the afternoon. He selected a bivouac area in a small valley by a stream. Because of the confusion we had experienced during the day of having German cars and trucks drive right into our position, Capt. Adams or someone wanted a tank and some doughboys to go up a long hill to our front. We were to stand guard there while the troops were getting dug in for the night. My tank and two or three jeeps of the I&R platoon pulled up to the top of the hill. We took positions covering the road to the east. Not long after we had taken our positions, we heard the motor of an approaching vehicle. Each jeep had a .50-calibre machine gun mounted on it. The tank had three .30-calibre machine guns: one mounted coaxially with the 75-mm gun, one for the assistant driver called the 'bow gun' and one on the tank commander's hatch – normally used as an anti-aircraft weapon (originally this was a .50-calibre gun, but some tank commanders substituted a .30). All of these guns were trained on the road as we listened to the motor coming closer and closer. It was getting dusk, which made it hard to see more than 100 yards ahead. Finally a small German staff car came into view moving directly towards us. It came to within 40 yards of our position and nothing happened. I decided that I didn't want the car to pass us and go on down the hill into the bivouac area. I squeezed off a few rounds of my machine gun. Apparently everyone had been waiting for some such signal. All the guns opened fire and really riddled the little car.

'(Andy) Rego had been watching the proceedings through his periscope. He yelled that a man had got out of the car and had gone into the road ditch. After the firing stopped he wanted to be one of the first to go up to the car. Rego had been wanting a souvenir watch pretty badly. I let him go. He told how he had found one German in the car. He said that when he tried to pull the German out of the car he was only partially successful. The body had been hit with so many machine gun bullets that only the top half of the body came out when Rego pulled. The next morning as we were moving past this spot, Rego said that the second German had been found a short distance away. Having been brought up with an average amount of Christian training, this affair bothered me some because of the very low value we had for a human life. This swept away any illusions I might have had about the true nature of war. I realised that wars are not fought under the Marquis of Queensbury rules. Rather, war is a dirty, rotten business. I suppose all GIs going into combat soon make this painful decision. We would all like to think that wars are exciting or romantic affairs. It is not so.'

Fred Putnam was a bow gunner/assistant driver in C Company. Edwin Jarusz, a gunner, 'was sitting in the gunner's seat and Putnam climbed up on the back of the tank to get his Tommy gun' while on Task Force Weaver, Jim Gifford recalled. 'When he reached down to get it and lifted it out, the damn thing went off, right in the back of Jarusz's head, killing him. He never knew what hit him. And Putnam was all upset about it. I was told about it. I was in another area and they said Putnam's in bad shape, he's just killed Jarusz. So I took him aside. I said, "Look, it was an act of God. You were just the instrument of God. That was his time to go. Don't blame yourself, I don't want to hear about it." That's the way I talked to him and it kind of straightened him out.'

Jule Braatz, the A Company sergeant, lost his third lieutenant, Arnold Lund, on Task Force Weaver during the approach to Le Mans. 'Second platoon started out as point and hit the enemy at Aron at approximately 1800,' reads the after-action report for 6 Aug. 'Deployed through fields and over hedgerows after the enemy... Lt Lund's tank knocked out, possibly by 88. Tank burned. Crew evacuated, but Lt Lund wounded as he ran across field. Tank driver killed by enemy machine gun fire. Remainder of crew badly burned.'

Ironically, although Braatz was the platoon sergeant, he was leading the platoon while Lt Lund's tank was in the platoon sergeant's position at the head of the second section, which comprised the fourth and fifth tanks. Braatz said Lund asked him to lead the platoon until he was better acclimated. Lund would die of his wounds and Roger Guay, an original cavalryman, would die of his burns. Percy Bowers, who had been a horseshoer in the cavalry, was the driver killed by machine gun fire. At Fort Benning, Bowers got a 'Dear John' letter from his fiancée and lost all of his money in a crap game. Braatz did pretty well in the game. Afterwards, he bought the engagement ring Bowers had planned to give his girlfriend. Braatz's wife, Lark, was still wearing the ring when I visited them in Beaver Dam, Wisconsin in 1994, although Braatz had long since bought her a fancier replacement.

Bob 'Big Andy' Anderson, who like Bowers was a horseshoer in the cavalry, said he did not witness it himself, but heard at the time that Bowers was waving a white handkerchief when he was gunned down. 'We were going through these hedgerows,' Braatz recalled, 'and we're firing and the infantry's with us. Then pretty quick there's no infantry and when the fourth tank came through. *Wham!* They got it.'

'Everything happened so darned fast,' Ellsworth Howard, who was then the company commander, said about the loss of Lund's tank. 'We got into a fight we didn't know we were gonna get into. And it had everything under the sun. If we went around this way to outflank the Krauts, they came around that way to outflank us and we ran into each other. It was a real brawl. Lund's tank was way out there. You've got the platoon scattered all over the darn place and I couldn't keep track of all of them. Then we got word from Randolph that we're pulling out, get your platoon down here right away. I had Dixon (Forrest Dixon, the maintenance officer) looking for Lund's tank and I left him stranded up there.'

'He left me up there with two medics, trying to get Lund and the crew out of the tank,' Dixon recalled. 'Here's the tank afire. Guay was one of the crew. Guay, Percy Bowers and Lund, and I don't know who the other two were.'

Colonel Randolph decided there was one way to prevent Braatz from losing more lieutenants: put him in for a battlefield commission. Braatz turned the offer down because such a promotion would mean being reassigned to a different outfit. The Army did not want officers leading men whom they had fought beside as enlisted men, so Randolph got permission to give Braatz a commission without having to leave his platoon. Such a move was apparently a big deal and was the reason officers such as Dixon were justifiably proud. By the time the war in Europe ended, the battalion had fourteen battlefield commissions.

Braatz led the second platoon from August until the battalion was fighting in the Siegfried Line in February when he had to be evacuated due to a serious case of the 'GIs' (diarrhoea). However, his reputation for losing lieutenants did not end there. Hank Schneider, one of the original A Company sergeants, took over the platoon when Braatz was relieved. Schneider's commission came through early in March 1945 as the battalion was crossing the Moselle River for the second time in combat. The day he was commissioned, Schneider was killed by a sniper as he rode with his head exposed out of the turret.

At Mayenne, Ray Griffin wrote that the first platoon of Company C was bivouacked directly across the road from the battalion command post when 'suddenly all hell broke loose in the form of a shelling from high-velocity guns (tank guns or 88 mm). The men of the company scurried inside their tanks or dove underneath them. Of my crew, Henry Lochowicz, Milwaukee, Wisconsin; Andrew Rego, Beaver Falls, Pennsylvania; and Calvin Bolden, Birmingham, Alabama, were in the tank with me. Bob Gladson, Galesburg, Illinois, was outside somewhere.

'It was during this heavy shelling that I was privileged to see a very courageous act on the part of our battalion C.O., Lt Col George Randolph. He saw that our whole company was jammed into this small field and that some of the men were outside their tanks and that we were pretty snafued in general. He came running across the road and told Jack Sheppard (the C Company commander) to get some tanks moving. Jack called me over the radio and said to get my platoon together. I told Lochowicz to "turn it over." Soon after the motor started, Bob Gladson came flying up the front of the tank. He had been under the tank. I had Lochowicz pull over to the side of the bivouac area. I tried to spot the other tanks of my platoon. Only one had moved out with me. Sgt Cecil Brock, Buffalo, Oklahoma; Art Mencer, Fresno, Ohio; Forrest Owen, Kittrel, North Carolina; and Kenneth Jurgensen, Council Bluffs, Iowa, were the members of the crew as best I can recall. There was a tank from another platoon moving, so I called him on the radio and got him lined up with Sgt Brock and myself.

'The three tanks then took off in a general direction from where the shelling was coming from. I automatically used the tactics that had been hammered into us for so long during our training days – that of moving by "leaps and bounds." This very satisfactorily answered for me the question of why there were so many dry runs in training. After we had gone a mile or so from the bivouac area, we came to a farm. There were two women moving about apparently doing chores or something. I remember feeling a little foolish charging in with three tanks while these women were going about their business as though nothing was amiss. The shelling of the area had stopped meanwhile, thanks to some work by some of our P-47s, so Jack Sheppard radioed for us to return.

'Soon after getting back to the bivouac area, my platoon and Lt Charlie Lombardi's (third) were attached to Charley Company, 1st Battalion, 357th Regiment, 90th Infantry Division. The mission was to be the advance guard for Task Force Barth, which was part of Task Force Weaver. The mission was to capture Le Mans. Capt. Adams, Arkansas, was the infantry company C.O. and Major Hamilton (Ed Hamilton) was the 1st Battalion C.O. Adams told me where we were going and that this move wasn't going to be "by the book." We were just to take off and go as far and as fast as we could. When our tanks were loaded with as many doughboys as possible, we lined up on the road behind the I&R platoon of the infantry. We were ready to take off on what turned out to be a pretty wild ride.

'Up to this point on the move out of Normandy, our company had been positioned so that someone else had been leading the way. Now it was our turn! I found it to be quite a different matter to move down a road with the knowledge that we and the doughboys within the range of my sight were the first Allied troops to have moved over this particular road. Before it had been to just follow someone else's route. The feeling of high tension relaxed after we had passed a number of small towns without any activity outside of the cheering of the French people.

'This was to change as we approached a town of greater size. The I&R platoon was held up at the edge of town. We waited while they went to do some checking on the situation. Soon, Frenchmen were showing up. Some were members of the FFI (Free French of the Interior). Others were just plain civilians. They were all so excited that they could hardly keep one foot on the ground. It developed that there were some Krauts in the town. The decision was made to enter the town and to clean them out before continuing our advance. As we got to the main part of town I noticed an excited group of people pointing to something on the street and then pointing up a hill that led out of town. Some Krauts had just gone along this street with some sort of a vehicle in an effort to get out of town before it was too late. Their radiator had sprung a leak so that it left a trail of water on the street. I very hastily spotted four of my tanks so as to watch the different streets leading in or out of town. Along with some doughboys, I then took off up the hill following the trail of water on the street.

'When we reached the edge of town at the top of the hill, I saw a vehicle moving away from us at a range of a half-mile or so. I gave Gladson a range estimation. He fired a round of HE (high-explosive). Rego quickly reloaded. We were about to fire again when an infantry medic came running up. He had been off to the side of the road when we fired the first round. The medic said that he could see exactly where our first round had landed. It had been short. He said that he would go back and tell me where our rounds were landing. On the next round, he reported that it was over. On the third round, I saw a puff of smoke and a blast of fire come out of the vehicle. It started to burn and soon there was a big black column of smoke rising into the air. This was my crew's first "kill." I'm also sure that it was the medic's first try at directing tank fire. He was in effect a forward observer for an artillery unit. Medics are supposed to go around unarmed and refrain from all aggressive action. Despite this medic's violation of the rules of conduct, I will always have a warm spot in my heart for this spunky guy.'

As for the medal Red Rose saw General Weaver place on Colonel Randolph, that had to be one of his two Silver Stars. Randolph did receive the Distinguished Service Cross, but it was awarded posthumously. Colonel George B. Randolph was killed during the Battle of the Bulge.

12

The Deadly Pea Shooter

Bill Holt, the gunner who was injured in the tank that ran over the string of mines outside Perier, remarked that the light tank's 37-mm cannon was 'good against bicycles.' On one occasion, however, it was effective against a Mark V Panzer. When Harold Heckler was killed accidentally by a member of his crew, his place was taken by another former cavalry sergeant, Everett McNulty. 12 August would be a day marked by both tragedy and humour in D Company's history.

'The 1st Platoon moved north through Alencon with the 90th Division Reconnaissance Troop, moved through the French 2nd Armored Division and met enemy resistance at a crossroad south of Les Ragolieres,' the D Company log for that day begins. 'Sgt McNulty's tank was hit by a shot from a German Mark V Tank. Tec. 5 Ezerskis, the driver, was killed and the remaining members of the crew, Sgt McNulty and Pfc Jezuit, were seriously burned and evacuated. Sgt Lutcavish's tank, which was leading the column, immediately opened fire on the enemy tank and destroyed it by placing about eight rounds of A.P. into its side. Sgt Lutcavish's tank had meanwhile been set afire by an enemy bazooka charge in its rear.'

I never met George Mauser, another D Company veteran, but I spoke to him briefly on the phone while I was visiting Andy Schiffler. When asked about Sergeant McNulty, Mauser wept and said that McNulty was burned so badly that when he was removed from the tank, he begged to be shot. All four crew members including Pfc Arthur Roselle, who was not mentioned in the D Company log, died from their burns. Two days after the incident on 14 August, the second narrative appears in the D Company log. This one even has a title: 'Another Mark V Bit the Dust as told by S/Sgt Lutcavish.'

'While moving in the lead vehicle of a platoon of light tanks up a road north-east from Alencon, France,' the narrative begins, 'the following action took place on the 12th August 1944. Upon rounding a curve, we suddenly came upon an enemy truck loaded with Germans. Before my gunner, Cpl (Fergus) O'Farrell, could fire, the truck stopped and backed around the curve. We pursued it and directed fire with the 37-mm and coaxial guns at a group of dismounted Germans by their truck. About that time, I heard a terrific explosion. I looked to the rear and the tank directly behind me was in flames. I caught a glimpse of a whirl of dust caused by a muzzle blast to my right. Immediately, I spotted the position under an apple tree at about 125 yards away. I didn't know for sure what it was or whether it could be knocked out with my 37 mm, but knew I had to do something quick because it was already traversing its gun on to me. There was no cover or no way to go back because of the burning tank behind me.

'Again I heard an explosion and felt my tank lunge forward. A bazooka had hit me in the rear and set the rear end of the tank on fire. What a position for a church going man to be in! There was nothing else to do but to dish it out, so I directed fire on the gun position that looked like that of a tank. That gunner of mine was plenty fast. In less time than it takes to tell, he threw eight well placed rounds of A.P. into that position and had it on fire. Now we could definitely tell it was a tank, a huge one with a gun that made our 37 look like a pea shooter. While we were wiping the cold sweat from our brow, another enemy tank crossed the road about 400 yards ahead of us. We swung the turret in that direction hoping that we could chalk up another one, but the tank disappeared in the brush before the gunner could fire on it. By this time my tank was burning badly so I ordered the crew to abandon it disregarding the numbers system and we made our way back to the rest of the platoon, toot-sweet, on foot.'

As Ray Griffin's platoon approached the outskirts of Le Mans, 'I noticed something in the road ahead of us 1,500 yards or so away,' he wrote in his memoir. 'Everything that had been coming from that direction so far had been German. I had Gladson lay our 75-mm gun on it. I told him to be ready to fire at any time. Our luck of meeting cars, trucks, motorcycles, etc., had run out. Ahead of us were what we later discovered to be three self-propelled guns. A better description of a self-propelled gun would be a tank without a turret. The gun could be raised and lowered to increase or decrease its range. It couldn't be turned sideways without turning the tank chassis on which the gun was mounted.

'The Krauts fired first. I heard a nasty sharp crack right over my head. Their round hit a tree branch over our tank. I learned later that this "air" burst had wounded a doughboy on the back deck of our tank. I told Gladson to fire. Rego was on his toes and immediately reloaded the gun. I had the boys fire 10 or 15 rounds as fast as Rego could load and Gladson could fire. I told them later that our tank sounded like a big machine gun as the shells really came out in short order. Rego was injured by the recoil sometime during the fracas. He didn't let me know about it until it was all over. He had his hand inside the guardrail when Gladson fired and it was smashed a little...

'Lt Lombardi called me on the radio and wanted to know what had been going on with us. I told him the best that I could. Not much later a lot of firing of all kinds opened up behind us. So as soon as there was a lull, I radioed to Lt Lombardi and asked him what had been taking place with the third platoon. "Lom" told me that I'd have to come back and look or I wouldn't believe him. Here is what happened. There was a sharp V-junction in the road where his platoon had been sitting. The two main roads into Le Mans from the west came together at this road junction... Lt Lombardi's platoon was right at the road junction on the north road. A good-sized German unit of armor and artillery had been retreating on the south road ahead of Task Force Weaver. When it came to the road junction, Lt Lombardi's platoon and the doughboys opened fire. In a short time a flight of our good friends, the P-47 boys, showed up. The combined firing of Lombardi's platoon, the doughboys and the P-47s had wiped out the Germans.'

Stanley Klapkowski, Lieutenant Lombardi's gunner, was awarded the Silver Star for his role in the incident. Klapkowski would earn a Silver Star, a Bronze Star, and would later have to be pulled off a machine gun and placed in a straitjacket. Later in life he was a recluse, but I felt drawn to interview him as his name came up in so many stories told by people like Tony D'Arpino, Bob Rossi, Ed Spahr and Jim Gifford who were in a crew with him when their tank was knocked out in the Battle of the Bulge. The way D'Arpino described the action outside Le Mans, Lieutenant Lombardi stopped the tank at the crest of a hill with only the barrel of the 75-mm gun pointing over the rise. Down below, a column of German vehicles was approaching. Klapkowski knocked out the lead vehicle and then kept elevating the gun a little at a time and firing again. In all, some thirty vehicles were knocked out, although artillery and the P-47s took credit for some of the destruction.

A popular saying at the time went: 'Did you ever have the feeling that you wanted to stay but you had to go?' On 9 August, while A Company was moving from Le Mans to the village of Coulaines, the tanks came under artillery fire and Sam MacFarland's driver headed for the shelter of some apple trees. As he passed under one, MacFarland's head brushed up against a branch and it knocked his glasses off, breaking them. Later that day, a batch of mail caught up to the company and MacFarland learned that his wife, Harriett, had given birth to a daughter in Pittsburgh. He gathered the members of his crew and asked them to help him come up with a name. They decided on Lucky. Then, according to Tom Wood, a member of the crew, MacFarland remarked, 'Did you ever have the feeling that you wanted to go but you had to stay?'

13

They Shoot Horses
(The Falaise Gap)

Ellsworth Howard became the A Company commander when Clifford Merrill was wounded on 13 July. Of the company's original platoon leaders by the second week of August, George Tarr was killed and Ed Forrest and Frank Miller were wounded. Sgt Jule Braatz had already gone through three lieutenants. The company saw heavy fighting on the road to Le Mans after which it finally had a couple of days to regroup. The battalion after-action report for 17 August begins, 'First platoon moved in to relieve one platoon of B Company so they could refuel, etc. After moving into position, one company of infantry plus the first platoon launched an attack to take the town of Le Bourg St Leonard. The eastern edge of the town was held during the night during which time the enemy infantry infiltrated to the east flank of the platoon and to the rear.'

The way Howard remembered it, Colonel Randolph told him he needed to send a platoon of tanks to relieve a platoon of B Company tanks and that everything was quiet. After the B Company tanks pulled out, 'we had to fight our way in,' recalled Howard who was wounded in the stomach during the battle. 'Come to find out,' Howard said at one of the battalion reunions, the B Company platoon leader, Lt Jack Galvin, may have been drinking and this was possibly the reason Randolph wanted his platoon relieved.

Sam Cropanese, Joe Bernardino and Edmund Pilz were crew members in an A Company tank commanded by Eugene Crawford. At some point, George Bussell was Crawford's driver. Bussell said Crawford had perforated eardrums and was so hard of hearing that 'he couldn't hear himself fart,' and that the fellows would sometimes fall to the ground just to see him hit the dirt.

There was nothing humorous, however, on the morning of 18 August 1944. Pilz was of German descent and was calling to the Germans in the woods to surrender. Some did. During the night, he began biting his nails which made Bernardino nervous, so he told Pilz to stop it. The two argued and Bernardino said to himself he would apologise in the morning as it was a stupid thing to argue about. Cropanese said he was outside the tank having coffee with a couple of infantrymen when the first shell came in. It exploded in the air and rained shrapnel, tearing off a piece of Cropanese's lip. About the same time, an armor-piercing shell penetrated the tank, striking Pilz in the neck and killing him instantly. Bernardino, who was wounded, would be haunted for the rest of his life as he never got to apologise. Later, at the aid station, a nurse came over to Bernardino and said there was a fellow nearby who said he knew Joe. It was Cropanese, but his head was bandaged and his jaw wired shut, and Joe did not recognise him. When Sam managed to communicate who he was, Joe said with a lump in his throat, 'Oh, I knew it was you, Sammy, I was only kidding.'

While A and B Company were fighting in Le Bourg-St-Léonard, the tanks of C Company were on a hill above the valley looking down on what was probably the largest killing field of the Second World War, a sight the tankers would compare to the televised scenes on the road from Kuwait to Iraq during Operation Desert Storm. Instead of a miles-long skein of abandoned and destroyed mechanised vehicles, the Falaise Gap was filled with dead horses and soldiers. 'It was a mess,' Bussell recalled. 'After we got through, Dixon said, "Come on, boys. Down here to the road and see what you've done." So we walked through the hedgerows and fields and got down to the road. And no matter which way you looked, there were German vehicles just bumper to bumper, burning, and oh hell, we wiped out the whole Seventh Army. And two of the guys in my outfit got the damn Seventh payroll and I didn't know what it was. One guy says, "Here, you want some money?"

'"I don't want none of that damn paper," I said.

'Sheee! Finally, Patton called it all back in. But boy, some of them got away with it. I think this fellow sent enough money home that his old lady bought a big fur coat.'

I never met Jack Galvin, the B Company officer who was credited with going down into the Falaise Gap and returning with 1,100 German prisoners. But at the 1996 reunion in Pittsburgh, I was speaking with Cleo Coleman who had been a gunner in B Company and I asked if he could tell me anything about it. 'I was right there,' Coleman said. 'Sergeant (Les) Vink, he was my tank commander and there was one German soldier who came out with a white flag. He comes up to Captain Galvin. He said, "I believe there's 200 or so over in the woods there wanting to give up." They were throwing in artillery, everything they had, in that little forest. And he said, "They will surrender if you'll go back with me." And he agreed to do it. He takes two or three doughboys with him. And Vink told me, "Now you keep your eyes right on them. After they get inside the woods, if they're not out within ten minutes, we're going in after them."

'I was really scared. I said to myself, "You're crazy going in there with all those Germans in there."

'Well, before ten minutes, here comes Galvin and the officer with the bunch. He must have been a German colonel. He comes out marching them in ranks and up there are tanks. It must have been two or three hundred yards from us. And he's marching them up there and he gives them orders to halt. In the meantime, there was an American boy. He comes out of the ranks over to us. He'd been a prisoner of the Germans and he was going under that barrage. He was taking the same thing the Germans were and survived. As soon as they hauled him in front of us, he steps out, he was tickled to death. He said you don't know about what I went through. I went through as much as they have. I was right there, scared to death.'

I met Orlando 'Lindy' Brigano and his wife, Lucy, at the first reunion I went to at Niagara Falls. On my drive home, I saw them at a service plaza and we chatted. Several years later I visited Brigano, who was a radio operator in Headquarters Company, and his buddy Paul Wannemacher, who was a loader in the Headquarters Company tank with a bulldozer attachment. 'Tuesday, Aug. 22. Bivouac north-west of Nonant le Pin ... Section 1 made patrol of investigation in valley of captured German vehicles,' Brigano said, reading from a report he had brought home from the war. 'They were knocked out and everything. We had to go in there and make they didn't use them as booby traps. I'll never forget the time at the Falaise Gap I saw this German soldier, an officer, laying on the side of the road. His gun was there. He was fully dressed and everything. Nobody made an attempt to go over and get a souvenir because it was too obvious at the time that this guy was too easy picking, because it was nothing for them to booby trap a person. We just left him alone.'

'What other things did you see down there?' I asked.

'Well, I'll tell you, it got to the point and I think the weather was kind of warm at the time, wasn't it?'

'It was brutal,' Wannemacher replied.

'The animals were bloated right up. See, we had to close up the gap. That's what our job was and that's what we did. We closed it up. And while we were going through the animals, cows, horses, just bloated. And I don't know who it was who took his knife and took a poke. I think it was a cow that was there. Oh my God! The stench was so bad... We grabbed hold of him and we went like hell to get away, that's how bad it was. They had horse-drawn vehicles. It got to the point where they were losing all their mechanised stuff. A lot of their artillery was horse-drawn. All these dead animals, plus the German soldiers, too. And they were really puffy because of the heat. It was really, really hot.'

'Is there anything later in life that you can compare the smell to?' I asked.

'I don't think so. To me, the stench was so bad that you can't explain it.'

'In later life,' Wannemacher said, 'if you might see one dead animal, that's not unusual. But if you saw a field with hell, I don't know, it might have been 300, for example, in that kind of heat, and the stench of 300 dead animals that have been lying there for a couple of days, it's just stifling.'

'Let's put it this way, if you're driving along the road in the summertime and you saw a raccoon or something that's been bloated up, that's just how these animals looked, but naturally bigger frames.'

'Huge.'

'I wouldn't suggest for you to go over and poke a dead animal just to find out what it smells like,' Brigano said. 'It's pretty bad.'

'You don't remember who did that?'

'No, but we could have killed him.'

The day after the battle, Jim Gifford recalled, 'It started to drizzle and we organised a whole bunch of guys, and their job was to just go down into the Falaise Gap and shoot wounded horses. The Germans were using horses to draw their caissons, these towed guns, and these poor horses were catching hell. Some of them died instantly, some were injured and some were just laying down with their heads up. It killed me to see that. I remember one horse, he had a shell in his shoulder. It was sticking out, a big round shell. It was about ten inches long and four or five inches of it were sticking out of his shoulder, and he's standing there. He had a shattered leg and he's eating the grass. He's not even jumping around or anything. He's just standing there.'

'At Falaise, I remember sitting alongside C Company tanks and just watching those tanks, the gunpowder, the firing,' said Major Clegg 'Doc' Caffery, 'and these Germans going from west to east along that road, and the tanks were just shooting. The next day we went down there, you could almost walk from corpse to corpse there were so many bodies. And horses. I went down there and it was complete destruction. It was awesome to see what our artillery, our tanks and everybody else was shooting down there. There were several horses. I said, "Let me put this one horse out of his misery," because it was in pain and just out of it. So I got out my .45 and I put it up to his head and I shot it, and he shook his head and ran off. Either the shell was bad or I didn't hit the vital spot, but the horse was shell-shocked, out of his mind. And I thought I was going to be kind to him. I don't think the .45 calibre slug went into his head. He just shook his head and left. I said damn, "I'm not gonna try this again."'

Although C Company spent much of the battle on the high ground overlooking the Falaise Gap, it encountered hard fighting on the way to Chambois. When the lead tank of the second platoon was hit, one badly wounded crew member, Rex Smallwood, was left in a ditch by the side of the road where he was found the following morning. He was still breathing according to Don Knapp, the tank commander of the second tank, but died soon after. The tank's driver, Sidney Henderson, was listed as missing in action and would later be declared dead. The platoon leader, Lt Leo Hellman, took over Knapp's tank and Knapp rode on the top. Hellman apparently was badly shaken. Three weeks later, he would be reassigned due to battle fatigue.

As A Company's third platoon was leaving the Falaise Gap, Duane Miner of Duluth, Minnesota, a loader, became the third battalion member to be killed by an accidental burst of machine gun fire. 'We were right ahead of that particular tank,' said Neal Vaughn, the tank's gunner. 'We were heading back to the company area. Miner and I were both standing up in the turret when the battle was over. I suppose anything could have happened as far as the gun that shot him. The gun was still loaded and somebody just barely hit that solenoid.'

Dess Tibbitts was the driver of the tank behind Vaughn's. Roy Sharpton was the assistant driver/bow gunner, but he was up in the loader's seat in the turret. 'We had our hatches open because the fighting was all over,' Tibbitts recalled. 'The coaxial machine gun was still loaded and Sharpton accidentally stepped on the solenoid. And when he did, it went *bup-bup-bup-bup-bup!* Five shells or three went through Miner just that quick. With that machine gun you touch that solenoid, you can't get off quick enough. I thought when Sharpton got killed, well, that ends that story. Nobody will ever know what happened. Who told you that story, Goldstein?'

'As a matter of fact we had a driver in my platoon, Duane Miner,' Goldstein said when I interviewed him and Tony D'Arpino at D'Arpino's home in Milton, Massachusetts, in 1992. 'He was married, tall, a handsome-looking kid. In back of the driver, up above, in the turret, you've got your 75 mm, you've got your gunner, tank commander and your loader. Sometimes the machine gun would get so hot from firing that if you don't open up the cover, she's gonna keep firing. And he's sitting down below. He got up, opened up the hatch and someone left the cover on the machine gun in the tank behind him and it fired. It killed him. That's how accidents happen.'

Goldstein was in the third platoon and was wounded the day before, but learned of Miner's death after he returned to the battalion. 'He and I were standing up in the turret together,' Vaughn said. 'The last words he said were, "Get me out of here," and I ducked down in. I told the tank driver to stop and I got him out, and a medical jeep came by. It was right after they closed the Falaise Gap.'

14

Mairy

After the Falaise Gap, the 712th Tank Battalion headed toward Paris, but when they were near Fontainebleau, 'we opened up our lines and let the French under Charles de Gaulle go through,' Jim Gifford recalled. 'We let them take Paris for two reasons. One, for French morale, and secondly, they could talk French.' He was kidding, of course. I think. While Paris was being liberated by the French 2nd Armored Division, the 712th and the 90th Division headed towards the First World War battlefield of Verdun and the towns of Hayange and Briey. The battalion was 'moving, moving, moving,' recalled Forrest Dixon, the maintenance officer, and each of its five tank retrievers was towing a disabled tank. Dixon told Colonel Randolph that if another tank broke down it would have to be abandoned as there was nothing left to tow it with. He pleaded for a few hours so the mechanics could get to work. Ed Stuever, the Service Company sergeant, often bragged that his mechanics could change the engine in a tank in three to four hours. Sometimes, it was simply a matter of removing the engine from a tank and replacing it with a new engine shipped from the States. When the crate was opened, Dixon said the engine was accompanied by a pack or two of cigarettes for the boys performing maintenance on the front. Although I did not attend the 1986 battalion reunion at Fort Knox, the keynote speaker was Col Vladimir Kaye (who changed his surname from Kedrovsky after the war), the battalion's third and final commander. In his speech, he described Dixon, the maintenance officer, as usually having his shoelaces untied and having three lit cigarettes on the go: one in an ashtray, one in his hand and the other dangling from his lips. The part about the shoelaces was not true, Dixon insisted in the hospitality room at a later reunion.

On the evening of 7 September 1944, Colonel Randolph told Dixon to get his men ready as the battalion was to stop for the night. On one tank, Dixon had his crew remove the engine in the evening, so that in the morning it could be replaced. A little after 2 a.m., however, a battle that the battalion's unit history refers to as the 'night counterattack' broke out. One veteran said he looked at his watch when the firing started and it was 2.11 a.m. The firing subsided after one to two hours of chaos. Dixon then laid out his bedroll and closed his eyes. 'I'd been up for nearly 48 hours straight,' he said when I pressed him for details of the incident for which he was awarded the French Croix de Guerre, 'and the Service Company boys were very shaken up, so I thought if they saw me go to sleep it would help to calm them down.' That, of course, is not why he received the Croix de Guerre, but more about that in a moment.

George Bussell, the tank driver, was standing guard when 'I heard this stuff coming down the road,' Bussell recalled. 'I could tell by the tracks it wasn't ours. The noise was altogether different. They had steel tracks and we had rubber. I squatted down there by a tree and this outfit came down the road, and they stopped. And the commander, he was sticking out of the hatch. The 90th Division had a sign there, Christ, as big as this wall. Red and white, it read 90th Division artillery C.P. and that's what the tank stopped and was looking at. And some doughboy, I don't know who he was, took a shot at this guy in the tank, but he missed him. And boy, when he missed him, hell broke loose and tanks started rolling in.'

'We heard tanks coming,' Jim Gifford said, 'and pretty soon here in the moonlight there was a column of tanks. There was a blacktop road there and we had tanks on both sides of it. I ran up to the road with E. L. Scott and I told him to grab a bazooka. He and I ran up to the edge of the road and we were going to wait for that one tank as he came down and blast him. And as he came down, Scott was pretty cool, he had it on his shoulder and we fired. The tank stopped and tanks on both sides of the road started firing at him. He turned and started firing at us, and the next thing there were tanks firing all over the place in the moonlight.'

The German armored column, which turned out to be the 106th Panzer Brigade with tanks and armored personnel carriers, passed through the tanks of A Company. Lieutenant Harry Bell, the officer Joe Bernardino confused with George Tarr, often chided his assistant driver, John McDaniel, of Paragould, Arkansas, as McDaniel took his shoes off before going to sleep. Obviously, McDaniel had never seen the movie *Battleground* – the Battle of the Bulge had not yet been fought, less a movie been made about it – in which a grizzled soldier reaches out of his foxhole for his boots and is killed by a sniper. 'For one reason or another I just couldn't sleep with them on,' McDaniel said at one of the battalion reunions. 'Lieutenant Bell would say, "We're gonna get into it, we're gonna get attacked sometime and you're not gonna have your shoes on." I said, "I'll put them right here beside me and I can put my shoes on in a hurry. I don't have to lace them up." One of the kitchen people from this little command post fired on these tanks and when he did, boy, there was just a terrible commotion and it woke us all up. I reached for my shoes where they ought to be and they weren't there. So I got in the tank barefoot.'

Bell told the driver, William Swartzmiller, to 'fire it up.' McDaniel continues: 'and when he fired that tank up, we had an advantage in that we had an electrical turret and they had to traverse theirs by hand. But they were facing right straight towards us so they didn't have much turning to do. They fired and hit us in our suspension system. We couldn't move the tank and Bell said, "Bail out!" I took off across the field because I knew about where Lester was.' (Lester O'Riley became the third company commander of A Company after Ellsworth Howard was wounded at the Falaise Gap.) While McDaniel was running, he said, 'Somebody hollered at me and said, "Are you American?"

'"Yes," I replied.'

'"Come over here." (Pointing towards a woodland area, it was General Devine, the artillery commander of the 90th Division, accompanied by his colonel.)

'"My company commander is right up here."

'"You just stay here with me."

'Then he and the colonel were talking. He said, "When I woke up, I reached to wake up my driver and he wouldn't move. He was dead."

'As soon as it got light, I went over there and that boy was laying there just like he was asleep. He had a little hole right in his forehead.

'There was no more blood than there'd be on the end of your little finger. I guess that hot shrapnel pierced his skull and seared that blood. He looked like he wasn't twenty years old. I had heard General Devine tell his colonel about the driver. So I stayed with Devine, and boy, when you get in combat like that, it will really work on your nervous system and your stomach, too. I told him, "I've got to use the bathroom," and he said, "Go right back over here." And he said there's some digging equipment. So I went over and dug a place, used it, covered it and came back. I stayed with him till it got light and when it did I asked him, "Do you reckon we're gonna get out of here?" It was cloudy at that time. He said, "Just as soon as these clouds clear out, we'll get 'em." He was so cool and calm, I was really surprised. After it got daylight, I started toward the tank and met old Bell. I said, "I couldn't find my shoes this morning."

'"These are not mine I've got on," he said.

"They're mine! I thought they look like them." And he pulled them off and gave them to me and then he went barefoot."'

Many battalion veterans I spoke to over the years thought the 106th Panzer Brigade unwittingly stumbled into the artillery command post, which was well behind the front lines, while travelling at night. That was not the case. According to the Dutch military historian Ruud Bruyns, the 106th Panzer Brigade was formed in the summer of 1944 with some of the latest German equipment. It had a strength of thirty-six Mark V Panzers, eleven Panzer IV tank destroyers, anti-aircraft guns and armored infantry personnel carriers. The commander of the 106th was Colonel Franze Bake, a legend among German tank commanders who was awarded the Knights Cross for valour on the Eastern Front. In civilian life, Bake was a dentist.

According to Bruuns, Patton's 3rd Army was looking for a way to cross the Moselle River and the Germans had fended off several attempts to cross the river on 5-6 September. 'After this little success,' Bruuns wrote, 'the commander of the (German) First Army, Colonel-General Otto von Knobelsdorff, felt confident enough for a counter-strike on the stalled American forces. When Hitler approved to release Panzer-Brigade 106 for forty-eight hours, Knobelsdorff had his armored fist with which he wanted to attack the exposed flank of the US 90th Infantry Division north of Thionville. Knobelsdorff and Bake were both seasoned officers who gained vital experience in Russia. They were confident that an armored blow on the exposed flank and deep infiltration within American ranks would cause enough panic to make their units collapse and run, like the Russians would in similar circumstances.' However, 'instead of fleeing in confusion when confronted with this night attack with tanks,' Bruuns wrote, 'the Americans rallied and started to counter the threat.'

Following the initial encounter with A Company, the German armored column entered the C Company area in darkness but for the light of the moon. 'C Company was on one side of the road and we were on the other,' recalled Eugene Sand, the Service Company mechanic. 'Service Company was in a low area and kind of a flatter area than C Company, but there was this pretty tall hill with small evergreen trees on it between us. We went up on this hill to stand guard that night. We just took our bedrolls and our guns. Six of us went because we always stood two hours on and four off. We had an old windup alarm clock that had a white face and black hands. We always took it when we stood guard because without making a light you could almost distinguish the time unless it was an awful dark night. After you've been out there for two hours, your eyes were adjusted to the darkness and you could see that in a tank pretty well.

'When that column came through there, C Company started shooting at them and everything they missed in that column landed on that hill where we were. We decided in one big hurry we're gonna get off of this hill. We didn't even roll our bedrolls up. We just jumped up and gathered them together. Adam Kochan picked up the alarm clock and started running as hard as he could to get down off that hill because the fire was coming in. He's got the alarm clock and is running through those trees and he tripped the alarm, and he never stopped to shut it off. He ran all the way down that hill with that alarm clock ringing in the middle of a black night.'

Ray Griffin wrote in his memoir that on 6-7 September, C Company was '...patrolling through the Argonne Forest in search of German troops and ammunition dumps.' On the afternoon of 7 September, he received orders to rejoin the battalion. It was dark by the time they arrived at the bivouac area. 'Not long after we settled down,' he wrote, 'a fierce battle broke out about a kilometre away... I believe that one A Company tank was knocked out during this night battle. The fighting lasted two or three hours. It was either during or soon after this night battle that I received orders to move my platoon to the 90th Division (artillery) C.P., which was located in the woods on top of a hill. We moved into position along the north side of a wooded area. It was still night time. We camouflaged the tanks with tree limbs and branches and then waited for it to get light.

'When it did get light enough to see that the tanks at the bottom of the hill were indeed German (Mark V Panthers), I had my gunner, Bob Gladson, lay our gun on the closest German tank. He fired. Our 75-mm AP round bounced off the German tank. My loader, Andy Rego, reloaded and we fired again with the same result. I believe we fired three or four rounds of armor piercing ammo at this German tank. None of our rounds caused him any damage. In the meantime, the German tank had picked up our position from the muzzle blast of our tank gun. He laid his gun on our tank and began firing. After my tank was hit, it began to burn. Gladson, Rego, Calvin Bolden and myself were able to get out.

'Henry Lochowicz, the driver, couldn't get his hatch open as our tank gun was directly over his hatch. I ran around in front of the tank and yelled at Lochowicz to crawl back through the turret and get out through the tank commander's hatch. He did this. Outside of some minor cuts and bruises everyone was OK. Sometime after our tank was hit and started to burn, my platoon sergeant, Frank Bores, came running up to the tank and crawled up on the back deck to see if anyone was still inside. The tank was burning fiercely by now. I called to Sergeant Bores and he came over to my foxhole. I later wrote up a recommendation for an award for Sgt Bores for his action. It seemed to me that it had taken a lot of courage to crawl up on a burning tank while it was still under enemy fire. The award was not approved because I hadn't shown any definite accomplishments.'

'Thirteen German tanks came down this road and they spied us on a hill,' John Zimmer, the loader in another C Company tank, recalled at the 1992 reunion. 'Out of five tanks, they got two of us. Those guys came down this road at night, pitch dark night, and when it got daylight, then they spied us. The tank I was in got hit twice while I was in it and twice after I got out. There was a ditch there and I got in the ditch, and I saw it hit the second time after I got out.'

Back in Normandy, when Harold Heckler was killed by a burst from the machine gun of his own tank, his entire crew, including the member who accidentally shot him, was killed a couple of weeks later. Roy Sharpton, the tanker who accidentally shot and killed Duane Miner after the battle of the Falaise Gap, was killed later on. It seems to be a statistical anomaly, but Fred Putnam, the loader who accidentally killed Edwin Jarusz in Normandy, was killed in the second C Company tank to be knocked out at Mairy. George Peck, the tank commander, was wounded in his legs and evacuated.

'We were in a copse of woods around Briey,' recalled Don Knapp, the commander of another C Company tank. 'Good tank country because of a lot of visibility and little patches of woods. I had guard duty. It was a bright moonlit night and I hear this equipment coming. I said, "That doesn't sound like ours," and all of a sudden yonder they come. It's an armored German outfit with a lot of their self-propelled stuff and armored personnel carriers. Not infantry. There was nobody walking. They're all talking away in German in the middle of the night and the tanks are rolling by so I bail out quick. I went and got Sheppard (Capt. Jack Sheppard, the company commander). He was partially awake and I said, "Shep, there's some Krauts coming down here, a whole mess of them." So we run back to my tank, which had the best visibility, then there's another one alongside of it. And he says, "We've only got about three tanks with field of fire in that direction. They're going past our position. We'd better let them ride." So then they went and shot up the headquarters outfit to hell. And the next morning, that's when Tambaro caught it." (Ralph Tambaro was the driver of the second C Company tank to be hit, the one in which Putnam was killed.)

'We were on the side of a hill and we were putting brush on to camouflage the tank and I heard *Whang!* His tank was just above mine, higher on the hill and sideways. And I look out and in the mist I see a German tank, maybe 2,000 yards away and I saw another flash. And as I saw the other flash, Tambaro goes running by and he had blood and stuff all over him. And I said to myself in my subconscious mind, "How the hell is he running with his guts all over him?" But it wasn't his. It was the guy next to him, Putnam. I said to Babe (Wes Harrell, Knapp's driver), "Never mind this goddamn brush, let's get the hell out of here." So we pulled out with brush and all because I think if we'd have pulled up on that hill we'd have got nailed too. I don't think a 75 would have taken him out and he was shooting an 88 and an 88 will take us out. If you catch him on the side you can get him, but he was aiming right at us. It looked like a Panther to me and that was one of their good tanks. And it had a hell of a gunner, he was laying it in close to us. So we pulled out of there and took up another position. We went down a road and took a position with hull defilade. Okay, so here come some more tanks down the hill and they didn't even see us. And we nailed them. We were all firing. And this is another picture in my mind's eye. I think we caught a Panther, somebody did, and it was on fire. And there was an explosion. There was a smoke ring coming out of it and at the same time out of the turret was a German in that black outfit. It blew him right out of the tank and he almost went through the smoke ring.

'About that time, Major Kedrovsky showed up in his jeep. He was so happy that we nailed them and he looked up at me and I think he said "Knapp, well done." But I hadn't done most of the shooting. Maybe it was Montoya or whoever it was, some gunner really nailed them. That's what I remember about that breakthrough. We were involved, but there must have been some bigger stories in the back there where they shot the hell out of headquarters. But that was our little part of it and I remember Tambaro. I said to him I wanted it cleared up. "You were the driver, weren't you?" And I said, "Who was your bog?" He couldn't think of it and it finally came to him. And he said "Putnam." And you know, when he left here, he's not a very demonstrative person, he wrapped his arms around me. Right here, today. After all these years.'

'Mairy was a little crossroad in France,' recalled Clegg 'Doc' Caffery. 'We went into a bivouac there one afternoon. The artillery command post was about 2 miles to the north of us and they had two tank companies protecting them. We were in a wooded area. Early the next morning, about 3 o'clock, I heard a 75 mm go off. And minutes later, Les O'Riley (the A Company commander at the time) comes on the tank radio telling Colonel Randolph that he is firing on a German armored column. Things quieted down and then at daybreak, two of these German vehicles, they were light tanks, Mark IVs, came into our area. I was in the wooded area with the headquarters vehicles and Dickie (Forrest Dixon) was not too far away with Service Company. I was hiding behind a tree and I saw Dickie climb into this inoperable tank with no engine and with battery power, he knocks off one of these tanks.' The Service area was in the centre of the battalion as, 'we had all the gas and ammunition with us and we needed the protection,' Dixon said when I pressed him for details about the Croix de Guerre.

'The shooting started about 2 a.m. Of course, we were all alert and wondering what was going to happen. I don't remember why but the Service Company boys were just very, very excited. It looked like they just didn't know what was going on and they didn't know what they should do. I had been awake for two days practically and I thought, "Well, I'm going to just put my bedroll down by the halftrack where the radio is and see if I can get some sleep," and maybe that would at least quiet them down a little bit. This was probably 4 o'clock. The shooting had stopped. Nobody knew there were other tanks in the area. So I got my bedroll and told the sergeant in charge of the radio, "If anything happens, wake me up quick." He said okay. And nothing happened. I got up the next morning, I think it was about breakfast time. Our crew was working on a tank – they had the motor out – when someone yelled "German tanks!" And everybody took off. I can't blame them for that. I thought, "Oh, shit." So I got in the tank. Besides, all the gasoline and ammunition was in our area. One boy stayed with me. I don't know who it was, but he was next to me and I said, "Do you know how to load a gun?"

'"I think so," he replied.

'"You get the gun loaded and I'll see if we can't get one of those tanks." There was one round of ammunition in the ready rack and he couldn't get it out. I said, "Let me try." So he took off. I put the round in the gun and I then thought, "I won't be able to turn the turret," because the boys were supposed to disconnect the electricity when they took out an engine. When I hit that traversing box, I didn't expect to hear it groan. It kind of groans when the gun turns. I was a little bit surprised. I thought my boys obeyed me better than that. But I'm glad they didn't. I had the round of ammunition in and the turret turned. I then got to thinking, "I'll bet the sight isn't lined up with the barrel." So I thought I'd just better wait. I kept it pointed at the lead tank and when it got about 50 yards from me, that's when he saw me and began to turn to get his gun in my direction, and I let him have it. I then grabbed the radio and I hollered, "Sam, I need your help!" That was Sam Adair. He had the assault guns and I knew that the assault guns were just up a little ways. The Germans saw the assault guns coming and they stopped right quick and everybody got out with their hands up. I stayed right inside the tank. I didn't want them to know I was the only damn fool there.'

'They just came attacking right across a field,' said Capt. Jack Reiff, one of the battalion's two medical officers, 'and there was a tank sitting there. Dixon jumped in this tank and he starts shooting at this German tank. This German lieutenant gets out, one of his arms was badly injured. I'm speaking to him in broken German. I said, "Alles kaput." He replied, "Nein, nein." We're still speaking in broken German. "Well, you're certainly out of action." And he said, "Which bone is it, Doctor? The radius or the ulna?"'

Although its performance under harrowing circumstances was exemplary, the 712th Tank Battalion alone cannot claim sole credit for the victory. The 773rd Tank Destroyer Battalion, which, like the 712th, was attached to the 90th Division, contributed heavily to the rout as did infantry bazooka teams. Nevertheless, according to Bruyns, 'at the end of its first day of combat, Panzer-Brigade 106 was routed and had lost most of its tanks and infantry in the process. At least 750 men were taken prisoner and twenty-one tanks and tank destroyers of the initial forty-seven were lost, next to more than sixty halftracks.' The brigade, he wrote, 'ceased to exist as a unit capable of any offensive operations.'

15

Gypsies and Blueberry Pie

'Dear Mom,' Flora Brantley inscribed in a blank notebook that she gave her mother, Vera Louise Forrest McCarthy Beckley, for Christmas in 1977. Vera Forrest was the younger sister of Ed Forrest, the A Company lieutenant. 'Consider this not a gift for you, but a gift from you to your great-grandchildren someday.'

'About five months before I arrived into this world,' Vera began her memoir, 'early one September morning, my mother baked two blueberry pies and put them in her pantry. She kept the shade down so the pantry would stay cool. Now at the time this event took place, those pies were cold and the door was shut so that no one outside of Dad and Mother knew those pies were in there. Dad was sitting on the front porch of our home in Hartsville, Massachusetts, late in the afternoon. Mother was standing inside the screen door talking to him, when some gypsies came along in several horses and buggies. Dad told Mother to lock the screen and also the back door, which she did. Then she came back and stood inside to listen to what they had to say.

'One short, fat, dirty woman gypsy got out and waddled up to the front steps and said, "I'll tell your fortune for one of those two blueberry pies you've got in your pantry."

'Mother and Dad were dumbfounded. Mother asked, "How do you know I have two blueberry pies in there?"

'"I know many things and I'll tell your fortune for one of those pies."

'Mother said "No," but Dad said, "Yes, tell mine." She did and here's what she said: "You were married to this woman, Flora is her name, on 19 February 1909, and you have one child, a sickly boy. You lost one, about two years ago, and now you'll soon have another child; a girl this time. She'll be a healthy one, blue eyes and brown curly hair; a different child from her blond-haired sickly brother."

'Mother was so astonished and said, "Go on."

'The old gypsy continued, "Four years after the girl is born, you'll have another child, a boy, and after that your husband will be very sick. And the sickness will keep him out of the war."

'Mother laughed and the old lady scowled at her.

'She went on, "Hard times will be in those days. Then after he recovers, good times will come. Then your fifth child, another boy, will be born."

'Then she turned to Dad and said, "Something terrible is going to happen."

'No more would she say, so Mother went and got her a pie and gave it to her and she went on her way. Forgotten was her tale until many years passed.'

Ed Forrest, Vera's brother, was drafted in April 1942 and was an officer when his kid brother, Elmer, was inducted two years later. 'If you want to get ahead in this man's army,' Ed wrote in a letter to Elmer, 'you've got to be a screwball.' He may have used slightly stronger language. A third brother, Warren, his parents' fifth child, died at the age of thirteen of peritonitis that set in after he was struck in the stomach during a snowball fight. When Ed was fourteen, he moved out of his parents' home following the death of his mother. He blamed her death on his father's drinking. Ed was working for an Episcopalian minister in Stockbridge, Massachusetts, doing odd jobs, and the minister – the Revd Edmund Randolph Laine – gave him a room in the parish house of St Paul's Episcopal Church and proceeded to raise him like a son. He tried to adopt Ed, but Ed's father would not allow it. Elmer referred to Revd Laine as an 'old batch' – or bachelor – when I met Elmer at his home on a Sunday after church in Lee, the town next to Stockbridge in 1995. He said Laine never married and lived with an elderly housekeeper, Jessica French, who was known as Aunt Jess.

Ed transferred to Williams High School in Stockbridge and went on to attend Clark University in Worcester, Massachusetts, Laine's alma mater. Stockbridge was the summer resort community of many important and wealthy people and when Ed had to drop out of college for a year because he could not afford the tuition, Laine convinced one of the parishioners, Mrs Merwin, to sponsor the remainder of his education. After graduating, Ed taught high school at Williams for a year or two and then went to work as a clerk at the local bank.

'Wishing one was never born is rather foolish,' Vera Forrest wrote in the notebook her daughter gave her, 'but I have wished I could of been born with a little more luck and happiness. I was born on 23 February 1913 in a very small town called Hartsville near Lake Buel. The day I was born, my Dad helped recover the body of one of his best friends. The men had been ice fishing and drinking hard cider to keep warm when this man fell in and went under the ice. One life passed away as another entered this world. I was the third child of my parents' marriage. Mother had lost one between my oldest brother, Edward Lester, and I ... I was a healthy young one, more so than Edward, who had stomach trouble all his life.'

What Ed lacked in physical prowess, he made up for with persistence, determination and intelligence. At Williams High, he played on a state championship basketball team. At Clark University, he was the goalie on the soccer team, managed the tennis team and won a basketball free-throw shooting contest. Ed looked 'totally out of place with a steel helmet on,' his platoon sergeant, Bob Hagerty, said when I visited him in Cincinnati in 1992. Ed 'was so thin his Adam's apple would bob up and down when he spoke. He wanted to do his job and do it well, but he wouldn't strike fear into you if you looked at him.'

One night in Normandy, only a couple of days after the 712th was committed to battle, Hagerty recalled, Lieutenant Forrest gathered his tank commanders together. He had a map and went over the next day's objectives. The commanders in his platoon at that point would have included Reuben Goldstein, Hagerty and the platoon sergeant, Charles Fowler. Then Forrest asked Hagerty to 'take a little walk' with him to reconnoiter the territory they were going to cover. 'We almost ran into an armored vehicle,' Hagerty said. 'All of a sudden there was this dark hulk and I thought, "God almighty, what have we done? This is the end of it for us." The thought went through my mind, "It must be awful being a prisoner." All we had were little sidearms and we're in front of this vehicle. It was a reconnaissance vehicle with a 37-mm gun and it was German. You could tell from the markings. Ed studied this vehicle and he realised it had been knocked out. But we didn't know that right away and it scared the hell out of me.'

A few days later, Ed volunteered to take his first section – three tanks – to see if he could 'stir things up,' according to his captain at the time, Clifford Merrill. The three tanks, with no infantry support, probed nearly 3 miles into enemy territory. When they turned to come back, they came under fire. 'Buddy, we was coming to hell,' is the way George Bussell, Forrest's tank driver, remembered the mission. Bussell had spread the governor on his tank and 'could outrun a jeep,' he recalled. Neal Vaughn, a gunner, was also on the mission. One of the tanks ran over a mine and Forrest's tank was hit in the suspension by an artillery shell, but all three tanks made it back. On the way, they knocked out one German tank, disabled another and killed at least twenty-five of the enemy according to the battalion's after-action reports. Bussell, upon turning a corner, saw three parked motorcycles. 'I ran over them,' he said. When I realised that both Bob Hagerty and Reuben Goldstein were in Lieutenant Forrest's platoon, I asked them for details of the incident, but Goldstein was in the second section and Hagerty's hand was injured by a hatch cover falling on it, a common injury among tank commanders prior to the mission.

'As I grew older and learned to talk and walk,' Vera Forrest wrote in her memoir, 'I found one has to fight for what one gets out of life. Edward had learned that if he fussed or cried, he got what he wanted from Mother. Dad saw through this and many times spoke to Mother about it and told her she favoured Edward too much. She, of course, denied it. Later, if Edward did something wrong, he'd blame me and she would spank me. One incident, one of the first I can remember, was when we were playing outside. Mother was preparing whitewash to do over the walls in the chicken house. She had to go inside for a few minutes, so she put her pail of whitewash down and told us to be careful, not to get any dirt in it. If she hadn't of said anything it probably wouldn't of occurred to Edward to do it. But as he was playing in the dirt, he got up and put two great handfuls of dirt in her pail. He was quietly playing with something else when Mother came back out and discovered it. She was furious. She asked who did it. Edward shrugged his shoulders and pointed to me. I was still playing with dirt. I still hadn't learned to talk very plain. Well I was spanked, which delighted Edward.'

'On 27 July 1944, we were up near some apple orchards and we got a barrage,' said Reuben Goldstein, who was caught outside his tank with Lieutenant Forrest. 'The first thing you do is take cover. The safest place is under the tank, but Ed couldn't get back fast enough to his tank, so we went in the bushes in the hedgerow. I jumped in. I've got my arm around him and they were still shelling. We're getting it and you're praying nothing hits you. But Ed got hit and I didn't know it, because when I said, "Okay, Ed, everything's okay, let's get going," he was hurt. So we put him on a stretcher and we got him on the road near a first aid station and they took him away.'

About a month later, while Elmer Forrest was in England with the 30th Infantry Division, he received a cable from his father stating Ed was wounded. 'I went to a Catholic priest and I said I had a brother that was wounded. He's somewhere in England, but I have no idea where. He said to give him Eddie's serial number and rank. Then he said, "I'll see what I can do." That night, a runner came over and said, "If you'll be in the chaplain's office tomorrow morning, the chaplain will tell you about your brother." The next morning I was there bright and early. The chaplain got on the telephone and he called the hospital where Eddie was and they got hold of him. He had seventeen pieces of shrapnel in his body, but he was able to get around. "Can you get a weekend pass?" he asked.

'We arranged to meet in Bristol. I got a truck ride in and he got us a hotel room, and we spent that weekend together. And I have to laugh. We'd be walking down the street and somebody would salute, because he had on an officer's uniform and he'd say, "Same to you."

'"What do you mean, same to you?"

'He's thinking "You no good SOB," and I'm saying "Same to you."

'He told me he was headed for a slit trench and they had a mortar barrage come in and a mortar exploded. Some of the shrapnel was still in his side and some in his arm because he had his hand up. He said they're gonna leave the shrapnel in until after the war is over because he volunteered to go back to his outfit.' The brothers agreed to meet at the hospital the following weekend, but 'I got back to my outfit and we were alerted to ship out. I tried to call him, but couldn't get an answer.'

A few days later, Elmer Forrest was on a British ship out of Bristol crossing the English Channel. 'Then the strangest thing happened. This guy came down and said, "Hey Forrest, what rank's your brother hold?"

'"He's a lieutenant. Why?"

'"They were just talking over the loudspeaker and asking for Lieutenant Forrest."

'So I went up to the orderly room. I saluted the captain and said, "Do you have a Lieutenant Forrest aboard?" I gave him Eddie's serial number.

'He looked it up and said, "Yeah. Why?"

'"That's my brother."

'So he called for Lieutenant Forrest. "Report to the orderly room." He commented, "Stand right there, soldier."

'So I'm just inside the bulkhead. I'll be goddarned before long Eddie came in and I tapped him on the shoulder and said, "Where the hell are you going?"

'"Holy Jesus! And I thought I left you in England."

'"Come on up to the stateroom." He had a stateroom with six officers in it and the stateroom's number was 13. Meanwhile, every officer had a quart that they brought aboard and we got plastered. So I spent the night in the stateroom. The next morning we went across the channel.'

16

'So Long, and If I Never See You Again, Goodbye'

'Dear Mom,' Billy Wolfe wrote in a letter dated 24 August 1944 from Fort Meade, Maryland. 'I don't know how long I will remain here. I am in Uncle Sam's Army. We got in here about 9 o'clock this morning. We rode almost all night. I washed windows in the barracks this afternoon, went for my meals and slept. A real busy day. Give my best regards to the friends and I will write a letter later when I get an address where you can write...' Billy Wolfe was one of the 400 replacements who would be assigned to the 712th Tank Battalion in the course of the war. He was eighteen years old when he was drafted.

'Dear Mom,' Billy wrote the next day. 'While I think we get our uniforms tomorrow, I think I will get an overnight leave this weekend, too. I am on guard duty from 12 to 3 o'clock tonight. I just watched a parade and I'm waiting for supper or chow. I wrote a card yesterday. I suppose you received that. We haven't taken any shots yet. We will get some tomorrow. I just went over to the PX to get some stationery. I didn't bring any along. I will try to write more after chow.

'Saturday afternoon – I got back from chow. We have good food but it don't taste like it does at home. I am sending some important papers. Save them for me. Tell all the folks back there hello, and I will write to them when I get time. Well, news and time is scarce, so I will say so long. I am going to send my clothes home, Monday I think. We were in line for a pass this weekend, but we go on KP. Love, Bill.'

'31 August 1944 – I received your letter "A" yesterday. I wrote to Hubert, Peg, Gigi and you the other day. I had to cut Peg's card short and go scrub barracks,' Billy's letter continued. 'I didn't go to church Sunday. I was on KP. I have been on day KP twice and on guard from

111

12 to 3 o'clock once. By the time you receive this I will be on my way. I am shipping out at 3 p.m. today. I will write the first opportunity when my destination is reached. Vic Fleming and Doug Bennett are going, too. Love, Bill.' (Peg and Geneva 'Gigi' Wolfe were two of Billy's sisters. He also had two younger sisters, twins Maxine and Madeline, who were sixteen when Billy was drafted, and another older sister, Mary. I met Maxine and Madeline at the first reunion of the 712th Tank Battalion I attended at Niagara Falls in 1987 and visited with them in Quicksburg, Virginia, in October 1993.)

A few days later on 2 September, Billy wrote: 'Dearest folks, We left Fort Meade 6.20 p.m. Thursday, arrived in Indianapolis, Indiana, about 11:30 p.m. Friday. We got in Louisville, Kentucky, about 7:30, had dinner, and arrived in Fort Knox, Kentucky, where I am now stationed at 3 a.m. Went to bed about 4 and got up at 5.45. I am to begin training in the tank corps week after next. I don't know where Vic and Kenny Fleming went. They were with us a while. I think they went to St Louis, Missouri, and hard to tell where after that. I hate to think of that rough tank business. That is really rough. I just watched (here the letter is illegible, but he probably referred to a training film) and saw enough to turn my stomach. We just had a physical check-up this morning. I received your letter "A." I don't believe I have mentioned the twins in any of my letters. Are they still awfully fat? Are they ready to go to school? I am to start training with the infantry about tanks, then shift to a medium tank.

'I haven't written to anyone except you and the family since I left. I bet Miss Cleda (a neighbour) wonders what happened to me, but I have been too busy to write much. Will you please give Mary, Gigi, Dad and Hubert my address? It seems like I can't find time to write. Boy, twins, you should see your handsome young brother in his uniform. I have most everything dirty, that damned train...' Billy's mother taught Sunday School and although he would never use such language at home, he liked to place an occasional epithet in his letters just to kid his mother, the way he kidded his sisters about their weight, one of the twins told me.

'We just had a fire drill and a lecture on military courtesy. It is about time for chow so I will have to cut this short. Be sure to have my adress/address, you know what I mean, even if I have forgotten the spelling. P.S. I just got back from chow. White beans, cooked tomatoes, buttered bread, coffee and Jell-o. It was good. Well, I think I will close and go to the PX.'

'3 September,' Billy wrote the next day. 'Dear folks, Are you old, fat twins ready to go back to school? I'll bet both catalogues are worn out by now. How about that, Mom? I just got back from a trip to the swimming pool with Doug Bennett. We couldn't go in because we didn't have bathing trunks. How about sending me mine? I haven't written to Peg yet, only a card from Meade. I wrote to Gigi and Miss Cleda yesterday. The camp is right in the mountains. Big trees and hills. It is *almost* as pretty as Virginia. Indiana is pretty too. The soil is almost black. It is level as a walk and pretty big farmhouses. It isn't quite as pretty as Virginia.'

Two weeks later on 18 September, Billy wrote, 'Dear Maxine and Mom and Madeline, Maxine, I received your letter just before chow. I just got back from eating and am going to try to answer it... I had KP yesterday from 7 a.m. to 6 p.m. Just my luck to have it Sunday. And Mom, I thought of you Saturday and Sunday almost all day. We haven't been having so much rain down here. It has rained about twice. We had grenade and gas mask drill so far today. Also a film on camouflage. So far, we go on an 8-mile hike with everything tomorrow. We are supposed to have a gas attack and everything just like real battle. A lot of boys got gigged Saturday for not having their shoes greased or dubbed as we call it. Polish is strictly forbidden. I will have to get a pair of brown slippers for dress. They have to have plain toes. If I ever get to Louisville I will, but I will need a stamp. Oh well, I don't really need them. Miss Matt (Madeline), what is wrong with you? Are you miffed? I will add your name to the salutation, but you had better write next time. I suppose you have the boys on your mind. How about that, Maxine?'

Billy wrote in another letter with an unknown date: 'Dear Madeline, Here is your pin. Take care of it and no boys are to wear it. Also, I want a big letter of thanks, understand? That costed me a big pile of money, you old soak. You never write. Maxine does. Well, don't be too bad now. I am in a hurry. So long, Love Bill.'

Billy came home on a furlough in January 1945. On 30 January, it was time for him to leave. 'When we got to Route 11,' one of the twins said during my visit in 1993, 'when Billy said goodbye to us, he said, "So long, kids, and if I never see you again, goodbye." And he waved all the way down the road. But going out that road, that mile, he walked between us and there was snow on the ground. And that snow laid for it seemed like weeks. And every day, when we went to school, we would walk in his tracks. That's how sentimental we were.'

17

Marshall T. Warfield

For a battalion that was on the front line virtually every day of its first two months in combat from 3 July 1944 to 8 September, the rest of September and most of October, the collective memory of the 712th is understandably a blur. September was the period when the battalion was used for 'indirect firing' and October, for the third platoon of C Company, was the time they spent almost a whole month in Maizières lès Metz, a town that was so hotly contested that there was a schoolhouse with Americans in some rooms and Germans in others.

It was the period when General Patton's tanks 'ran out of gas' according to some of the tankers. In the words of Lt Dale Albee, precious fuel was diverted to 'Montgomery, that glory happy bastard, so he could run his tanks up the dike' during Operation Market Garden. However, it simply may have been that Patton advanced so quickly across France that supplies could not keep up with him. At one point, B-24s of the 8th Air Force flew fuel in to a hastily reconstructed airfield at Reims. The delay would prove costly as it gave the Germans sufficient time to bolster the lightly defended network of forts along the Moselle River around the city of Metz.

With one tragic exception – the loss of one of the best officers in the battalion, Lt Marshall T. Warfield, on a scouting mission – September offered the battalion a respite from the day-to-day existentialism of war, a chance to think about tomorrow instead of wondering if there would be a tomorrow. Pfc Bob Rossi, the skinny nineteen-year-old kid from Jersey City, New Jersey, crossed the Atlantic on the *Ile de France*, rode for several days in boxcars, transferred to a truck and then heard the ominous instruction to 'lock and load' as he was dropped off at the

712th in September. He was assigned to Lt Charles Lombardi's third platoon of C Company as a loader. His driver was Tony D'Arpino. The assistant driver was Ed Spahr who Rossi knew from Camp Myles Standish before going overseas. The gunner was Stanley Klapkowski and the tank commander was Lieutenant Lombardi.

During this time, the battalion was sending small parties across the Moselle River, probing the German defences in search of a place to cross in force. This would explain why when I interviewed Fred Steers, a sergeant in Headquarters Company's reconnaissance platoon, at the battalion's reunion in Medford, Oregon, he said he crossed the Moselle three times, whereas the battalion in general crossed it twice. On 15 September, according to the battalion's after-action reports at 8.45 a.m., a message was received from Lieutenant Warfield, the leader of the reconnaissance platoon. 'Have made contact on right flank,' the message read. 'Everything OK. Will be back shortly.' Two days later, Warfield made contact with the enemy again.

Marshall Warfield was 'very reserved and serious,' said his widow, Olga. Warfield, who never remarried and still lived in the house in Oakton, Virginia, that she bought with a VA loan, when I visited her about a decade ago. 'Whatever he had to do, he wanted to do it the best way he could.' The Warfields were a prominent Maryland family and Olga came from a prominent Jesuit family – her cousin, Robert Ignatius Gannon, was president of Fordham University. One of Marshall's ancestors had been governor of Maryland and his brother Albert was the commander of the Maryland National Guard during the turbulent 1960s. Wallis Warfield Simpson, the Duchess of Windsor whose husband, King Edward VIII, abdicated his throne to marry her, was a cousin. And although no Warfield ever became president, the SS *President Warfield* – better known in its later incarnation as the *Exodus* – was named after the president of the Baltimore Steamship Company, another of Marshall's relatives.

I asked Olga what the 'T' in Marshall T. Warfield stood for. She opened one of her albums to Marshall's obituary in the *Baltimore Sun* and it read 'Marshall Turenne Warfield.' That's an odd middle name, I thought. I would later learn, as if it were his destiny to be a great soldier, that Henri de la Tour d'Auvergne, Vicomte de Turenne, marshal of France, was arguably the second greatest French general behind Napoleon, and that Napoleon studied the campaigns of Turenne closely.

Fred Steers was a corporal at the time and Warfield was 'assigned a daylight reconnaissance mission,' he recalled at the Medford reunion. 'Ordinarily he always asked me to go with him wherever he went because he liked the way I handled my rifle. I was a pretty good shot, I guess. But this day he wouldn't take me. He said, "I don't want you to come with me." He took another corporal and Tim Reilly. (Joseph) Patrick was the corporal. And they took off on this mission. And later that afternoon, Patrick came back. He's the only one that came back. Tim got killed right on the spot. Warfield was shot there, too. Patrick got him back to the aid station, but he died there.

'Warfield always said, "I know if I get hit I'm gonna die." Later, Smitty (Eugene Smith) and I were assigned to go out there and see if we could find Tim. We went out and found where they'd took off and Smitty wouldn't let me go with him. He said, "You wait here." He was a staff sergeant and I was just a corporal. He anchored me right there and made me stay there. So I waited for him. He was gone for a good half hour and I heard a rifle shot. And I just was so afraid it was him. I was just getting ready to take off and go down there, and here he comes back. He'd picked up Tim's pistol and he handed it to me, and I carried that for quite a while. He'd found Tim and they finally got him out of there, but Smitty couldn't get him out then. I asked him about the rifle shot. He said he heard it, but it wasn't fired at him.'

One day, Steers recalled, he, Warfield, Tim Reilly and Phil Felinsky were out scouting. They came to a rise in the highway and left their jeeps below the rise. Across the valley, about a mile away, they could hear Germans moving around in vehicles. 'Pretty soon, here come some motorcycles, messenger carriers.' Warfield and Reilly 'laid down in the ditch alongside the road while I sat upright behind an apple tree, probably about thirty feet from the road. Phil Felinsky was behind me, behind another tree. And here comes this bike, it had two riders on it. Warfield jumped up and held up his hand and the bike rider just laid on the gas and was coming around him. Lieutenant Warfield and Tim each had Tommy guns. Phil and I had M-1s. They emptied those Tommy guns and they just shot the air, they never touched them. And they were going to get by us. I fired and at the crack of that gun the bike hit the ground instantly. It went sliding down the highway. And the guy on the back jumped up and started to get his weapon and Phil killed him. The guy I shot wasn't killed. But that one bullet, I put six holes in him. Two in one arm. It went in his side, out the other side and out the other arm. Six holes. And he was up walking around. He wanted to go to a doctor. So we loaded him up on the jeep and took him to the medics.'

18

'Kill All the Sons of Bitches'

An author once contacted Paul Wannemacher, the battalion association president, and asked him to send a list of key words to battalion veterans to spark their memories. I did not think much of such an approach until a few days later when I was in the cafeteria of the Lyons VA Medical Center in New Jersey before the start of a prisoner of war group meeting, which Bob Levine – a 90th Infantry Division veteran who was behind one of Jim Flowers' tanks on Hill 122 and was wounded and captured – invited me to attend.

In the cafeteria, I was seated at a table with a former prisoner of war and I decided to experiment with the key word approach. I asked him what he might think of if I said the word 'potato.' I do not remember the story that ensued, but it gave me a great deal of respect for the use of key words in sparking memory. I was telling the key word/potato story at the battalion's 1997 mini-reunion in Florida and I asked a group of C Company veterans – Tony D'Arpino; Dave Toland, who was a replacement; Grayson LaMar, a driver; and Buck Hardee, a gunner – what they thought of when I mentioned 'hand grenade.' Hardee, who owned a variety store in Randleman, North Carolina, spoke up.

'We were trying to cross the Rhine River and they were floating mines down blowing up the pontoon bridges. (This would have been a different river, most likely the Moselle, which the battalion crossed in November as Hardee was seriously wounded on 29 November.) We were held up in this town. I can't remember the name of it. Our tank was sitting in the street. They were just waiting to cross the river and we were right in front of an old home, sitting back off the street, a big old colonial type, beautiful home. There was a walkway and we were sitting there right in front of the walkway. You could see straight up the walkway right into the front door. And this guy, we saw the front door open... You mentioned hand grenade, that made me think of it. We saw the front door of that house open, real slowly and a civilian walked out of the front door. He came out real slowly with his hands down at his side.

'We observed him closely and he came walking right on out to the street, real slowly, right on towards our tank. We didn't know what this guy was up to and he kept on coming. He didn't make any moves. We had him covered pretty well. If he'd have made any false moves he'd have been gone, of course, and I'm sure he knew it. He kept walking, coming right on up towards us. And the closer he got, the more concerned we got. What's this guy up to? We were afraid that maybe he was going to walk up and get up there close and suddenly toss a hand grenade into the tank. That was my real concern. He came walking right to the sidewalk, right up close to our tank where he could speak with us. He didn't make a move. I guess he knew he'd better not. Anyway, we were so curious. What is this guy up to? And he walked right up close to us, and when he spoke, he talked in English. Do you remember that, Grayson?'

'Was that when Lombardi was our platoon leader?' La Mar asked.

'I think so. Anyway, when he spoke, he spoke in English and I'll never forget the words he said. He said, "Kill all the sons of bitches. They've been fucking my wife." I never will forget that. When you mentioned the hand grenade, I thought of that.'

19

Maizières lès Metz

Battalion veterans were often unaware of the 'big picture.' Similarly, authors who put the 'big picture' in perspective often do not know the snapshots, stories of the riflemen in the foxholes or loaders and drivers in the tanks. All the veterans knew about the big picture in September was that the tanks had run out of gas. This was when they were used as stationary artillery pieces in an attempt to penetrate the impenetrable forts in and around the city of Metz. The names that came up most frequently in my interviews were Fort Driant and Fort Koenigsmacker. The battalion after-action reports for much of the month state that the target of indirect firing was Amanvillers. Amanvillers was a strong point in the defence of the fortresses at Metz. I doubt that any of the tankers in a position below the command structure knew this.

Following the battle at Mairy, Jim Gifford said, 'We moved toward the Maginot Line and we got up near the Moselle River. And then we were told to pull back and to hold up in this area because we were out of gas. So this whole massive force stopped. We dispersed ourselves around that area and while we were waiting for gas to come up, we were almost three weeks not moving. And we could have walked in through the Maginot Line. But they came back into it. They evacuated it and we went into it and came back, but then later it had to be taken.'

According to Forrest Dixon, the fortress city of Metz was only lightly defended when the battalion arrived on the west side of the Moselle in mid-September. The 6th Armored Division had an advance party near Metz with the 90th Division right behind them, Dixon recalled in 1992. 'But the Sixth couldn't go into Metz because they were down to one unit of gas. So they bivouacked maybe 25 or 30 miles from Metz. Their advance unit got into Metz, but they were told to come back. Then that night and the next day, Patton flew in gas and the following day we advanced. In the meantime, the Germans came back and reoccupied Metz. And then the unit from the 6th Armored didn't get into Metz, so they parked outside, and the next morning the Germans knocked out a good portion of this combat unit's tanks. I believe it was right under Fort Driant is where they parked. And then the war stopped for several days until we got adequate supplies. But that was when they flew the gas in, just before we advanced into Metz.'

'When we started out again,' Gifford added, 'our particular unit had to go down with the 357th Regiment to take a town called Maizières lès Metz, which was by the Moselle River, and this is when the whole thing started up again.' The attack on Maizières lès Metz began on 7 October 1944 and it would take nearly three weeks to capture the town. According to *The Lorraine Campaign* by Hugh M. Cole of the Center for Military History, the houses in Maizières lès Metz 'were strongly constructed, generally of stone and strengthened by wire and sandbags so as to form a succession of miniature forts which had to be reduced one by one. The pivotal point in Old Maizières was formed by the heavy masonry of the Hotel de Ville, around which the fighting surged indecisively... A platoon of tanks was brought in from the north after the roads were cleared of mines, but there was little room for manoeuvre in the narrow streets – down which German bazookas and anti-tank guns were sighted – and the tanks played only a minor role in the fight for the town.'

According to the battalion after-action reports for the period of 7-10 October, 'A bulldozer tank was borrowed from Battalion Headquarters Company and used to clear a roadblock into Maizières. This was done under fire. Third platoon then moved into the town. The bulldozer tank was taken to another part of town under cover of two accompanying tanks. One tank was knocked out, but the crew remained inside and used it as an armed pillbox. The platoon was under heavy enemy artillery fire. An additional tank was taken into the town and engineers blew a hole in a house to permit it to fire on buildings across the street. The tanks remained in town at night not withdrawing.'

Maizières lès Metz 'was a big railroad junction with four or five tracks going through it,' Gifford replied. 'It was a small town that straddled the railroad tracks. And there was a slag pile there from ore. It was a mining town or it had something to do with iron there. So we dispersed our tanks along that town and while we were there for almost two weeks we had a lot of action going on. Every day it was something.'

In 1991, I was working on research for an oral history of the 712th Tank Battalion. I had been to three reunions and came to the fourth with a list of veterans I wanted to interview. Forrest Dixon was one but he had recently been diagnosed with rectal cancer and was unable to attend. Another was Jim Flowers who was having some difficulty with his prostheses and could not attend. Most of the other great storytellers including Wayne Hissong and Reuben Goldstein were in attendance, but I was disappointed that my agenda was thrown off. And then I met Ed Spahr. Spahr was small in stature and was from Carlisle, Pennsylvania. He had recently survived an aortic arterial aneurism, which only had a 10 per cent survival rate at the time. When asked if he was wounded, Spahr showed me one of his hands, which had a couple of whitish spots. 'These scars on my hand... They had anti-aircraft guns. I think they were 20 mm and they hit our tank I don't know how many times. They didn't penetrate, but on the inside of the tank a little round spot would get cherry red and the paint would sometimes catch on fire. We got the piece of equipment that was firing at us. I think there were four guns mounted on it that they used for antiaircraft fire, but they turned it on our tank. That's what made these little white spots on my hand.

'I was wounded on the inside of my left arm. Lieutenant Gifford was our tank commander. Our tank got knocked out and we luckily got out of the tank. They hit us somewhere in the track, so that if we'd have kept going we'd have just gone around in a circle because it only had one track to pull it. After we got hit, Lieutenant Gifford stuck his head out and a machine gun bullet struck him around one eye. He had blood all over. When he got out of the tank, I don't think he thought he was hurt as bad as he looked and he stepped behind the tank away from the incoming. They were firing machine guns on us but we were behind the tank. Lieutenant Gifford tossed me his camera and said, "Take a picture of me."

'So I'm standing there with my hands up taking the picture. That's the only way I could have got hit in a spot like that. I had to have my arms up. It felt like a bee sting. I felt the same thing in my face, but that was just a little piece of metal, something out of the machine gun projectile that hit me there. It was no bigger than a small match head that they picked out. It was probably the shell casing off of a .30-calibre bullet. It was no big deal to me. I really didn't think I was hit until the medic asked to see my hand because when I dropped my arm the blood would drop off my fingers. He said, "I can't see where the blood's coming from. It's coming down your arm. Take off your shirt." And then there this was. I was bleeding like a stuck pig. I haven't seen Lieutenant Gifford since. He was all right, but he never came back to the company after that.'

That was at the 1991 reunion of the battalion. The 1992 reunion was held in Harrisburg, Pennsylvania. A highlight of the reunion was a guided tour of the Gettysburg battlefield on which the tour guide explained that there was no such thing as 'shrapnel' in the Second World War. Apparently, shrapnel was strictly a Civil War term for the metal from exploding cannon balls. And here was a circle of elderly gentlemen standing around the guide, many of them with small slivers of no such thing as shrapnel embedded in their bodies.

But I digress. There I was standing in the hospitality room at the 1992 reunion talking with Ed Spahr when who should enter but Lieutenant Gifford. Also, two members of the tank that was knocked out on 10 January 1945 during the Battle of the Bulge were at the reunion. As they sat around a table discussing the horrors of war, this is when the subject of Maizières les Metz came up, not to mention stories about Sergeant James Warren and Corporal Stanley Klapkowski, the crew's gunner that day who did not attend the reunion. I never met Sergeant

Warren, but I later interviewed Klapkowski at his home in McKees Rocks, Pennsylvania, just outside of Pittsburgh.

'I want to relate a story about one of our real characters of the third platoon, Sergeant Jim Warren,' Rossi said as the four former crewmates sat around a table. 'He was a career Army man. And just prior to the Bulge we were in Kirschnaumen (France). We were standing around one evening and we had this one room where the stove was. The mother and father and daughter lived in one room and there was a GI blanket covering a hole where a shell had hit. So it was pretty cold in this house. And we were standing around kibitzing this one night. There was a kerosene lantern hanging down from the ceiling on a cord. And Jim Warren, he always had a half a load on, and he's shadowboxing the lantern. And we're laughing. He's playing around, he's boxing the lantern and he throws a haymaker at the lantern, misses the lantern and hits me. I went flying across the room. I come up with the biggest lip you ever saw. This was late at night and the next morning we're getting up and I could hear him saying, "I never touched the kid." And I showed him the lip. He believed it then.'

'Sergeant Warren was the type of guy,' Tony D'Arpino, the tank driver, added, 'that was really military. His tank crew wouldn't eat unless he said so. He was that kind of a guy.'

'When I joined the third platoon,' Rossi said, 'I arrived with a Koon Leong Moy, who we automatically called Chop Chop because of his Oriental heritage. Right away, when Lieutenant Lombardi was assigning the crews, Warren says, "I want him." He thought Chop Chop was going to cook for him. Chop says, "The hell with you. You cook for yourself."

'But I'll tell you one thing about Sergeant Warren. Sergeant Warren – and we weren't used to it, Lieutenant Lombardi even told me this himself – he wasn't used to having a guy like Warren in the Number 2 tank, because if Lieutenant Lombardi had something hot in front of him, Sergeant Warren rode up on his backside. You could count on him. He was very dependable. He wasn't one of these guys who would sit back 400, 500 yards.'

'He was a good tank commander.'

'The only trouble Sergeant Warren had was he liked his "tea" a little much. But other than that, he'd been a first sergeant and busted. He could remember MacArthur when he was a major. We were discussing that a little while ago today. He had some kind of antique guns that he'd break down, paint and everything else down in the islands there, and MacArthur came to make an inspection. And he told Sergeant Warren to take off his shoes and socks. He wanted to see if he'd cut his nails square. He didn't even look at the guns that the guy broke his back cleaning and painting. He wanted to see how he cut his nails.'

'He made the battery that they were attached to break ranks to crowd around Sergeant Warren,' Rossi said.

'He was from Flat Lake, Oklahoma, and his wife was from Crows Nest, Kentucky,' Spahr added.

'They can say what they want to. I think from the time you were with us,' D'Arpino said, speaking directly to Jim Gifford, 'you could probably say the same thing. Sergeant Warren was one of the best Number 2 tanks because when you were in trouble he was right there.'

'He was dependable.'

'You could never tell whether he was excited or not.'

'If you had a fast tank like I had in reverse, you'd always bump into him because he was still there.'

'He didn't shirk from anything.'

'He had other faults like all of us.'

'There are more Warren stories than you can shake a stick at,' Rossi said. 'He had pots and pans galore on the back of his tank. I used to say his pots and pans make more noise than the tank itself coming down the road.'

'But he was the type of man that you'd want, especially when you're a Number 1 tank,' D'Arpino added. 'I can say this now, I think the driver of a lead tank is the worst goddamn job God ever created because you're looking through that periscope. You ain't got no gun to shoot to keep you busy. You're looking to see if anybody's aiming at you. The gunner's busy. The loader's busy loading. At least the bow gunner, he had a machine gun that he could spray, play with a little bit.

The driver just sat there waiting. But one thing I always did when they told me to stop, the first thing I'd do was put it in reverse.'

'Tony, in Maizières les Metz, were you driving the tank when we went up on the sidewalk and scraped that building?' Gifford asked.

'Oh, yeah.'

'I was up in the turret. Up ahead there was a split in the road and there was an anti-tank gun in the lobby of a hotel, so I hollered for white phosphorous. We fired a white phosphorous shell into the lobby and later we saw the gun in there, and there was a guy behind it, and there was nothing but his boots. That white phosphorous wiped him right off the face of the earth. But when we went up on the sidewalk and started scraping that brick building, something made me look to the right and here was a second story window. There was a Kraut standing there with a gun right at my face and he fired it. I looked at him, he looked at me and he fires the gun. It went either to the left or the right of me and then he disappeared back into the room. That was the damnedest thing I ever saw.'

'You know what I remember?' D'Arpino said. 'We were in the hedgerows, one of our first days over there. Klapkowski was the gunner. He saw a guy and he wanted to fire the machine gun. The solenoid for the machine gun and the 75 mm were close together. He hit the 75 mm. I'm looking up the periscope and I see this German machine gunner. And all of a sudden, Jesus, I don't see nothing but dust. The whole thing disappeared: the gun, the guy, everything. Klapkowski stepped on the solenoid for the 75 mm instead of the machine gun.'

'I remember the day,' Spahr said, 'and this was not long before Klapkowski really went haywire and they took him back. You remember the guy that went running across the field about five or six hundred yards away from us and a 75 round went after him? Remember, he shot at one man? I knew he was completely cracked then. When you do tricks like that, you know you've got a killer instinct then. You ain't just fighting a war.'

'I saw them doing that when we were up in the Sudetenland,' Rossi said. 'Light tanks were shooting at one German soldier in the field in the snow. It was like a game.'

'I think Sergeant Warren used to have the right idea,' D'Arpino said. 'I can remember him, God rest his soul, saying, "Listen, if you ever become a tank commander, never mind getting the high explosive shells. Get the white phosphorous." He says it does the same job and twice the damage.'

'I hit a Tiger tank one day at least three times with an armor-piercing shell and never touched him,' said Spahr. 'He just kept on coming. Then my loader accidentally threw a white phosphorous shell in and I hit that tank right in the front end and he stopped. They thought they were hit and penetrated and they thought they were on fire. We used the white phosphorous shell for markers. It burns and a puff of white smoke explodes. They were good for hunting range. We had the old type sights where you guessed the range and we used to use what we called bracketing shots. Some gunners would use high explosive to get their bracket. The first shell, you could see it hitting. Now if it would hit, say, 200 yards short, the gunner would raise his elevation 400 yards, and if he shot over the target, then he would drop down 200 yards. That's bracketing. And if you didn't get him the third shot, you'd better find a hole to get into because he was then going to be shooting at you.'

1. Lt Jim Flowers, centre, with Dr William McConahey, left, who treated him when he was rescued after the battle for Hill 122 in Normandy, and Lt Claude Lovett, who found Flowers after he lost both of his feet and lay in No Man's Land for two nights.

2. Olga Warfield and her husband, Lt Marshall T. Warfield.

3. Six A Company officers at Amberg, Germany, after the end of hostilities in Europe. Five of the six earned battlefield commissions. Front row from left: Lt Bob Hagerty, Capt. Ellsworth Howard, Lt Howard Olsen and Lt Jule Braatz. Back row from left: Lt Morse Johnson and Lt Sam MacFarland.

4. Three of the six A Company officers at a reunion in the 1990s. From left: Pete Borsenik, Ellsworth Howard, Dick Bengoechea, Jule Braatz and Howard Olsen.

Above: **5.** Bob 'Big Andy' Anderson of A Company butchers a cow that was put down as it had a broken leg. 'That cow's leg was no more broken than yours or mine,' Big Andy told the author during a 1992 interview. (*Signal Corps*)

Right: **6.** Eugene Tannler, one of the nine members of Jim Flowers' platoon who was killed in the battle for Hill 122.

7. Steve Szirony, who was a mechanic in A Company, at a reunion in the 1990s.

8. Sgt Harold Heckler of D Company who was killed accidentally by a member of his own crew.

Right: **9.** Reuben Goldstein who was a tank commander in A Company. He was wounded at the Falaise Gap.

Below: **10.** Major Forrest Dixon, the battalion maintenance officer, who on 8 September 1944 climbed into a tank with no engine and knocked out an approaching German Mark IV panzer.

Above: 11. A Company third platoon tankers at Amberg, Germany. Top from left: Eugene E. Crawford, Roscoe D. Treadway, Lt Harry F. Bell, William Swartzmiller. Bottom, sitting: Earl E. Hollingsworth and John H. McDaniel. With the exception of Crawford and Swartzmiller, this was the crew at Distroff, France, where McDaniel was wounded after crossing the Moselle River in November 1944. (*John McDaniel*)

Left: 12. 2nd Lt Maurice Elson, the author's father.

Above: 13. An anti-tank ditch in the Siegfried Line near Buren, Germany. (*Jim Gifford*)

Right: 14. Jack Sheppard, the C Company commander, at his home in Bartow, Florida, in 1992.

15. A photo of Colonel Randolph's body lying beside a tank destroyer after he was killed during a barrage of **Nebelwerfers aka** 'Screaming Meemies'.

16. A German tank of the 106th Panzer Brigade that was knocked out by the 712th on 8 September 1944 at Mairy.

Above: 17. A platoon of A Company tanks in Bavigne, Luxembourg, heading into the Battle of the Bulge. The driver of the lead tank was Dess Tibbitts. The tank commander (left) was Lt Wallace Lippincott Jr, the platoon leader who would be killed days after this picture was taken. The tank commander silhouetted in the second tank was Sam MacFarland who would receive a battlefield promotion. The third tank commander was Olen T. Crawford and the commander of the fourth tank was Sgt Henry Schneider who would be killed by a sniper on the day he received his battlefield commission.

Right: 18. Lt Jim Gifford at Kirschnaumen, France, prior to the Battle of the Bulge.

Left: **19.** Jim Gifford's tank days before it was knocked out near Berle, Luxembourg, on 10 January 1945.

Below: **20.** Dan Diel and John Essenburg of B Company. Diel was wounded on his first day in combat. On returning to his unit, he later received a battlefield commission.

Above: **21.** Sam MacFarland (left) and Quentin 'Pine Valley' Bynum of A Company. MacFarland received a battlefield commission. Bynum was killed during the Battle of the Bulge.

Right: **22.** Ed Forrest, a lieutenant in A Company, in Stockbridge, Massachusetts, before going overseas. (*Dorothy Cooney*)

23. Railroad tracks at Heimboldshausen, Germany, following an explosion on 3 April 1945. (*Jack Roland*)

24. One of four houses that were demolished by the explosion in Heimboldshausen. Lieutenant Forrest's headquarters were in one of the houses. (*Jack Roland*)

25. Another of the four houses destroyed at Heimboldshausen. (*Jack Roland*)

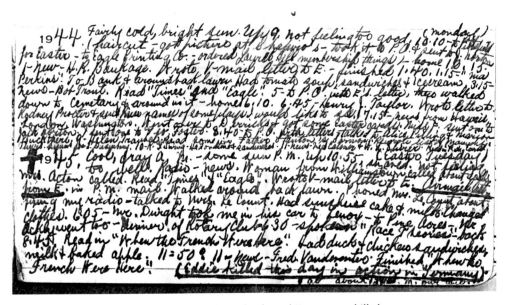

26. The entry in Reverend Laine's diary the day Ed Forrest was killed.

Left: **27.** A propeller blade from his Bf 109 marks the grave of the pilot whose plane caused the explosion at Heimboldshausen.

Below:
28. Heimboldshausen in 1999.

Right: **29.** Jim Gifford in the crematory at the Flossenburg concentration camp. (*Jim Gifford*)

Below: **30.** Some have questioned whether there should be snow on the ground, but the date on the picture states 5 May 1945 and gives the location as Czechoslovakia. (*John Zimmer*)

May 5 1945 C

czechoslovakia

31. B Company at Amberg, Germany, where the 712th was stationed following the end of the war in Europe. (*Louis Gruntz, Jr*)

32. A shell crater made by a 'railroad gun' at Hof, Germany. Some thirty-two service personnel were in the house at the time.

20

Time to Do the Dishes

In Maizières lès Metz, 'they had a schoolhouse where in one room were Americans, the next room were Germans and there were tunnels underneath,' Tony D'Arpino said when I interviewed him and Reuben Goldstein at Tony's home in Milton, Massachusetts in November 1992. (Goldstein was in A Company, but since he lived nearby in Hull, Massachusetts, I met the two together.) 'Our tank stayed in the same position for three weeks. We were guarding a couple of roads and they used to drop off the rations in the centre of town.

'They had five sets of railroad tracks and the Germans had that place zeroed in, so the jeep could only come down so far with the supplies. They'd dump them there and we'd have to go get them and lug them back to the tank. I've got a five-gallon can of water on my shoulder and Klapkowski's got some frozen chickens, and a few other rations. And I dropped that can of water so many times. I'd hear *ding!* and I'd drop the can and hit the ground. And finally when I got back to the house – the house where our tank was on the corner, there was no roof on it, it was blown off – down in the cellar was a bin full of potatoes. So I told the lieutenant, "This is it. You guys want to eat, you go up there and get the rations, I'm not going up there no more. I'll eat the potatoes down in the bin." That's a story I've told about Klapkowski. We get food, it's chicken and he wants to fry it. All the stuff was in the house. As a matter of fact, they had a lot of dishes, beautiful dishes. So Klapkowski is looking for flour. He wants to roll this chicken and fry it, and he starts a fire in the stove.

'"There's smoke going up the chimney. For Chrissakes, they can see us," I said.

'"Aww," he says, "we've been here so long they know we're here anyway." So he goes down in the cellar and he gets this bag. It had a bunch of German writing on it. He says, "Is this flour?"

'"No, that feels like plaster of Paris, the stuff you patch walls with."

'"No, that's flour."

'So he rolls the chicken in this stuff. And he's saved the bacon fat from the 10-in-1 rations. He fried this and it came out the prettiest golden brown you'd ever want to see. But you couldn't eat it. It was tough. So he just banged it against the wall and knocked the plaster off. The plaster came off in one piece and the chicken underneath was cooked. He then set the table. He got the tablecloth and set it with five dishes. Then he said, "Okay, fellas, time to do the dishes." And he opened the window, tablecloth, dishes and everything else out the window. I don't know how many plates we broke in that house. But that place was really something. They had it zeroed in. I can still see the slag piles all across the way there. And down at the end of the street, it was like a dead end street. There was a pasture and the cows were dead.'

'You know what happens when a cow is dead?' Goldstein said. 'They go belly up, feet up in the air and they blow right up.'

'As a matter of fact,' D'Arpino said, 'I was driving the first tank when we first got into position in Maizières. I was just easing into position and I'm going, "There's a gun pointing at us down there! There's a gun pointing at us!" All I could see was this leg. I didn't know at the time it was the leg of a cow pointing down the street. So we put one round into this dead cow.'

21

'I Think I've Been Shot'

Following the group interview with Jim Gifford, Tony D'Arpino, Ed Spahr and Bob Rossi, I interviewed Gifford individually and D'Arpino along with Reuben Goldstein. I already had interviewed Spahr and Rossi, and I eventually visited Klapkowski.

'In Maizières,' Gifford said during the one-on-one interview, 'I was walking across a field with an infantry officer and he looked at me and says, "I think I've been shot." So we both ran over this ridge and we got on the other side, and his jacket had a small hole in the right shoulder, like a pencil hole. I pushed his jacket up and there was a bullet that went in his back, right there. But that's the reaction. He didn't get knocked down. He just said, "I think I've been shot." There was a jeep on the road. I flagged it down and told the jeep to take him back, and I never saw him again.

'We never heard a thing. We were just walking across the field toward this slag pile when he said that. He looked at me, startled like, and said "I think I've been shot." Sometimes a bullet will enter you, it comes in so fast I guess you don't realise it. I know I never felt the bullet enter me (when Gifford was wounded during the Battle of the Bulge). I got the Bronze Star at Maizières. We were getting ready for an attack to take the town (on 27 October) and the infantry was there. On the morning of the attack, there was Colonel Barth, Major Henry and myself. We were standing by the side of my tank and as we were going to move out, we didn't realise it, but the Germans had moved in during the night. Now it was daylight, it was just about the time to move out, all of a sudden this German soldier crossed the railroad track and threw a hand grenade at us. I got hit in the left leg, but I had a very small wound, it wasn't much. But Colonel Barth got hurt bad. As for Major Henry, a piece of shrapnel went through his legs and he died a little later. But that was the beginning of the attack. I checked later to see how he'd made out and they said he died. Then Colonel Mason took over from Colonel Barth, so I had to deal with him and he was really a good line officer. So I told him we could still do the attack because we were lined up all night getting ready. So he said, "Okay."'

'This is while you have fragments from the grenade?' I asked.

'It wasn't much, just a lot of blood on my leg. A medic patched it up. So then we started out with the tanks and we headed out across the railroad tracks. As soon as we made our turn to go up the main street, these houses were all old cement houses – they go back probably a hundred years and they're right next to each other. There are no alleys and the houses are usually two storeys high. Tony was the driver. I'm not sure who the gunner was because we shifted crews a lot, but Spahr was in the bow. As we drove down the street, the shell fire was real heavy. They were dropping everything at us and the whole street was boiling with dust and explosions. I was in the turret and our tank, because of the shell fire, it was blinding the driver and he went up on the sidewalk and started grinding the side of the building.'

After knocking out the gun in the hotel lobby and surviving the near miss by a German soldier in the second story of a building, Gifford said, 'Tony got the tank straightened out and he's pushing the tank out into the street. Then we continue up to the end of the street. We got towards the end of the town and we stopped and reconnoitred. The infantry came behind us, we took the whole town and held it. Everything happened quickly. In the meantime, we got orders to move further to the north, I forget what the next town was. (According to the after-action reports, three tanks from C Company's second platoon took part in the attack.) He wanted to take it with infantry, but I offered him tank support and he really appreciated it, so I led the attack into the town. And we shot up a lot of guys and kept going through the town and took it. They gave me the star over that. When you're shooting at guys, you don't really know how many you hit, but at least it helped us take the town.'

Again, according to the battalion after-action reports, 'one platoon continued on Maizières lès Metz under constant enemy shelling and firing at 50-70 yard ranges. The other two platoons (of C Company) continued indirect fire support mission from positions in Hagendange. On 28 October, a sandbag emplacement was erected for the command tank. Ammunition was moved into the town in preparation for an attack the following day. On 29 October, three tanks in Maizières fired on enemy position (50-70 yard ranges) from 07.15 to 07.30 to neutralise two positions for friendly infantry to assault. Enemy fire was heavy. Opposition fair. By 16.00, 90 per cent of the town was taken. At that time, the attack stopped to permit consolidation for the night. By 09.00, 30 October, the remainder of the town was taken.'

22

'Hands on Place, Hips'

Judd Wiley, the tank commander who was injured the day before Jim Flowers' platoon was wiped out in the battle for Hill 122, recalled the day Lt Charles Lombardi joined the battalion at Fort Benning. 'Let me tell you a funny, funny, funny,' Wiley said when I interviewed him at his home in Seal Beach, California in October 1994. 'See, he was a 90-day wonder, but he was a real nice guy. Everybody always liked Lombardi. Do you know enough about the Army? A preparatory command is "Hands on hips." They're giving you an exercise and a lieutenant always does this. The right thing would be "Hands on hips, place!" Well, he said, "Hands on place, hips!" And we all fell down in the dust where we were laughing so bad. And he was laughing right with us. He says, "What'd I say?" And then we told him. He says, "God almighty, no wonder you're laughing at me." He was a heck of a good guy, he was a nice officer. "Hands on place, hips!"'

'Lieutenant Lombardi was wounded several times,' said Tony D'Arpino. 'It all started back in Fort Benning. I was in the third platoon and we had a different platoon leader every other week. We used to get all the crap. I don't know why. Kedrovsky was our company commander at the time. He was a second lieutenant, then he made first lieutenant. And we kept getting different platoon leaders all the time. And every time there was a strength test to be taken or some 10-mile hike, it was always third platoon. Third platoon, third platoon. Third platoon had K.P. every Sunday. So finally, one day we get this guy and he looked like a sad sack when he showed up. He was built kind of squatty and he had a moustache. And there was something about his lips, I don't know, that made him look like a sad sack, especially when he started wearing his helmet and it came down over his eyes.

'And they gave him the third platoon. Well, the first thing he did when we got down to the motor pool was to maintain the tanks every day: clean the guns, wire brush and scrape the connectors. There was nothing on there, but we'd do it anyway. He gets the platoon and sits us down in the shade and says, "You know my name now, my name is Charles Lombardi." He says, "I don't know a goddamn thing about a tank. I was a company clerk in the Air Corps and I went to OCS and here I am." From that day on, everybody liked him. We became the best platoon in the company. Anything you want, old Lum there would take care of you. In combat we had a Number 2 tank. I can't think who the sergeant's name was, but Lombardi says to me one time, "Jesus, I've got to get rid of him and put somebody else in the Number 2 tank." Lombardi would always lead the way. He never let anybody else go. He'd always take the mission himself. Something happened one day and he told the Number 2 tank to cover us. I'm the driver. The loader's got the guns to load. The gunner's got the guns to fire. The commander's busy looking around. The bow gunner, he's got that gun he can play with. But the driver, once you start, all you've got is that periscope. So you're looking around making sure nobody's sneaking up on you and Lombardi would say "Everything all right?"

'"Fine."

'"Okay." The bow gunner was shooting a couple of rounds. And then everything settled back.

'He had told the Number 2 tank to cover us and I'm looking in the periscope, and he's back over a hundred yards. He couldn't cover nothing. So finally, we got a replacement and it was Sergeant Warren. He'd been in the Army for years. He'd been a first sergeant and busted. He said he came from Barnyard, Kentucky. He'd been married more times than I have fingers on my hand. He took over the Number 2 tank. And when Lombardi said "Cover me," I'd look and Jesus, his gun was practically touching the back of our turret, that's how close he was.

'Sergeant Warren had one problem. He used to drink all the time. So Lombardi used to get his liquor rations – all the officers had liquor rations – and anything he didn't like, he would give to Warren. One time, we were waiting for our flanks to catch up or something. We were sort of in reserve and Warren was drunk. He'd drunk the last of Lombardi's beer and whatever else was around. So all of a sudden there's a counterattack and we've got to move out. And Sergeant Warren said to Lombardi, "I've got to have a drink."

'"I don't have anything."

'"I've got to have a drink."

'"Mount the tank and let's go. We've got to move out."

'So Lombardi never buttoned up. He might duck down inside, but he never closed the hatch. Then I hear *clunk-clunk*. Then I hear on the radio, "That sonofabitch is shooting at me."

'And we all say, "Who? Who?"

'It was Sergeant Warren. He had his .45 out. Of course, you couldn't hurt the tank. He had his .45 out and he was hitting the turret because Lombardi wouldn't give him any booze. Warren had a smile from ear to ear all the time. But he was a good man in combat. I remember I was driving Warren's tank and there was a counterattack and I can still see it, like a little lake or a pond and there was a road coming alongside of it. We were supposed to guard that road. And Warren was standing in front of the tank guiding me into position. Now he's behind this little scrub brush tree and he's telling me, "Go on!" I don't want to go because I'm gonna hit that tree and knock it over on him. And I'm going like this, pointing at the tree. "You sonofabitch," he says.

'So I says, "All right." So I gunned the engine. When I got right to the tree, I pulled back the levers. I snapped that tree off and it comes down and knocks him out cold. He never said a word to me about that afterward. But all his tank crew liked him. He took care of his crew and made sure that they didn't do anything crazy.'

23

The First Moselle Crossing

While the third platoon of Company C was fighting in Maizières les Metz, much of the battalion was in reserve or used for indirect firing on the fortresses. In the beginning of November, that was about to change. The 90th Division was about to cross a flooded Moselle River that was as much as a mile wide. Before the crossing, Patton addressed the troops. Arnold Brown recited the speech almost word for word nearly fifty years later when I interviewed him in Owensboro, Kentucky.

'We got a message from the regiment, "All officers report to the division rear." So we don't know what's up. We all go back and they had a building there, kind of like a sports arena where they can get all of the officers of the entire division in the building. I thought that's taking quite a chance if somebody dropped a bomb. You can imagine how many officers were in that building. With a stage up front and we're all waiting to see what's going to happen. The first thing, here comes General Patton walking across the stage. He walks from one end of the stage to the other and he walked back and stopped. And he said, "Men, this is it!"

'I'm not going to quote all his curse words. He said, "We're going to cross that damn Moselle River at 2 o'clock in the morning. I want to tell you a little bit about the enemy over there. Now, in these fortress battalions, the Germans don't have their best troops. Their armored forces, their crack troops, they're back in reserve. But some of the fillers in these fortress battalions, some of them are old men. Kill the sonofabitches. Some of them have been slightly wounded in combat or maybe they've got a cripple leg or one arm missing, but they can man those machine guns in these forts. Kill the sonofabitches. This business

137

about taking prisoners. When you accept an enemy as a prisoner, you've searched him and disarmed him and he's in your possession, you treat him according to the Geneva Convention. Now there's nothing says you can't shoot the sonofabitch before you've accepted him as a prisoner. What I mean is, some of their snipers. They'll take camouflage in a tree and some of them are going to let you pass and are camouflaged behind you, and they'll kill a few of your men. Then when you locate his position, he wants to come out and surrender. Don't accept that sonofabitch. Kill him."'

Dick Bengoechea, the replacement Pfc, also remembered seeing Patton prior to the Moselle crossing. 'At Metz, when we were all out of gas,' he said at the 1995 reunion in Louisville, 'they made us stand in the rain, miserable, in our raincoats waiting for him for about two hours. And he drives up in a command car and he says, "You're the sloppiest bunch of goddamn soldiers in this whole Third Army." And then he said, "That outfit I just came from was a sharp bunch of soldiers." He went all the way up the line and told that same story each time.'

The infantry crossed the Moselle in assault boats and it was two or three days before the engineers could complete a bridge for the armor and other vehicles to cross. A platoon of tanks from B Company and a platoon of tank destroyers were the first across. They arrived just as the infantry was in danger of being pushed back into the river. Jim Gifford recalled, 'We were crossing the Moselle at night and I had on the back of my tank a little artillery trailer, a small thing but it was a big box. It had a German machine gun and some other stuff. And when we brought the tank up to cross, Patton was standing there with a couple of his aides watching us go by and damn, this trailer was too narrow, so it wouldn't go into the tracks. If it was going to be dragged across it was going to be a problem. So I pushed it off into the river and let it sink as we weren't supposed to have all that loot.'

Lex Obrient, who was Andy Schiffler's lieutenant, recalled that 'Sam Adair with his three assault guns and my platoon crossed the Moselle at Thionville at night. My tank was on one of the engineer floats, the rafts they made up, and very quiet. Everybody was quiet as a church mouse. Off in front of me, a German gunner fired and it seemed like the thing came over my head. It was orange and I saw it coming right towards me and I thought, "Oh, this is it." But it was overhead and it missed. So we got across the river and we're north and east of Metz. And Sam Adair with his three assault guns and my platoon, we assembled and then we went right on out onto the road. We went down the road to a junction and right at that junction there was a guest house. It had a high wall all the way around it and I figured that's a wonderful place to stop.

'We were very good to the people. We said, "Listen, we need to be here. You can have half of the house for yourselves, but we need the other half." We weren't rough with them. So I positioned my tanks and Sam kept his assault guns up on the high ground, but we were all aiming for that road that came out of Metz. And sure enough, we could see the little cat eyes of vehicles moving and they were coming right on into us. I had a squad of infantry with me. I've forgotten where those guys came from, but they had mortars and they could fire flares, so I said, "Okay, now hold what you've got. Don't do anything yet. I want the first vehicle sitting right out there in front of me until he can't turn around and get away." So that's exactly what happened. There was a lieutenant in there. He had all clean clothes hanging on his vehicle and he thought he was headed for Strasbourg, and he didn't even know we were there. Then I told the guy, "Okay, flare. Let's see what we've got here." So the flares were fired all over the place and we could see them real good. Radwan was the guy that I depended on a lot. So I said, "John, yell out there to them to surrender. We're not gonna hurt them." But we had no takers. And then all of a sudden we started firing. I didn't really know what all was in that column except we took the lieutenant right away and I think we probably didn't get more than ten or twelve people at the most. We took them into that guest house and somebody stood guard over them.

'The next morning we saw what we had. There were horse-drawn vehicles, wagons, brand new Luger pistols and supplies. They had been holed up in Metz and were trying to get out and get home, but they never made it. We wiped that column completely out. And then sometime later on in the morning, here comes a major from the Air Corps and he had his pad and he's making notes.

'"What are you doing here?" we said.

'"I'm assessing all these casualties that our Air Force did."

'"Wait just a minute. The Air Force didn't do this. We did it." So he didn't like that and left.'

Dess Tibbitts, the cowboy from northern California whose buddy Phil Schromm was killed the first day in combat, remembered the fighting that took place after crossing the Moselle. Tibbitts was a driver in A Company's second platoon that had a new lieutenant, Chauncy Miller. 'Right on the first hill after we crossed the Moselle River we had a hell of a fight on top,' recalled Tibbitts. 'They blew two or three tanks up then we went into another tank. I remember there was a German tank that had a wounded soldier in it. They didn't get around to get him till pretty near morning. You could hear him moaning in there but we didn't go in after him. Their medics finally came and got him. But there was quite a bit of shooting right afterward.'

The lead tank of Tibbitts' platoon (its driver was Pine Valley Bynum who gave my father a lift to the front in Normandy) was knocked out with no serious casualties. Lieutenant Miller returned to Tibbitts' tank – which was the first tank of the second section – as it had a two-way radio. 'So he could get headquarters or anyplace else,' said Tom Wood, the gunner in that tank. 'Miller was in the motor pool and the way I understood, somebody wanted to get him out of the motor pool. So they told him you ought to get a platoon so you can get a chance to get a promotion,' Wood recalled at the 1995 reunion. Miller was standing in the turret of Wood's tank with the hatch open when shrapnel from a tree burst penetrated his helmet. 'I was holding him when he died,' Tibbitts said, 'and it seemed like I wasn't holding him very long.' The lull in the action was over for the 712th Tank Battalion.

At the 1994 reunion in Fort Mitchell, I spoke with John McDaniel, the A Company veteran who could not find his shoes during the battle at Mairy. McDaniel drove for Lieutenant Bell whose platoon took over for Miller's platoon.

'We were talking yesterday about Lieutenant Miller getting killed at Evange,' McDaniel said. 'I've been back to the big church building just as you go into Evange. I remember almost the exact bullet holes there.

When we were back 40 years later they were exactly the same. But we took the town of Evange after Lieutenant Miller got killed and the next day we were taking Distroff, France, and that's where we fought all day.

'Ellwood McCord from Washington State and I went back there. It was a little area that had changed none, but the curve that went around into the town, even to the front of the building where they shot the bazooka into us was exactly the same. And the area that we had to run back through the field. At that time, there was an anti-tank group there. They had all been shot. Some of them were dead, others were trying to get help, but we were all wounded too. That's the route that we went back and they had a holding area back there taking the wounded. We were all taken to it. That curve and everything is exactly the same except that they built a highline across that field. That was the only difference. There wasn't a new building. Every building was exactly like it was and that was forty years later.'

'What's a highline?' I asked.

'Oh, I'm sorry. I'm an old electrical guy. A highline is a distribution line, one that feeds the businesses and the homes. A power line. They had a big transmission, double structure. They didn't have any wood over there, their structures were concrete. I was wounded in the neck and then I was burned. My hair was burned. I've even got some on my fingers. I've got a little bit of shrapnel in my leg, too. It went through and they couldn't take it out the front way because it was lodged right against the main artery and they had to enlarge the wound to take it out the back way. It had gone almost all the way through. And I remember my head being numb until after the operation and they had to cut some of the nerves to get it out the back way as it was lodged against the artery.'

24

Gross Hemmersdorf

You will not read much about Gross Hemmersdorf in books or documentaries about the Second World War, perhaps a line or a few paragraphs in the many memoirs written by veterans of the 90th Infantry Division. Gross Hemmersdorf was one of a thousand villages whose names are logged in the unit histories and after-action reports of the 712th Tank Battalion and 90th Infantry Division. It was the place where Buck Hardee was seriously wounded and his tank commander, Sergeant Wesley Lochard, killed. It was the place that after the battle Jim Gifford recalled shooting and killing a pig that was devouring Lochard's remains. And it was the town where Ed Spahr asked me to turn off the tape.

'1st platoon captured Guerfanger 29 November while 2nd platoon took the high ground east of that town,' the C Company after-action report for 29-30 November 1944 reads. 'One tank knocked out en route by enemy artillery. 3rd platoon captured Gross Hemmersdorf. One tank knocked out by bazooka, the tank commander being fatally machine gunned by the enemy as he got out of the tank.'

Ed Spahr died on 15 January 1997. According to his obituary, he was awarded five Bronze Stars, none of which he mentioned when I interviewed him in 1991. Stanley Klapkowski, who, according to his crewmates, received two Silver Stars, passed away on 10 February 1998. When I interviewed him, Klapkowski claimed he was awarded the Bronze and a Silver Star. Jim Gifford, Bob Rossi, Grayson La Mar... they have all passed away. One of the generic questions I asked Spahr that afternoon in 1991 was 'What was the toughest thing you had to do?' It would be the first of many times that I would see a grown man get choked up.

'There was this one incident near the end of the war. The Germans were getting hard up. They had horse-drawn artillery and there were three pieces of artillery coming down the road. They saw us and stopped. They turned an anti-tank gun around on us and fired. They must have been poor gunners because they fired three shots at us before I fired and I could see in my sights that I hit this anti-tank gun. I hit it with H.E., that's high-explosive, and I could see a body flying up in the air. I saw a horse get hit at the same time when the shell exploded on the front end of this German field piece. The horse was hit in the backend, I guess, because his front feet were trying to drag around. I believe there were four horses attached to this field piece or maybe it was only two, I forget. But one horse was all right and the other horse was trying to get away, and dragging this other horse... (Spahr's voice begins to break) And my next shot, I took to put those horses... out of their misery. I didn't know whether the other horse had been hit, but it probably had some shrapnel in it. I had seen a horse before that was hit and he was all blown up. He was laying in the field. He looked like he was going to burst and I thought to myself, those poor horses, I'm not going to let them suffer. So the next shot, I sent a high-explosive into those horses... That's hard... In fact, that's harder than enemy soldiers. But I had to do it.' After a pause, perhaps taking a moment to reflect on whether he should continue, Spahr said, 'Turn off the tape.'

What he said next took a hammer and a chisel and engraved itself in my mind. And although he did not remember the date or the place, a corroborating interview placed the incident in Gross Hemmersdorf. At some point according to Spahr, a woman in a German uniform, possibly that of a boyfriend, emerged from a house and opened her jacket, baring her breasts to show she was a woman and not a combatant. Klapkowski, who at this point was on top of the tank, then cut her down with the tank commander's .50-calibre machine gun. Klapkowski had jumped off of his tank, climbed on another tank, most likely Sergeant Lochard's, and resumed firing the .50 that was mounted on the turret. He continued firing after the battle was over and had to be pulled off the gun.

Sometimes the line between a decoration and a court martial is a thin one. Bob Rossi was furious that Klapkowski had left his tank without a gunner, although this was presumably the incident for which Klapkowski got one of his two decorations. (The other was for almost singlehandedly destroying a German mechanised column outside of Le Mans.) Jim Gifford likely would not have witnessed the woman being cut down, but he did recall that Klapkowski had to be pulled off the machine gun. Spahr said the medics tried to sedate Klapkowski by giving him two pills that were called 'Blue 88s.' Spahr said they had no effect on Klapkowski and he had to be taken away in a straitjacket. However, although Klapkowski would eventually be sent back to the States with battle fatigue, this was in November and he was still with the tank in January when the tank was knocked out and Lieutenant Gifford wounded. When I interviewed Klapkowski at his home in McKees Rocks, Pennsylvania, in May 1996, he had no recollection of gunning down a woman. On the other hand, he did say he was credited with 236 days in combat, which would mean he was with the platoon until February 1945 when the battalion was fighting in the Siegfried Line.

At the January 1997 mini-reunion of the battalion in Bradenton, Florida, I was sitting with Grayson La Mar and Buck Hardee. I asked them about the incident. Hardee was wounded that day and La Mar was driving another tank in the third platoon.

'Klapkowski shot a woman running across a field with a .50 calibre machine gun,' La Mar said.

'Was it clear she was a woman?' I asked.

'Yeah, Lombardi chewed him out for shooting a woman. He didn't care. He was crazy. He was a good gunner, though. That was down where you all got hurt,' he said to Hardee. 'You and Lochard, when Lochard got killed and I was driving for Lombardi, do you remember any of that? Dead-end street at the end. We went as far as we could. I went back down there and got y'all's tank. They didn't bother the tank.'

'It had a hole through it,' Hardee added.

'Yeah, well, it was still running. I went down and got it. Drove it up by where we was.'

'Of course, I didn't know anything about that. That was after...'

'They had Lochard laying on a sidewalk and an old hog biting him,' La Mar said. 'I saw him and one boy shot the hog.'

'I was looking straight at Lochard,' Hardee said.

'Straight at him when he was hit?'

'Yes. He was taking cover by a building over to the right, back off the street. He got out of the tank and fire was coming at us from everywhere. After we were hit, the first thing was get the hell out of that tank.'

'That's when you and Lupe (Guadalupe Valdivia, the loader) crawled out of the tank, wasn't it?' La Mar asked.

'Yes. Lochard got out of the tank and he got over by this little building. It looked like an office building. It was back off the street and he was out there with that submachine gun. That's all he had. He had got out of the tank and we could see tracers. There was all kinds of firepower coming at us from every direction. You could see those tracers just flying everywhere and my leg was so paralysed I couldn't move fast. I looked back around trying to figure out where am I going with all these tracers going everywhere. How can I get out of here? So I got myself down the side of the tank, but while I was trying to get out the turret, I was looking to see where to go. Wes was over here and they were firing at him. The bullet hit him right in the forehead and he dropped right there. That's when I first saw all that firepower. There's nowhere to go and Lupe came right behind me, and we both went right down beside the tank.'

'Didn't a German crawl down there with you?' La Mar asked.

'I don't know.'

'Seems like it was and Lupe stabbed or shot him.'

'We slid on around the tank. There was firing coming everywhere. They were hitting us from every angle. So we slid around the front of the tank and crawled under to try to protect ourselves from some of that firepower. I was hit through the neck and lost consciousness. I left this old world as far as I knew. But some weeks later back in the hospital in England, I now know what happened after that. You said you had gotten the tank?'

'Yeah, I went and got Lochard's tank.'

'I was looking straight at Lochard,' Hardee said. 'He was a good guy. I heard someone made some such remark that Lochard was trying to run away or something. He definitely was not. He was there trying to protect us. He was doing his best. He was standing there with a submachine gun in his hand trying... "What can I fire at? What can I do to protect...?" And suddenly it hit him right in his forehead.'

'Lupe was loading, wasn't he?' La Mar asked.

'I believe he was loading. I've been out that way. I've stopped by to see him a couple of times when I went through there.'

'This is Lupe Valdivia?' I asked.

'Yes, Guadalupe R. Valdivia.'

'He was a whole lot older than we was, wasn't he?' La Mar asked. 'He was a little Mexican, wasn't he?'

'Yes, he was shorter than I am.'

'I thought he was too short to be in the service.'

'But he had the right position back there as the loader. He fit in there good. We stopped by there. It's been years ago (Valdivia lived in Topeka, Kansas). You know, one I'd like to see is old Raymond Seymour. I had a card from him at Christmas. He said he's had some heart problems. I would really like to see him. We were travelling through Humboldt, Tennessee, and I made some calls. I found the name in the phone book and called a couple of numbers to see if I could locate him. I didn't find a Raymond Seymour listed but I found a Seymour and called him. It was an attorney and he didn't know anything about him, so evidently he lives out in the country somewhere. I thought certainly somebody would know where he lived. He was real tall, skinny, at that time. I imagine like the rest of us he's put on considerable weight. We used to give him a hard time being from Tennessee. We teased him about the way he got into the service, he swung out on a grapevine to get the mail or something like that and the draft board caught him. He was a typical Tennessee hillbilly.'

25

Dillingen

While listening to the stories of the veterans of the 712th Tank Battalion, I have even become the subject of a few stories. For instance, Jim Flowers was telling the story of Hill 122 and he took a little longer than usual to reach for a detail. Having heard the story several times, I supplied it for him. Jim fixed me with a stare and said, 'Who's telling this story, me or you?' Another time, at the 1993 reunion in Orlando, Florida, I asked Otha Martin a question that resulted in a story Paul Wannemacher likes to tell. 'If you were in Snuffy Fuller's platoon,' I asked, 'were you at Pfaffenheck?'

Otha, a rancher from Macalester, Oklahoma, who looked every bit the former Macalester State Penitentiary prison guard he was, said 'Pfaffenheck.' Just that one word. He then paused and said, 'The 16th day of March in '45. I was *there*. I can tell you every *man* that was there.' Paul Wannemacher watched in awe as Otha proceeded to name the five crew members in each of the five tanks that took part in the battle for Pfaffenheck when the second platoon of C Company fought elements of the 6th SS Mountain Division North. The third story Paul likes to tell also took place at that 1993 reunion in Orlando. Caesar Tucci, who was then the battalion association president, brought a D Company log to the reunion. I was sitting at a table in the hospitality room leafing through it and opened to the portion describing the battle at Dillingen, Germany, where my father was wounded a second time. My father was a lieutenant in A Company and the log was from D Company, so I did not expect to see his name. At the first reunion I attended in 1987, all I remembered from my father's stories about the war was the name of one fellow officer, Ed Forrest, and the place where my father was wounded for the second time: Dillingen. At that reunion, I found many more veterans who remembered Ed Forrest as he was one of the battalion's original officers whereas my dad was a replacement. When I mentioned Dillingen, I discovered that I had tapped into one of the significant events in the battalion's history.

Dillingen was an industrial city on the Saar River, south of Saarbrucken. The Saar stood between the Moselle, which the battalion crossed in November, and the Rhine. It was also the subject of two of Forrest Dixon's favourite stories, although the numbers of the first tended to change as he repeated it over the years. In the story as Dixon told it, the battalion had crossed the Saar and was fighting in Dillingen when Colonel Randolph heard on the BBC that the Germans broke through north of Dillingen with ten thousand men. So Colonel Randolph called Colonel Stillwell on the phone and said, 'Is it true that the Germans broke through with ten thousand men?' To which Colonel Stillwell replied, 'It's true, but it wasn't ten thousand men. It was ten divisions.'

That first reunion I attended was in 1987 and I knew little about military history. So I was surprised when other people at the table gasped. 'How many men are in a division?' I asked. The answer was 13,000 men. Sometimes when I subsequently heard Forrest tell the story, the Germans would breakthrough with 13,000 men and Colonel Stillwell would tell Colonel Randolph it was thirteen divisions.

In actuality, the Germans broke through with sixteen divisions and the Battle of the Bulge had begun. The 90th Division had crossed the Saar a few days earlier and was fighting to expand the bridgehead. The Nied River where the battle of Gross Hemmersdorf took place was a tributary of the Saar. But back to the story Paul Wannemacher likes to tell about me. When Lieutenant Elson arrived at battalion headquarters, all three platoons of A Company had officers, but an officer was needed to lead a patrol bringing material across the river. As I was reading the D Company log under the entry for 10 December, which coincidentally is the date in 1949 that I was born, I came upon the following passage:

'10 December 1944 – The 357th Inf. Regt had crossed the Saar River and had penetrated into the enemy lines. Their position was rather precarious due to enemy forces and pillboxes to their direct front and on both flanks. All their available manpower was needed to hold the ground they had. Supplies were needed very badly so 40 men were called from the Battalion to act as the carrying party. Ten men and one officer were chosen from the Company and included 1st Lt (Lambert) Hiatt, 1st Sgt (William) Thompson; Sgt Kwiatkowski, Tec. 5 (U.Z.) Roderick; Pfcs Sparks, Vincent and Pvts Kittelson, W. Doyle, Murray and McLesky. The carrying party left the Company area at 18.30, proceeded to the C Company area near Buren, picked up the men from the Company and parked at a chateau about a half-mile west of there. A guide was picked up and the party was marched to the river and to the row boats stowed with the food, ammunition and medical supplies needed by the Regt. Great care had to be exercised in making the crossing because of the nearness of the enemy and very swift current. The boats were rowed by our men because there was also a shortage of engineers. The supplies were unloaded on the beach and the forty men started carrying them to a large chateau located 1½ miles west. The terrain between the two points was low and marshy and was covered on the right flank by two German machine gun nests located in the outskirts of the town of Pachten.' I was fascinated as I read this as it was the first description I had of the circumstances of the patrol on which my father was wounded, although I had not yet come across his name nor did I expect to since this was a D Company document.

'Guided by fire from the partially burning chateau and by following the railroad tracks for part of the way, the party reached the chateau and dumped the first load after being subjected to heavy searching mortar fire. The time was now about 24.00. The return trip was made without event except that the point was missed by about a half mile to the left. A wet and heavy snow began to fall that made travelling conditions even worse. A group consisting of Kwiatkowski, Sparks, Mallak, Kittelson, Roderick, Doyle, Murray, Vincent and twelve others formed a party to carry bundles of litters, two men for each bundle of litters. About eight minutes after the party left, Vincent reported back to the 1st Sgt after his partner was unable to continue from exhaustion. The balance of the men from the group reached the chateau with the litters.

'An enemy pillbox had been captured several days before and was being used as a forward medical station. The position had become too hard to hold with the available forces and that section was forced to retreat. There were 25 litter patients in the pillbox that would have to be left behind to be captured by the Germans unless evacuated by forces other than the holding forces. The litter carrying group at the chateau was asked to, and agreed to, try to evacuate these patients. Each man took a litter and placed under the command of Lt Elson. (In my third year of attending reunions, I had just discovered the first official mention in a document of my father, and unexpectedly at that, but this is not the part of the story that Paul likes to tell.) They started toward the pillbox around 03.00 (A heavy snow was on the ground. I remembered my father saying there was snow on the ground when he was wounded, taking cover advantage of trenches wherever possible. Heavy artillery, mortar and small arms fire was encountered along the way. The following is the part of the story that Paul likes to tell.)

'While crossing a road, Lt Elson was hit three times by small arms fire believed to come from our own troops. (Paul happened to be looking in my direction when he saw me jump out of my seat. Each time he told the story subsequently, I seem to have jumped a little higher.) The group was ordered to drop the litters and return to the chateau to check on our own firing and to wait until the enemy fire moderated. Again, the group started for the pillbox, recovered the abandoned litters and proceeded slowly onwards. Progress was very slow due to the extreme darkness, thick woods, mud, rough terrain and heavy enemy mortar and artillery fire. The pillbox was reached about 07.00. The litters were loaded and the trip back started with the litter patients, about 40 wounded that were able to walk, the small group of medics and the holding force that amounted to about 15 soldiers.

'It was soon discovered that the group was heading in a slightly wrong direction and Pfc Sparks volunteered to carry the Red Cross flag and try to lead the group back to the proper place. He hid his weapon in the folds of a blanket and set off on a new course, waving the flag as he went. Fortunately, the Germans respected the flag and ceased small arms fire, but the men were still subjected to air and tree bursts from artillery. A German machine gun nest was passed that had just been knocked out by the infantry. This nest was passed on the way up to the pillbox and must have been in operation at that time. The chateau, or forward C.P. of the 357th Infantry, was reached with the 25 litter patients. The time was about 10.30. This group was released, but had to remain at this C.P. until the river could be crossed under the cover of night.'

On 5 December 1944, according to the battalion after action reports, 'A composite platoon made up of Headquarters Company, D Company and Service Company personnel left to join the 359th Infantry Regiment with ten .50 calibre machine guns.' Caesar Tucci of D Company was one of those personnel. 'They requested volunteers to man gun positions on the Saar River to kind of make a fake for the Germans, to make them feel that we were coming across in strength, so there was a lot of firing to be built up and I volunteered. They said this would be a mission of two or three days. I went down and manned a .50-calibre machine gun. We had .50-calibre machine guns and mortars that we set up inside the houses and various areas on the west side of the Saar to fire across at the pillboxes of the Siegfried Line. I travelled light because they said it would be two or three days. To get down to the firing position, we had to reach the top of a hill and then the halftrack had to make a mad dash because it was exposed to direct fire from the Germans on the other side of the river. It was like going through a gauntlet. They were firing at us but we beat it. We got into town and then we were out of their view.

'We set up our headquarters in a brick apartment building. My partner and I sandbagged the machine gun in a German home on a porcelain kitchen table and had it fixed to shoot out the back window of the kitchen across the river. The fire missions would be announced to us on the radio. When we were told to start a fire mission, we would run across the street, put the back plate on the machine gun (we'd never leave the back plate there because German patrols would come through the town at night) and when they gave us the word to fire, everybody – mortars, .50-calibres, everything – they'd fire across that river to give a real show of force. That would go on for four or five minutes and then the gun would get real hot, so when the fire mission stopped, I had to reach out with an asbestos glove, take the barrel off, ram an oil patch through it right away and then take the back plate off the machine gun and beat it across the street back into the building. That two or three day fire mission lasted two weeks. We were relieved from that position on my birthday, the 16th of December.'

On 9 December, according to the after-action reports, Lieutenant Lombardi and two enlisted men left to go on thirty-day furloughs to the States. This is likely when Lieutenant Gifford took command of C Company's third platoon. A day later, the night of which I had learned my father was wounded, the first tanks of the battalion crossed the Saar on ferries. This is when Bob 'Big Andy' Anderson, the horseshoer turned tank driver, earned the first of his three Bronze Stars. 'On our third platoon, we got all five tanks across,' Anderson said. 'Two tanks got mired down out in the mud. I took my tank. We had cables, oh, I might say 15, 20 feet long. I hooked three of them together and dragged them back, and hooked onto the tank back there in the mire. I then got back in my tank and got the two tanks pulled back out. Of course, I pulled my tank. We got in there right up in front of a store and we looted that.'

'For heroic service in support of operations against the enemy during the period 9 to 10 December 1944,' the citation for Anderson's Bronze Star reads, 'when the tanks of a platoon were mired in the marshy soil on the far side of the river, Technician 4th Grade Anderson, tank driver, with companions, subjected himself to heavy enemy artillery and mortar fire and laboured arduously to retrieve the tanks. His untiring efforts and complete devotion to duty were instrumental in saving the tanks and in enabling the platoon to accomplish its mission. His heroic service was in accordance with military tradition.'

By 14 December, the battalion had forty tanks, three assault guns, three quarter-ton trucks and one ammunition truck across the Saar and fighting in Dillingen. 'We kept one tank as an outpost,' in Dillingen said

Ed Spahr of C Company's third platoon. 'It was almost three-quarters of a mile outside of town overlooking the Siegfried Line. We would take turns manning the tank in case the Germans would come back through there. We'd go back into town to eat, but always, night and day, there was a whole crew in the tank. To get to the tank, we had to cross a zigzag trench that the Germans had built. One day, I was going up – we'd rotate people one at a time – through this open field and I thought I heard something going past close to me. It just sounded like somebody snapped their fingers. I couldn't figure out just what this was because you could see all around and I couldn't see anything. The second time I heard this, it seemed like it was getting closer, something just snapping going past my head. And at once I realised somebody was shooting at me, because after I'd hear this snap, a second or two later I could hear a rifle crack. It wasn't loud. It was way off. But he was shooting at me. I made a leap, rolled through the grass, came to this trench and dropped down in it. I didn't know which way I landed and I didn't know which direction to go in.

'The trench leaned a little towards the tank on one end and away from it on the other. So I thought I'll go down through these zigzags a little ways one way and then I'll look out and if I can't see the tank I'll go in the other direction. As I came around one of the zigs in the trench, I saw a German soldier sitting down and he had a machine pistol laying across him. The first thing that came to my mind was that he had that gun aiming at me. I had a Thompson submachine gun with the stock cut off slung over my shoulder. I had a 15-round clip in it and I swung around and pulled the trigger, and I could see the dust flying out of his uniform. I just emptied that clip. I stood still and didn't move. I thought he should fall over. He never moved. I put another clip in and I eased up to him. I kicked his foot. Nothing moved. He had probably been dead for two or three days. He was stiff as a board. I have to laugh at myself. I've only told one or two guys about this, me shooting the hell out of a dead soldier.'

Jim Cary, the C Company commander who was wounded by a booby trap on the battalion's first day in combat, returned in September and was now the B Company commander. 'We got in this operation closing up to the Saar. As I remember the plan, it was for the 90th Division to go across the Saar and establish a bridgehead, and then the 10th Armored would attack through that bridgehead and go up towards Frankfurt. Right where we went across was the first belt of the Siegfried Line. It was pretty rough going and the first assault that went across was strictly infantry. They got into a very bad situation. The Germans really wanted to wipe out that bridgehead and they threw almost everything they had in the area at it. They were rolling up on the flank and the only way the Americans could stop it was to turn all the artillery they had in the area loose on this German attack. I heard figures like 30 battalions of artillery. I really don't know how many battalions, but I saw what happened afterward and that was the most horrible sight I ever saw in the entire war, and something that I still visualise at times.

'We had this fairly shallow bridgehead across the Saar and the Germans were going up the left flank, and they were doing a pretty good job of it. There were GIs along a road here and this extreme intense artillery fire came down right in the middle of that concentration of troops, and it was very shortly after that that we got our tanks across. I had a platoon that was out here on this flank and I used to have to ride through that scene and there were bodies stacked one on top of the other. There must have been eight or nine hundred bodies in that area with parts of their heads blown off. I remember in one case, a German had fallen face down in the road and it was muddy. Cars were driving back and forth over him and I kept asking myself, "Why doesn't this bother me more than it does?" You get so immune to it.

'You could almost see what had happened. There were GIs in this shallow ditch along the edge of the road and some of them had got shot by the Germans, some of them were caught in the artillery barrage. They were frozen in position, some of them sitting up. It was a terrible thing to have to go through day after day. One of our tanks threw a track. It was on the side of a hill and we couldn't get it out. Eventually, we had to destroy it when we pulled back. But before that, I was back near the regimental headquarters and every day I had to go out to see these tanks. You couldn't drive up there and I had to go across an open space, and the damn Germans sitting up there would start dropping smoke markers. They would land maybe ten feet away from me and that meant that if they wanted to they could drop a mortar barrage and that would be the end of me. I had to get out there to see those guys. Fortunately, the Germans didn't want to waste the ammunition on one man.'

As the Battle of the Bulge intensified, it was decided to bring the 90th Division back across the Saar. The engineers completed a pontoon bridge and a chemical mortar company provided smoke cover, which resulted in the other of Forrest Dixon's stories about Dillingen. 'The engineers had put a bridge across and it was covered by a smokescreen. We put a tank destroyer platoon across the bridge and the next group to go across was the first platoon of A Company. Sergeant Bussell, who was my driver back when I was in G Company, yelled to me. I recognised him. I said, "Be careful." He was a good driver, but careless. One tank would be leaving the bridge, one tank in the middle and one tank going on. And just about then the wind changed direction. The smokescreen cleared and the bridge was wide open. I heard about three shots from the Germans and all of a sudden, my God, right behind Bussell's tank the bridge was cut. I picked up the mic and said, "Bussell, give her hell or you'll drown!" And his tank started to sink. Then he gave her the gas and he went across the rest of the river at an angle, but he got across.'

Big Andy was also a driver in A Company and may have been on the bridge ahead of Bussell, although he remembered the bridge being attacked by planes rather by artillery. 'We were sitting on the bank waiting to go across,' Big Andy recalled, 'and they came back and said, "Now, when you go across, go slow." Well, you know how it is with a 33-ton tank going across water. I was probably three-quarters of the way across when two German planes came in and started strafing across the river. And you ought to have seen me go across the river. I didn't go slow.'

'I might add a couple of other things about this withdrawal,' Jim Cary said. 'The American Army is not very good at retreating, I'm afraid. There came a stage when enough had been pulled out of that bridgehead where the control started to disappear, particularly after most of the infantry was gone. I was near the headquarters where they were directing this withdrawal and you couldn't get a straight story from anybody about what you were supposed to do. I was upset about it and I was sort of wandering around outside. It was at night and this MP came up to me. "What am I supposed to do with these civilians over in this church?"

'"I don't know. What were you told you were supposed to do?"

'"I was told to leave them, but I understand the building next to it is full of C-2 explosive and they're gonna blow that before they pull out of here."

'"Who do you take your orders from?"

'"They're gone. I can't leave those civilians there."

'"You sure can't. I don't care what the problem is, just get them out of there and if anybody comes back at you, tell them I told you to do it."

'So he moved them. And then we did get back across and I was standing on the other side of the Saar River when they blew that, the whole skyline lit up. Do you remember what the burning of Atlanta looked like in *Gone With the Wind*? Very much like that. The buildings were silhouetted against the sky and behind the sky there were all these flames and the sky was red. It was quite a scene.'

In 2010, I received an e-mail from Patricia Robison. 'My uncle was a member of the 712th Tank Battalion,' she wrote. 'He was killed on 27 February 1945 in Luxembourg (the battalion was in Germany by then). I have been reading one of your books about the 712th and was wondering if any of your interviews mentioned a Lee Miller, nickname "Punch."'

I remembered that the name of Patricia's uncle came up in my interview with Jim Cary, but it was I who supplied him with the name. Before I interviewed Cary, I was sitting with some B Company veterans including Juel Winfrey, Bob Vutech and 'Rip' Bardo. 'We had a young fellow as a tank commander named Lee Miller,' Winfrey said. 'Lee was another boy from Oklahoma. When they started the Bulge, they gave us orders to pull out of Dillingen. We had one tank that had been mired down in the mud and they wanted a volunteer to stay behind and blow up that tank after the rest of us got back across the river. We were going back across that pontoon bridge. He was to meet a couple of infantry guys and the three of them would come back together, because the infantry guys had a bunch of ammunition they had to blow up. And when Lee got back to this designated place that he was supposed to meet the two infantry men, they never did show up. This is in December. He swam that Saar River that December night, cold as the Dickens, and I don't remember the exact date, but it must have been a week or ten days before he was able to catch up with us.'

It was a short while later that I interviewed Jim Cary. I asked if he remembered Sergeant Miller.

'No.'

'There was one B Company tank that had to be left behind.'

'Yes, was he the guy that destroyed it?' Cary asked.

'Yes.'

'I've lost the name of the man, but I put him in for a Silver Star. I asked for a volunteer to stay behind. We knew that the infantry was going to pull out. Stay behind and put a thermite grenade in the barrel of the gun and strap one on the other part of the gun, then pull the plug and get the hell out of it. And he did. He did a good job. And came running back and he reached the Saar. As I got the story and he was supposed to go back on one of the barges they had going back and forth, and there wasn't anybody there, so he jumped in and swam across. I put him in for a Silver Star and I understand he got a Bronze Star.

'About destroying a tank, that was spooky business. That was way out on the flank. I felt like I had to go out there and see those guys every day, but every time I did, the Germans started dropping smoke mortars in on me. But the closest call I had was when some damn stupid tank destroyer on our side of the river spotted me moving over there and started shooting at me. And I had to dodge through all of these trenches trying to get away from our own guns. He could see me across the river.'

'How do you know it was a tank destroyer?' I asked.

'I think it was because it was a flat-trajectory shell. It could have been a tank. Besides, I didn't like tank destroyers. Every time you moved into someplace, they were always there ahead of you and they had picked out the best places for sleeping. And I never saw them do any fighting.'

'Not that I know of,' said Clegg 'Doc' Caffery, the Headquarters Company Major, who was sitting at the table.

'Me either,' Cary added. 'I'm revealing all my prejudices now.'

'They were so lightly armored, but they had a 76-mm gun.'

'I guess they did do some fighting,' Cary said. 'It was really a misconceived weapon. They should have put that gun on the tanks, then you would have had a versatile weapon. You could either use it to fight other tanks or you could use it as a tank. It's a high-velocity gun, a 76 mm. We could sure have used it. We had a shorter 75. The tank destroyers didn't have much armor.'

'I can understand why they were hesitant.'

'Yes, well, they weren't really an attack weapon, they were a defence weapon. Come to think of it, how the hell did you beat me in that tennis match?' And so, as many conversations in the hospitality room went, the content shifted from warfare to tennis or baseball, golf, grandchildren, hospitals, travel...

As for Sergeant Miller, in February 1945, according to Winfrey, 'The 6th Cavalry made arrangements with the 712th Tank Battalion to get one platoon of tanks in an area to support them. And they sent this lieutenant back to pick us up. This lieutenant led us by jeep with the tanks following to an area that was supposed to be secured. And when we got up there, our platoon leader, Lieutenant Gaggett, said, "Now you guys, one tank of you get your mess kits and your rations and go in this house back here and make an evening meal. The other two tanks, you keep a loader and a gunner in the tank just as an outpost, and the other three of you go." We climbed out of our tanks, got in front of it, and you know how wide the front of a tank is. We were lined up, me right in the middle and Lee Miller on my right side, and I can't remember who the assistant driver was, but he was on the other side. Aaron Craig, who was the loader, was on my left side and the other member of the crew was over here. And all at once we heard the German shell come. And Lee Miller said, "Look out!" and that's the last words the man ever spoke. The shrapnel caught him right in the back and it killed him like that. Standing right here at my shoulder. Aaron Craig over on this side was badly wounded. And the other three of us didn't get scratched.'

According to Forrest Dixon, Colonel Randolph was told if he could not get the tanks back across the Saar, he should destroy all forty tanks. One C Company tank had a bad clutch and Captain Jack Sheppard, the company commander, was driving it. 'I think he was still a first lieutenant,' Dixon recalled. 'I said, "Lieutenant, get this tank off this corduroy road." (A corduroy road was made from trees that were chopped down so that the tanks could traverse a muddy area without getting bogged down.)

'"Oh," he said. "I can manage it."

'"I've got orders to destroy the whole battalion if we can't get them across the river. Nobody's going to criticise me for destroying one tank."

'So we got the whole battalion across and he still wanted to bring that tank across.

'"That isn't your best tank anyway," I said.

'"But I've never done this."

'"If you don't want to do it I will."

'"No," he said. "I'll do it. What do I do?"

'"Empty a can of gasoline in it and take a hand grenade and put it in, but make sure you get the top shut before the hand grenade goes off. Then jump." So we left the tank burning and came on across. Colonel Randolph told me, "Use your judgement. If we can't get the tanks across I've got orders to destroy them all."'

After the bridge was blown, the remaining tanks were carried by ferry back across the Saar. Clegg Caffery was among the last to leave. 'We crossed the river that night at 3 o'clock. I was the last vehicle across, I think,' he said. 'My flashlight fell off my belt and hit the deck of the ferry and went on and I reached down to pick it up. A light colonel of the engineers stuck his face about two inches from mine and said, "What are you doing with that, soldier?" I was so pooped, really, I was just at a ragged edge and I just laughed in his face. I uncontrollably laughed in his face. And I turned around, got in the jeep and took off. About five minutes later, we went in battalion headquarters right across the river Saar in a little house there. Jim Cary and I hit the deck. Before we hit the floor we were almost sound asleep. We were just pooped out.'

'That would have been about the 20th of December,' Forrest Dixon replied.

26

'I Am in Company C and in Germany Now'

'Dear Mom,' Billy Wolfe wrote in a letter dated 12 February 1945. 'I am glad you heard from Hubert. I had a letter from Gigi, Peg and you today. The most mail I received in a long, long time. So Uncle Hukey is in Belgium? (Hukey is what the neighbour's children called Hubert Wolfe, Billy's older brother, as they could not pronounce Hubert.) I have written to him a number of times. About the next time you hear from me I will be overseas. We packed this morning. We will be leaving soon. Tell Mary I am awfully sorry about her cigarettes. Was Hubert's letter V-mail? It didn't take it long to come over considering the distance and all. I will have to close now. If you don't hear for a while, you will know why. All my love, Bill.'

On 16 February, Billy wrote, 'It seems like a long time since I last heard from you. I did get a letter on the 12th. How is everyone there? Oh, yes, I got the Valentines the other day. Thanks a lot. I saw in a newsreel a couple of weeks ago about a fire in the Norfolk Navy Yard. Was it close to where Dad works? I wrote to Hubert yesterday. I hope he gets it all right and before his birthday. Have you heard from him lately? We just had a physical check-up. They are a nuisance. Say, Mom, have you gotten my January war bond? I reckon you and the censor will have a hell of a time reading this, but the boat is sort of rocking and Jake is sort of shaking his bunk. I wish you all could see the ocean from a boat. The ocean is so blue it looks like I could dip my pen and write with it. We are on a nice boat, I think. Well, folks, I don't know what to say, so take things easy. Love, Bill.'

'5 March 1945, Dearest Folks, I wrote you a nice long letter the Third and lost the darned thing, so I will have to try another one. I haven't much to tell except that I have joined an outfit. As a lieutenant told us, "The best goddamned outfit in the world." I don't know much about its history as yet, but it played a major part in smashing the Siegfried Line and has fought since D-Day and drove the Nazis from France. It is the 712th Tank Battalion. I am in Company C and in Germany now. Have you heard from Hubert lately? I haven't heard a damned thing from anyone since the first of February. I am going to write to Hubert tonight, I think. I have written to him I don't know how often, but haven't heard from him. When my mail comes through I should get a bushel basket full. I wrote to Peg the other night and haven't sent it yet. Twins, I think you are having a birthday soon. Sweet 17, isn't that right? You can be glad you are not boys or there would be a possibility of you getting in this mess, although I don't think and hope it won't last that long. Happy birthday, Twins, and many, many returns of the day. I am sorry I can't do anything about it and I can't even send cards. I'll tell you what I will do. I'll bring you or send you some souvenirs. I already have some. Peggy, Brookie and Gigi have birthdays in March, too. What has Scorcher been doing? (Scorcher was a friend who acquired his nickname after accidentally setting his house on fire.) Tell him I have seen some of the German rifles and machine guns and would like to be back and talk about them. Has Alpen been over to see Mary yet? Is Mary still there? I haven't heard anything for so long. Maybe she is married and settled down. How about that, Mary? I don't know anything else to say, so I will close now. Love, Bill.'

27

The Finger of Fate

In general, the men of the 712th Tank Battalion were not religious scholars and most of them probably would not have known a brimstone from a gemstone. Come to think of it, neither would I. Nevertheless, it was not uncommon to hear the phrase 'All Hell broke loose.' Similarly, a common refrain among the tankers, as among most soldiers in the Second World War, was that if a bullet had your name on it, there was nothing you could do to avoid it. 'I don't know how many other people have got that opinion, but a long time ago, and some of it probably had to do with things that happened in the Army, I became a fatalist,' Dan Diel, the B Company tank commander who was wounded on the battalion's first day in combat said at the 1994 reunion in Fort Mitchell. 'I say when your time is up, you're going, it don't make any difference where you're at. And until your time is here, you can't do anything to hurry it. You might be able to commit suicide, but that is also maybe when your time is up.

'I thought my time was up a couple of times like the day that the tank got hit. I thought probably that before I got away from there with all the fire that was going on around there, that mine would come that day too, but it didn't. And then when we went back up there when we pulled out of that area where all the tanks got hit (one platoon of B Company lost four tanks in the Battle of the Bulge) and went around and relieved some other outfit that was on a hill. Vink (Sgt Leslie Vink) and Schmidt (Sgt William Schmidt) and I walked up on the hill to look the area over because we was gonna move in there at night and we wanted to go up in the daytime to see where we were gonna move into. We were doing the proper thing. We were walking along with our five-yard interval and here comes *Shhhooooomm!* A shot came in and threw dirt on us and never exploded. It wasn't time. It was a dud. The aim was perfect, it just wasn't time.'

For three members of the Headquarters Company reconnaissance platoon, it was time on Christmas Eve of 1944. One of them, Zygmund Wesilowski, was so shaken up on 3 July when the assault gun ahead of his was knocked out, killing Richard Howell, that he refused to get back inside a tank and was transferred. Wesilowski, Richard Newcomb, Ray DeLong and Dick Curran were riding in the first of two jeeps while Tom Chojnacki, Harold Raybuck and Bud Moore were in the second jeep. As they approached a field, the driver of the lead jeep realised he had run out of the territory he was supposed to cover, so he switched places with the second jeep, which had a better map of the territory. The lead jeep pulled over to the side of the road to let the second jeep pass and as it pulled in behind it set off a mine. Wesilowski, Newcomb and DeLong were killed while Curran was thrown off the back of the jeep and severely injured. For Wesilowski, who had asked for a transfer fearing he would be killed in a tank, there was no escaping the proverbial bullet with his name on it.

28

Into the Bulge

'Then we got into this wild march up to the Bulge over roads that were icy. We were all on our own. We knew where we were supposed to go but each company was on its own,' Jim Cary said. The battalion spent Christmas and the next few days in Kirschnaumen, France, west of the Saar and south of the Battle of the Bulge. It is not in the after-action reports, but Kirschnaumen is the town where Sergeant Warren shadowboxed a lantern and wound up knocking Bob Rossi halfway across the room. And where, according to Rossi, Tony D'Arpino, after receiving a package from home, told the grandmother living in the house that LifeSavers were good for her arthritis and traded some for a bottle of schnapps. The main threat during this period came from the air from both German and American fighter planes.

On Christmas Day, the after-action reports state, 'a group of P47s and FW190s flew over our area and bombed and strafed the tank destroyer battalion south of our area. It is quite evident the enemy was flying them.' This may have been the incident Jim Gifford spoke of when he said that on Christmas Day his platoon was strafed by an American fighter piloted by a major who mistook another river for the Saar and thought he was in German territory. 'We all went to Mass that morning,' Gifford said. 'The church was full. The townspeople were there and we were there. About 10 o'clock we came out of the church and went back towards the houses where our tanks were tied up. And the next thing an American fighter plane comes down about a hundred feet off the roadway shooting the hell out of everything. Then he came down again doing the same thing. There was a ridge on the right, then a long field with woods at the top of it. So we backed some tanks up there along the woods and we waited. We knew it was an American plane, but we had been alerted to look out for Germans using American equipment. About 2 o'clock in the afternoon, he came down again and we could look right into the plane. I was on the .50 shooting at it and I could see the bullets go straight into the fuselage along the side of the plane. They didn't hit the pilot. The plane smoked and started to turn over and headed right up out of sight into the clouds, and the next thing we saw was a parachute coming down out of the clouds.

'The guys jumped in a jeep and went to pick up the pilot, and I'll be damned. It was an American major who thought we were Germans because he couldn't see the Saar River up ahead. He had crossed another river and thought that he crossed the Saar, so he was shooting the hell out of us. He was lucky he wasn't hurt. Friendly fire killed a lot of guys. Today they call it friendly fire. Back then I guess we called it accidents.'

On 6 January 1945 at 11.30, the after-action reports note, 'Battalion alerted for move in conjunction with Division moving North to 3rd Corps area.' At 13.00, the report states, 'No maps available to cover route of march.' At 15.15 on 7 January, 'S-2 returns from Division with road maps covering route of march.' And at 00.30, 'Battalion closes in bivouac at Rippweiler. Distance travelled 51.4 miles.' At 15.20 on 8 January, 'Battalion moves out from Rippweiler to proceed to Boulaide.' On 9 January, 'Distance travelled 16 miles. One assault gun of Headquarters Company threw a track en route. A Company lost one tank, one retriever, one halftrack, one truck, two and a quarter tons. All to be brought up later.' The A Company tank that was lost on the march was most likely to be the one in which Steve Krysko was the gunner.

'As we drove north through Luxembourg toward Bastogne,' Krysko wrote in an account, 'the weather was horrendous. A blizzard made driving difficult and hazardous, and tanks chugged along slower than one could walk. Going uphill at night was an ordeal beyond comprehension – you had to be there to experience it. It was impossible for the driver to see the road. He was driving without lights and what he did see was nothing but white – in front, to the left and to the right. Wind-blown snow slapped at his face, making it necessary for him to press the bridge of his nose against the hatch rim and have his helmet pulled down to his eyebrows. His field of vision was reduced to a one-inch slit and was guided by a fluorescent reflector attached to the back of the helmet of one of his crew members who was walking in the left track impression made in the snow by the tank in front. A slip off the road to one side could plunge the tank into a ravine; to the other side, into a ditch, which would make it impossible to get back onto the road unless the tank were backed down to where ditch and road were on the same level. Needless to say, my tank slipped into the ditch. My crew and I had to wait until the convoy passed, then back down and start the hellish climb over again. It took more than two hours for us to reach the top of the hill. When we got there, we stood alone. The 712th had disappeared.

'About a mile to our front, the sky was ablaze with flames. Whatever town it was, it was a scene straight out of Dante's Inferno. Not knowing in which direction the others had gone, we decided to get off the main road and turned onto a side road that led us to a building that looked more like a lodge than a home. I pounded on the front door calling out – in German – to ask if anyone were inside. A frightened, elderly woman holding a lighted candle opened the door and I told her we were looking for a place to get out of the cold. She let us in and we gathered in the kitchen – the warmest spot in the place. We were soon joined by two other women, an elderly man and a teenage boy. They, too, stared in fright at us. My crew and I talked in English, and the man timidly asked if we were Americans. Even though I told him that we were, they still were doubtful until I opened my uniform and pulled out my dog tags. Their dour expressions turned into broad smiles.

'The teenager spoke fluent English and explained that my speaking in German made them suspicious. Donlingen had been caught in a tug of war between German and American forces, and they feared that we were Germans dressed as American soldiers for the purpose of finding out whether or not they were sympathetic to Americans. They were apprehensive about showing any sign of friendliness, lest they be killed.

In the morning, we moved the tank to the rear of the building, out of sight from the road. The place was a winter resort and we were its only guests, non-paying but most welcomed. Meals were meagre but hot and home cooked, and water was heated for us to bathe. We were even provided with under the bed potties when we retired. It was the third day when we were found by one of A Company's lieutenants. He bitched about my hiding our tank behind the building, telling me he had passed by a couple of times looking for my tank, which was presumed to be ditched somewhere. I told him we had to hide the tank so it would not be spotted from the air by German planes. It was back to the 712th and the Bulge.'

Just like when the battalion was leaving Dillingen and Clegg Caffery dropped his flashlight on the deck of the ferry to start laughing uncontrollably, Big Andy had a similar, albeit more perilous, experience on the drive into the Bulge. 'It was cold and a lot of snow,' he said. 'I would say it was weather like we have right here: summer it's hot, winter it was times when it got down to ten, twenty below zero. When we moved from Dillingen up through Luxembourg, I knew it was cold because I took and cut a sock up and made a slit for my eyes to see and I covered my head. I didn't have an assistant tank driver and I was getting sleepy. One time I hit an icy spot in the road and I sat on the edge of a cliff, and the tank rocking and going over, and just a laughing.

'"What's the matter?" Hagerty said.

'"We're just about ready to go over the cliff."

'I don't know how steep the cliff was. It could have been just a ditch or it could have been a mountain. I just remember that I sat on the edge and the tank was rocking. Whether it was far enough out that if you had put a 50-pound weight on the gun it would have gone over I couldn't say. A guy came up behind me and hooked his tank on and pulled me back. And then there was another time I ran General Patton off the road. I stopped. He said, "You did the right thing, Soldier. You had the road. Get them tanks up there!" And then another time I hit an icy spot and damn near went through a building. And then we pulled the tank back and we helped other tanks. That was cold that night and the road was icy and it was snowing.'

29

George Kitten

'I guess it took us two days to get up there, that's about the way I remember it,' Jim Cary said. 'The course we were supposed to follow was pretty well marked out. Part of it was mountainous. I remember tanks turning, hitting sheets of ice on the road, spinning around and ending halfway hanging over the edge of the road and almost falling in the gullies. I remember a long, narrow road with trees closing over the top. It's one of those things that just gets imprinted on your mind.

'I thought we were going a little too slow. We knew there was going to be an operation on 9 January and here it was January 8, sort of middle of the afternoon. There was a chain of hills and mountains here and the road was winding back and forth through this, and where we were supposed to go was about over here. And I went out ahead of the company, it was moving along, and I noticed a road outside of the mountains that looked like a very good road. So I went down in my jeep and ran all the way up there and then over it. It was a much shorter, more direct route. Everything was fine. I thought "Gee, that's great. I'll bring the tanks down here." So I took them out of the mountains down on this road and by the time we started down that road it started snowing, and the road was completely obliterated. You couldn't see anything. The only thing we had to guide by was a fence that ran parallel to it and that pretty well kept us on the road. But the second we came out on that open country, I didn't realise we were going to be under German observation. They started shelling us. Pretty heavy, too. We kept moving, deploying to scatter the tanks and then moving some more. We finally got through there. That was a mistake for me to do that, but it saved us about two hours.

'We got the tanks in. I remember coming down this rather steep road into an encampment area and Colonel (Ray) Bell who commanded the 359th Infantry was amazed that we had got there and was very pleased. He apparently said something to Colonel Randolph about the success of the movement. So we spent the night there in that bivouac area. In the morning as I was leading the company of tanks, the road curved around and then as you curved around there was a road junction. And the arrangement was that the 359th would have three guides there, one assigned to each of the three platoons in my company. They would guide that platoon of tanks to their battalion to support them during the day's operation.

'It was just as we were coming up to this road that Colonel Randolph was waiting. I stopped and talked to him briefly, and he expressed his pleasure that we had done so well in getting the tanks up there and he was real happy about that. He said I was doing a wonderful job and I said it wasn't me, it was the whole company. If I had a bad company I couldn't have gotten it up there. We shook hands. And that's the last time I saw him.'

'We had rubber pads on our light tanks,' said Dale Albee, the former horse cavalry sergeant who by now had received a battlefield commission and was a lieutenant in D Company, 'and rubber on ice, we skidded and everything. But through the efforts of our damn good drivers, we got darn near everything through. My platoon stopped at a barn. It must have been one or two o'clock in the morning and were going to bed down for the rest of the night. That's when I got orders to report to the 359th Regiment commander. And then we had to go up on the line, so we pulled out and went there. We pulled through Nothum. I had orders to go up to a crossroad and contact this commander out of B Company.'

Jim Cary, the B Company commander, was riding in an assault gun with a 105-mm gun as he led his company. 'We came around that corner and that exposed us to the Germans and they laid in on us awfully heavy as we came around. They had that road junction zeroed in and the shells were really flying. We came up to the road junction and the guides weren't there. So I jumped out of the tank and started running around looking for them. I started first towards the German lines, realised that was the wrong direction, came back, and by that time the guides had shown up and we were getting the platoons moved. And I didn't think anything about my tank because I was up trying to find the command post where I was supposed to report in. So I found the C.P. and I guess it was ten or fifteen minutes later I saw my communication sergeant who worked in that same tank. The tank had taken a hit, right in the side, a large high explosive shell. And as I recall, it ripped the weld open on the tank and gave everybody inside a terrible blow, but nobody was seriously hurt. They really got their bells rung. I wasn't very popular with them when I left that tank on that zeroed-in intersection. Dumb thing to do, but it was in the excitement of trying to get the platoons to where they were supposed to go.

'I found the C.P. over to the left. I've got a photo at home of that C.P. It was taken inside the C.P. Colonel Smith: they called him Foxhole Smith. He was anything but a foxhole type. He was a real tough guy and in charge of the assault. I was more or less directly under him. And above him was Colonel Bell. Colonel Bell was there, too, in this C.P. It was a shattered building. The front window was completely blown out and the roof was gone. And I saw this one solid wall, so I said that's the place for me. I got as close up against it as I could and that's where the picture was. One reason I knew it was me is because I could see how well I was hugging that wall.

'Anyway, General Van Fleet came in. And then the Germans. It wasn't because he arrived, but that was just about the time the attack really started moving and they laid in on us the heaviest artillery I've ever encountered in my life, really terrible. And an awful lot of it were 'Screaming Memmies/Moaning Minnies.' (The dreaded *Nebeltruppen*: batteries of six to eight mortars, three batteries per battalion.) With a regular artillery shell that goes up and down, you can hear it and tell by the sound how close it's going to land. With a 'screaming meemie' you can't. They fire these things like a shotgun, in barrages, whole squares of them. And they have this sound and the sound is all around you. You have no idea whether it's going to land right in the middle of you or off to the side. And it has a psychological effect on you, particularly after a while. Those things were screaming and coming in and pounding and hitting all around us. At one stage, Colonel Bell and I got caught outside the C.P. and there wasn't any cover except a concrete chicken house we both saw about 40 yards away. So we had a race to get to that chicken house and I beat him. I mean, rank had no privileges on that day. I dived in ahead of him.'

'Were there any chickens in the chicken coop?' I asked.

'I don't think there were. I don't remember any chickens other than my feelings. Anyway, General Van Fleet came in and was standing in the C.P. when we got hit with one of these artillery barrages and he just stood there. But people all around him were getting hit. One man standing next to him practically got his head taken off, killed. Colonel Smith lost his entire forward observation team. They got taken out in that barrage. It was during that chaotic situation where we were taking these very heavy barrages that somebody came into the C.P. and said that Colonel Randolph had been killed.

'"Are you sure?" I said.

'"Absolutely. I saw him myself. I saw the body."

'So I went outside and ran over to my tank, which by then had been moved right in back of the C.P., and got on the radio and called battalion headquarters. I insisted on talking to Major Kedrovsky because he was second in command. It wasn't the kind of message you could pass on through channels very well. And we had a very poorly disguised code that we used. Randolph's codename was "George" and the codename for killed was "kitten." And we hadn't used this code very much. I got Kedrovsky on the radio and I said, "George kitten. Do you understand what I'm saying?"

'"George kitten?"

'"Yes. George kitten."

'"Oh."

'And that was it. I know that he left then and I guess he went immediately to division headquarters to let them know what had happened to Randolph. If we'd been in a stable situation I would have gone and tried to find the body and find out what had happened, but we were in an attack formation and we had to move. Not too long after that the attack got moving and we got out of Nothum proper. That relieved the situation somewhat. Then the Germans didn't have the road junctions all zeroed in where they could really lay it in on us, but they were still putting a lot of artillery fire in.

'You know what the attack was all about? The 4th Armored Division drove a corridor up into Bastogne to help relieve Bastogne, but they were having a lot of trouble widening that corridor, so we were ordered to attack astride a road that came into Bastogne. We were astride that road and over here, this was sort of a high finger of ground. Then down in the valley you could see Wiltz in the distance. So we were attacking astride this road, got out of town, and Germans were falling out from the bushes right under our feet. We didn't even know they were there and surrendering. Most of them were Volkssturm troops: old men and young boys. Poor guys, you had to feel sorry for them.'

'Did you feel sorry for them at the time?' I asked.

'I felt sorry for the kids. We saw kids that were fourteen, fifteen years old. The rest of them I didn't have any great feelings one way or the other, except I saw one guy, one German up ahead waving a white handkerchief wanting to surrender. I motioned to him to come and he starts running down the road then some GI comes out of the woods and shoots him. You hate to see things like that. But we got up a fair distance astride this road. I was with Colonel Smith on one side of the road and I looked back and here comes a platoon of our light tanks barrelling down the road real fast. It's only then that I remembered that Colonel Randolph told me he might attach a platoon of light tanks to Company B. So I stepped out there and stopped them to ask them who they were looking for. They said they were looking for me and Company B and asked what to do. I said, "I haven't any idea, but I think it would be a good idea if you deployed your tanks along this flank over here." It was wide open and the attack had moved past. There wasn't anything on the right flank and it bothered me. There was a valley and they did deploy those light tanks and that's the last I saw them. But somebody told me that later that night the Germans did counterattack and ran right into those tanks.'

'I was sailing down the road,' Dale Albee said, 'and I noticed this German tank burning right over in the ditch. Up ahead is a curve and this captain stepped out and stopped me. And he said, "Where are you going?"

"'I've got to go up to the corner and report," I replied.

"'If you do, you're going to be in enemy territory. You're on the front line right now. Pull on over here. We want you to guard the flank." I think it was Wiltz over on the side there. So I pulled over there. And that night we had a firefight. The Germans went between us and the tank. They had two columns and the old German captain out there was hollering "Don't shoot! We're Americans!"

'This is in the Ardennes, I think it was the Ardennes,' said Walter Galbraith, who was Lieutenant Albee's gunner in one of the first impromptu interviews I conducted. 'That night I heard tanks moving and I said, "I can hear the medium tanks, I guess they're leaving." And all of a sudden I saw a flame go up. I said, "There's a tank on fire." I said, "Shit, they hit one of our tanks." We took turns sleeping and I happened to be awake. Lieutenant Albee was sleeping. So I'm looking out and I see somebody run across in front of the tanks, a silhouette, and I looked again. The Germans had a different helmet. There was something about the hook or something on the helmet that got my eye and I said, "Albee! Albee!" I woke him up. I said, "I think those are Germans running across the flaming tank." He got his binoculars out and in the meantime I got my turret turned facing right at that tank. He said, "Yes, they are."

'So we started shooting. I was firing the machine gun and the cannon, and he's firing the .50-calibre machine gun on top. And we heard, "For God's sake, stop firing. You're killing your own men!" And Jesus, my head shrank. Then Albee got his binoculars again and said, "No, they're Heinies." And he started firing again. And I started shooting like hell at them. And even then they kept hollering, "You're killing your own men!" Then all of a sudden we saw our pink tracer go this way and we saw a white tracer come back. And then we knew that those were Germans because we had a pink tracer and they had white ones. Then everything was quite for a while. I kept my machine gun ready for anybody who might come across. I'm in the tank and someone starts climbing up the side of the tank.

174

'"Who's there?" I ask.

'"Who's in charge here?"

'"Albee, wake up," I said.

'"I'm Sergeant So-and-So. You know what happened? You see that tank over there that's on fire? That's a German tank."

'I thought it was our tank that was knocked out. So he said what happened was, "You know how we are in the dark? You can't see shit. I had to climb out of the tank. This German tank is coming up the road. I had to tap the guy on the back to tell him to turn the turret and then when he got lined up, through his eye, he just kept firing and knocked the shit out of that tank."

'So that was over and he got off. A few minutes later, somebody else started climbing up on the side of the tank. And I'm ready to throw a hand grenade back, I had it all in my mind what I was gonna do. Anyway, it was a colonel. Now goshdammit, he gave us his name. "I'm Colonel So and So." And he says, "You know what happened? Had they gone by, this would have cut the whole advance." And then he left.'

'Galbraith was asleep, my gunner,' Lieutenant Albee said, 'and it just happened to be my turn on guard and I had a .50-calibre machine gun mounted on the turret of my tank. Between me and this burning German tank, I could see this column moving and they were wearing the Wehrmacht hat with the brim. Americans don't wear brimmed hats, they wear the helmet. So I opened up. I hollered at Galbraith. I opened up with my .50 and he jumped in on the coaxial .30 and we started firing this way. We got white tracer coming back at me this way. All of a sudden behind me I get white tracer coming at me too and then my second tank starts red tracer. And what we had was two columns. One was between me and the burning tank and one was between me and my second tank. And then out here in the distance came this voice, "Don't shoot! We're Americans! I'm an American captain! You're killing your own men!" Americans don't fire white tracer. So we continued firing on them. And then later on they gave up and came in. I forget how many we captured and how many we killed, but this was a German captain that could speak English that we got. If I remember right, I think we killed twenty that night.'

'Walter Galbraith said that an American colonel came up to the tank after the firefight,' I said.

'I don't know. One that came up was a .50-calibre machine gun that was dug in on the road right beside my tank and he didn't fire a shot. And later he apologised to me and I said, "I don't blame you a damn bit." With all the stuff going on, if he'd have stuck his head up there he'd have got killed, so I didn't blame him. I told this story to my two sons when we returned to Fort Knox for the 1986 reunion. We were sitting at the table and my son who was in the Navy at Norfolk, and my younger son who was in basic training at Fort Knox, all came to the reunion. And we were sitting at this table and across from me this guy says, "You're from D Company. I wonder who ever took over Coe's platoon."

'"I did."

'"I've always wondered, I was up on the line and here came this stupid ass down the line with these tanks. He only had four of them and he's on his way up into the German lines when I stopped him."

'"Oh?" And my two kids are about to crack up.

'"Yes. And I never knew what happened because about fifteen minutes after that I was wounded and I went to the rear and I never did find out."

'And I looked at the two kids and kind of grinned at them, and they grinned back. I says, "You know, you're looking at that stupid ass. I'm the one that was in those tanks when you stopped us right there. You had that German tank burning, didn't you?"

'"Yes."

'But the kids, they were real interested in the war and it just kind of brought it out. Well, Dad kind of told the truth once in a while.'

Earlier, when the B Company tanks pulled out of Nothum, 'We got maybe a mile out of town,' Cary said, 'and the attack bogged down. The Germans were very deeply embedded in strong positions and these were not Volkssturm troops, these were German paratroopers and they were really tough. They weren't going to move out. You'd have to move them out. You could tell the difference immediately in the amount of resistance we were getting. I didn't see any of the Germans, though they had distinctive uniforms as I understand, but I didn't recognise it from that. I could tell from the way the fighting was going because we were stopped. I had a platoon here and a platoon over here, and Bob Vutech was in a reserve platoon. There was a shattered building and I brought our company train up to that point and had them put the kitchen in that building.

'I got the kitchen set up and got the gasoline truck there, and went up to one of the platoons. Sergeant Schmidt was in charge of this platoon and I told him to send his tanks back. It was about 4:30 in the afternoon of 9 January. I told him to send his tanks back one at a time to get food and gasoline then come back and send another tank. The same with the platoon over here. There was a brand new officer in this platoon named Metzger. My 105 tank was parked right beside the road and I went back to the tank to find Colonel Smith and report to him to see what was going to happen next. I put my left leg up on the track of the tank and was throwing my right leg up over the back when this flat-trajectory shell came in. It was a self-propelled gun. I heard the motor start up and I could tell it was moving, and it was right after that the guy fired a high-explosive shell. Apparently there was a double column of infantry moving down the road. That was what he was shooting at. He wasn't shooting at me.

'As I was pulling my left leg up, the shell fragment came in and hit me right in mid-calf. It was still hanging in the flesh. I thought it took my foot off, that's what it felt like. It seemed that the whole shell hit right on my foot and exploded. But you had no time to think. I just dived off the tank to the ground on the other side. I looked down and was very happy to see I still had a foot. And I was laying there thinking about all this when heads started popping up out of my tank looking around wondering what had happened to me. I knew I was finished, so I got in the bow gunner's place in the tank, started back and ran into Vutech. He was bringing his platoon up and I told him what the situation was and turned the company over to him. I went back to the aid station and about two minutes later they brought Metzger in. He had been shot across the stomach. And that was my last day in combat. We were evacuated back to Luxembourg City. I remember going into this operating theatre and they had all these operating tables laid out. Remember the scene in *Coma*? It was just one operating table after another.'

At 10.28 on 9 January, the battalion after-action reports note, 'Received message from commanding officer of B Company. 'We have attacked.' At 11.10, the entry reads, 'Received message from CO B Co. that CO of Bn. was killed in an artillery barrage. Confirmed.' In the column where it reads 'Action taken' is the notation 'Bn Ex Officer notified.'

30

'Take My Picture'

Earlier, I wrote extensively about the actions involving the first platoon of C Company that lost four tanks in Normandy. When I began attending reunions, I heard about a similar disaster during the Battle of the Bulge involving a platoon of B Company tanks. However, I was only able to find two survivors of that action. Chester Martin, one of the survivors, declined to talk about it. Leroy Niehaus, another survivor, rarely missed a reunion, but he had suffered a stroke that wiped his memory of previous events.

Louis Gruntz Jr of New Orleans, however, took a trip through France and Germany with his father in which they retraced his father's combat route. Louis wrote an unpublished book that is as good a history of B Company as will ever be written. In describing the battle that took place during the Bulge, he wrote: 'The mortars and artillery that rained down upon the 359th Infantry Regiment also unmercifully pounded the tanks from B Company, which had also moved into the open field that morning several hundred yards ahead of the infantry. Dad described the fate of the tanks that morning with the 359th: "When we (Company B) attacked them during the daylight, we had four tanks knocked out. That's when Richard (John R.) Williams, David Dickson and Buck Lee were killed. Harvey Fowler was wounded and died of his wounds two days later on 12 January and I believe Dee Johnson was hit (Dee Johnson also died on 12 January). All in all there were 14 casualties that fateful day."

'On the evening of 9 January, Dad and other crews were rotated to the rear area for a hot meal and to be resupplied with ammunition and gasoline. During that time, Dad saw David Dickson Jr whom he trained with back in the States. Dickson was a comedian. He was a bartender from Philadelphia. During basic training, Dad and Dickson had a running gag. "We used to kid one another," he'd say. "When they bury you, I'm going to piss on your grave." And I'd say, "Yeah, well when they bury you they better bury you face down cause I don't want to piss on your face." That evening, there was no kidding because they both knew the battle that lay ahead. Dad related what Dickson said to him that evening. He told me, "Louis, if I make it past tomorrow, I am going to come see you in New Orleans after the war is over." Dickson must have had a premonition. He was killed the next morning.'

At 12.00 on 10 January, the after-action report reads: 'One of C Co. tanks knocked out by enemy action, Lt wounded. Lt Gifford after being hit and blood was pouring from his eye ran to tank next in column and had the tank Comdr take his picture (with his own camera). Then he put to bear all weapons on the MG until it was silenced.' I can only imagine that the clerk who wrote the after-action report had to restrain himself from adding an exclamation point. There is one discrepancy between the action involving Gifford's tank as it was told to me and the entry in the report. Tony D'Arpino and Bob Rossi both recalled the incident as happening in the evening, and according to the report word of Gifford's injury was received at noon.

'Just prior to the Battle of the Bulge, Jim was brought in as our new tank commander,' Rossi said as the four crew members and I sat around a table in the hospitality room at the battalion's 1992 reunion forty-seven years after their tank was knocked out. Only Stanley Klapkowski, the gunner, was missing.

'Gifford was our platoon leader,' said D'Arpino.

'We were in the Number 1 tank,' Rossi confirmed. 'We wound up in the town of Kirschnaumen in Belgium [sic]. I can recall so vividly how we wondered where Lieutenant Gifford was all day. We were in a hayloft and he came up the ladder. He said, "Come here, I want to show you something." He had draped the tank in white sheets. They weren't whitewashing the tanks at the time. There was snow all over the ground, so he scrounged these white sheets from all over and he draped our tank so we'd have camouflage. That same night, he had got a package from home and had some canned chicken. He shared his package with all of us. We were talking about home and he said, "You know, I'd rather lose an arm or a leg than lose my eyesight. There's too much to see in this world." And the next day he got hit in the eye (likely to have happened several days later). It was a hairy situation because we had gone into a pocket to flush out Germans and as fate had it our left track was knocked off.'

'Wasn't that the time we just took one section of the tanks, just us and the second tank?' D'Arpino asked. 'We were almost ready to eat supper when we had to go out.'

'We only had two tanks: us and Warren's. There was concentrated machine gun fire. Lieutenant Gifford got hit in the right eye. The bullet lodged in his cheek. I thought he might jump out of the tank and I yelled at him to keep down or they would blow his head off. He said, "I don't want to jump out. I want Warren to come forward to help us." Then he asked me, "Rossi, how bad am I hit?" And I lied. "You don't look bad, Lieutenant." But he looked like somebody hit him in the face with a sledgehammer.'

'I remember something else about that, too. He was great for having a camera around your neck, right?'

'I'm gonna get to that. So he says to me, "Fire the smoke mortar." In my excitement, when I fired the first mortar it came almost straight down. Then I fired subsequent mortars to give us a smokescreen. As we were abandoning tank, Lieutenant Gifford was firing his .45 and pulling Spahr out by one of his arms. Spahr's leg was locked. (When I interviewed Gifford individually, he would explain that Spahr was trying to reach into the tank to get his bag of loot.) Ed was the assistant driver. His machine gun was firing by itself it was so hot. And I said "Twist the belt! Twist the belt!" so he could stop the bullets from feeding into the machine gun. And Klapkowski, who was our gunner, he and I were running in a zigzag. We could see the snow being kicked up around us. As we were running, a recon truck came toward us and Lieutenant Gifford ordered, "Fire that .50 and protect these boys!" And the guy yelled out, "It's our last box!" He says, "Fire it anyway, you sonofabitch!" And that's when they started firing the .50 to give us cover. As we got out of the line of fire, he handed his .45 to me. "Hold this for me till I get back." And with that he says, "Take my picture." I says, "Lieutenant, I can't take your picture."

'I took it. That's the only way I could have got hit right here (on the fleshy inside part of his arm) when I was holding the camera up to take his picture,' Spahr said.

'And there he was,' Rossi said, 'having his picture taken. He had got a Bronze Star that morning. He had the ribbon, his face was all puffed up, blood all over his combat jacket. He says, "Take my picture."'

'I couldn't see out of my right eye, but I didn't know how bad it was,' Gifford said. 'It's a funny thing, I didn't feel any pain when the bullet went in.'

'I can remember plain as day one thing about that evening,' said D'Arpino. 'We were about ready to eat our meal and they said there was a small pocket that was holding the infantry down. They wanted the tanks to clean it out. You took two tanks. It was just supposed to be a small pocket and it turned out to be a little more than that, I guess.'

'After we were knocked out, Sergeant Warren's tank came forwards and under Lieutenant Gifford's orders he set our tank on fire,' Rossi added.

'We had ruined the radio. We put a grenade in the gun barrel. We did everything we were supposed to do.'

'So the Germans couldn't turn the gun around and fire on the town,' Rossi said.

'I had Warren shoot into the back of our tank because the Germans were stealing the tanks. They'd use them against us. The track was blown off so it was useless anyway.'

'But the gun was still good.'

'So we immobilised it by hitting it in the back.'

'We had the best working escape hatch of anybody in the platoon,' D'Arpino said. 'I used to oil that thing up good so when you touched the lever it would fall right out. Sometimes that was the only way of escape. If you're inside the tank and the hatches are down and the gun is traversed over your hatch, you can't open it to get out. You have to go out the other way. I can remember always telling Klapkowski, "You sonofabitch, if we ever get knocked out make sure that gun's in the centre because if it's traversed over my hatch I can't get out and I'll haunt you. I'll come and pull the sheets off your bed."

'I'm sure there's a few guys that aren't here today because of that gun being over their hatch.'

'We subsequently got a new tank after that,' Rossi said. 'Sergeant Holmes became our acting platoon leader. When Lieutenant Gifford was wounded and we were knocked out, that was 10 January 1945 in Belgium... Luxembourg...'

31

Doncols

At 10.05 on 11 January 1945, according to the after-action reports, the first and second platoon of C Company were in Berle, Luxembourg, 'ready to move up on call.' At 12.30, the 'attack of 357 Inf. jumped off. Heavy fighting reported in Doncols.'

'I was in Doncols,' John Zimmer recalled in 1992, 'when we got hit with a bazooka or a panzerfaust. A guy hit the track and knocked it off. If it hadn't been for that we might not be here today as if the warhead hits the steel, it'll blow right through and explode inside. It came out of a cellar window. The driver, Leroy Campbell, was a good soldier, but he couldn't steer it. He ran it right into a manure pile. And the manure pile was over a big hole, four feet deep. The tank went all the way down and they couldn't get it out with another tank. I guess they did get it out with two tanks hooked on it.'

Larry Green of Webster, Wisconsin, was a sergeant who had a rear echelon job but asked to see combat according to Don Knapp, a tank commander in the second platoon. Green was in the tank by himself pulling guard duty when a mortar shell plummeted into the turret and exploded killing him instantly. The platoon leader, Lt Francis 'Snuffy' Fuller, was twenty-seven years old and managed an Acme grocery store in Buffalo, New York, before the war. His grandmother was from Koenigsburg and his grandfather came from Alsace-Lorraine, an area in France near the German border. Fuller took three years of German at North Tonawanda High School because with it spoken at home he figured it would be easy. One time in Germany, Fuller's gunner, Russell Loop, recalled that the platoon was moving at night and got lost behind German lines. All of a sudden, two German tanks joined the column. Fuller went back and convinced the German tankers they were behind the American lines and talked them into surrendering without a shot being fired.

The night before entering Doncols, Fuller said when I interviewed him at the bar he ran in a rundown section of Buffalo in 1994, 'We had been in the little town of Berle. This was towards the end of the Battle of the Bulge. We had terrific artillery going over up there. Then they told us the next morning we're heading for this little town of Doncols. Berle was up on a hill and Doncols is down in the valley. You could see across there all right, but it was too steep for the tanks to get down. And Berle was up on the side of a bluff. There was just one road going in there so the strategy was we'd just hit this road and barrel ass as fast as we could into the town. We had two platoons; Lieutenant Griffin's platoon preceded us. He got into town and pulled behind the first set of barns and was waiting there. I got down right behind him and said, "Well, what are you gonna do, Griffin?"

'And he didn't really know. We can't all stay here. So I headed into town. The tanks are in a string. It's a single road, you're in a line and we see this sucker off to our right with a panzerfaust. I couldn't get my gun around fast enough and he let go, but he didn't hit my tank. He hit the second tank, hit it right in the sprocket. The track came off and the tank rolled to the left, right into a goddamn manure pile. I kept going with the first two tanks. The third tank, that's the one Zimmer was in, he could probably tell you more about it. They were immobilised. Somebody came along and told them they had to guard prisoners. So he got stuck all night guarding a bunch of prisoners. We went up ahead and outposted the far end of town and that was a little hectic too because we had no infantry again this time, and we're waiting for them. We could see a car coming down the road. We didn't know what it was, but finally we figured it was one of our own recon vehicles. But then the infantry came across and they captured a whole German regimental headquarters.'

'I tell you,' John Zimmer had said at the battalion's 1992 mini-reunion in Bradenton, Florida, two years before I interviewed Fuller, 'that time the panzerfaust hit us, we were on the manure pile and the tank sunk. They said, "You guys stay there and guard the prisoners." I don't know who told us, but we did. And we had about 20 of them. And this Aaron Brown (whose nickname for obvious reasons was 'Souvenir Brown'), he stirred around the next morning and found a ham. I bet the thing weighed 50 pounds. And we fried the ham on our mess kits. I had a German blowtorch that would shoot a stream of blue flame. It was made so you could set it down and in five minutes you'd fry the ham. Then the kitchen moved in on us. They got the rest of the ham. That was during the Bulge. Griffin was down there. We didn't have any infantry for this deal. And I don't know why they couldn't get there. They were pinned down somewhere. I forget a lot of the points.'

After the panzerfaust fired from a basement window struck Zimmer's tank, Knapp, the tank commander of one of the two tanks following it, and Byrl Rudd, the platoon sergeant in another tank, fired their .50-calibre machine guns into the house. 'The house was starting to burn,' Knapp said at the battalion's 1994 reunion in Cincinnati. 'We got a white flag. Ceasefire. I don't know whether Rudd was firing also because I was kind of in his way and he didn't want to knock anything out. That's why he hollered, "Goddammit, are you going to open or not?" Which I did. And out came this priest and he had a long black robe and circular hat. And he was carrying something. He walks by and looks up at me like "You have sinned," and there's a little baby in his arms. I think it was a little girl and it was bleeding. It's in my mind's eye like she was shot in the butt or something. Maybe that's how I calmed myself in that I didn't hurt her fatally. And he went by and that was it. Then after that, Jack Green and I got into rousting out Krauts in a couple of houses.'

Jack Green (no relation to Larry Green, the member of the platoon who was killed in Doncols) was one of the less savoury characters in the battalion. Knapp, who described himself as a sensitive fellow at ninety-one, said he and Jack Green were buddies as if Green were his Jekyll and Hyde. 'He always used to come over to me and we had things to talk about, raise a little hell,' Knapp said. '"You got the GIs (diarrhoea), Knapp? You take some of this schnapps, that'll kill it for a while." And it did. Jack died in a van drinking booze down in North Carolina shortly after the war, asphyxiated by gas fumes somebody told me. The infantry used to say, "Oh, that Jack Green. Man, he'll cut a guy in half with that .50-calibre." He loved to kill Krauts.

'When we went into Doncols without infantry, we passed the first platoon with Ray Griffin. He was told to hold this position and he said to Snuffy, "Go in, it's yours." So Snuffy went in, infantry or not, and what makes me remember about Jack Green. I think that operation took all day and late at night. Some people came out and they said, "There's some Germans in that house," because we were only meeting scattered resistance. And I think the person said, "They won't come out." So Jack, he always carried a couple of hand grenades and I think he threw them down the cellar and we were hollering "Kommen se hier!" And we got them out of there and they're kind of arrogant. First we disarmed them as they came up. I think one of them had a pistol and one had a watch Jack wanted. And the guy's talking about the Geneva Convention. And it's hairy after that. I don't recall if Jack shot him or not, but he got the watch.'

32

The Two Deaths of
Pine Valley Bynum

Quentin 'Pine Valley' Bynum was the tank driver who gave my father a lift to the front in Normandy where my dad was wounded the first time. Jule Braatz, the A Company sergeant he reported to, said he could only tell me the story third hand as the person who told him about it, Bynum, was later killed. I have only seen one picture of Pine Valley and a double exposure at that, but he was tall, rugged looking with a shock of hair that his colleagues said made him look like Li'l Abner or one of the Duke boys. He was twenty-six years old. The tank drivers who remembered him – Big Andy, Bussell, Dess Tibbitts – said he got his nickname from the area where he grew up. Only one problem: there's no Pine Valley in Southern Illinois where Bynum was raised.

In 1996, I received an e-mail from Chris Bynum, Pine Valley's nephew, who inherited his uncle's dog tags and considered Pine Valley his hero. That September, I visited James Bynum, Chris' father, in Springfield, Illinois. Quentin was born in 1918. According to James, when Quentin was an infant he came down with diphtheria and was pronounced dead. This may have been diphtheria or the flu as it would have occurred during the global influenza pandemic of 1918. Quentin's mother, Mabel Claire Murphy Bynum, 'had the mouth of a mule skinner,' and barred the door, refusing to let the doctor leave until he brought her baby back to life. 'Wrap him in a blanket,' the doctor said, 'and warm him by the fire of the cook stove.' And young Quentin came back to life. As he grew older, Quentin loved to do chores on the farm but did not do well in school, while two of his older brothers would go on to become college professors as would James later on. But Quentin developed an almost superhuman strength. Once, Quentin and his brother Hugh got into an argument which they settled by each of them lifting an axle of a sprayer. Such an axle would normally be pulled by a team of Clydesdales and they both dragged it along to see who would quit first. (James didn't remember who won.)

'When Quentin was still going to school with his younger sister,' James said, 'it was a bitter cold day in January and we just had light jackets, and your hands got really cold. We all walked home from school together. Quentin was wearing a light tan jacket and a toboggan cap pulled down over his head, and I had on what we called a pilot's cap. The kids used to wear these leather things with earflaps and they were lined with wool on the inside. I think I had one of those and my sister probably had a kerchief tied about her ears. She and I were little and we were crying with the cold. And Quentin unbuttoned his jacket so that it made two corners and he had Betty hold onto one corner and I on the other. He said, "Now you'll have to pick your feet up." And he carried us all the way home.'

Quentin had a naive innocence that resulted in battle-hardened veterans of the Second World War recalling the pillow fights he started in the barracks at Camp Lockett. It was also an innocence that, combined with his good looks, some women found hard to resist. His parents had a friend named George Bean, James recalled, and Bean was a gangster who had been a member of the notorious Charlie Birger gang that controlled much of the area during Prohibition. George Bean's wife took a liking to Quentin who was about eighteen at the time. 'George and Ruth used to come to our house on Saturday nights for square dances,' James said. 'George was Dad's age and Ruth was probably ten years younger than George, and she was tall, pretty and redheaded. She took a liking to Quentin and Quentin liked her. Quentin probably had his first taste of sex with Ruth. Our mother didn't approve of it because George was a good friend of the family. But Mom had no influence with Quentin. You know how sex works on a person. So she got her coat – we lived a couple of miles out of town and we did almost everything by walking – and George lived in a house on the edge of town. She took her hat, coat and pocketbook and walked down there and said, '"George, I want to talk to you."

'"Well, Mae, what about?'

'"Quentin is chasing after Ruth. I've talked to him and it doesn't make any difference." And she said, "If it doesn't stop, I will kill Ruth."

'"Mae, if it doesn't stop, I will kill Ruth."

'"Wait a minute,' I said. "Wasn't anybody going to kill Quentin?"

'They both knew he was innocent. She was at least ten years older than him. I was a kid, but I recognised that this is a good-looking woman. And it stopped. Ruth stopped. Because George Bean was not a man you messed with. Soon after that, Ruth left George and I don't know where she went.'

While James confirmed that there was no place called Pine Valley anywhere in the area, there is a Pine Valley in the hills near San Diego, not far from Camp Lockett where Bynum trained with the horse cavalry in 1941 and 1942. And while it is pure speculation on my part, it is possible Quentin earned his nickname by spending much of his leisure time there. A query posted on an Internet bulletin board for the municipality of Pine Valley, California, several years ago, however, did not turn up any elderly ladies who remembered a rugged young cavalry man named Quentin Bynum.

Back at Thionville, Charles Vorhees, a tank driver in the 8th Armored Group, was sent with a tank to the 712th as a liaison. 'We were going across the Saar at night. The engineers were putting us across on pontoons,' Vorhees recalled when I interviewed him at his home in Ohio in 2001. 'There were five medium tanks going over, five jeeps, our light tank and a 6-by-6 truck with a trailer loaded with ammunition. The colonel of the engineers said each of the tanks was going to go over and tow a jeep out through the bottom. It was all flooded. And he said: 'You'll wait on the ammunition truck until we tow it out.'

'"Why don't you let one of the medium tanks tow that?" I said.

'"Oh," he said. "A light tank's the best towing vehicle in the Army."

'So we're sitting there all lined up waiting to go across and they gave me orders to move. As I put it in gear and started moving, somebody yelled. I'd run over somebody's foot. Then we got to the other side of the river and we waited until the truck came over and I hooked onto it and started out across the bottom. I ran into a shell hole and one motor quit. I tried to back out so I could unhook from that truck and broke the drive shaft on the other motor. So the tank commander and one of these guys walked clear into the 712th Tank Battalion in Dillingen and the next morning they backed a medium tank out. He hooked onto me and took me and the truck and trailer, everything, into town. The light tank had a great big radio in it and when we got there they said, "Just pick out a building and move into it." We picked out a pretty good-sized house and we no more got settled in than along comes an officer who says, "You're going to have to get out, we're going to use this for battalion headquarters." So we just went upstairs. Then the colonel sent word up that he wanted to know who was going to be on the radio last as we had a lantern upstairs for light. He said, "We're going to keep the battalion headquarters open all night and we want some light. Whoever's on duty last, bring the lantern down."

'That was me. So I went into headquarters and here's all these officers in there. Colonel Randolph asked me what my name was and I told him Vorhees. And he says:

'"Are you any relation to General Van Vorhees in charge of the 5th Corps area?"

'"Well, Sir, all I know is my father told me all Vorheeses in this country were related. There's only one family that came over from Holland originally. I guess I'm related to him in some way, I don't know how."

'"How come you've got so much rank in that tank? What's your rating for?"

'"The staff sergeant, he's the platoon sergeant. I'm a T-4 and that's for a medium tank."

'"Oh, you're a medium tank driver? Did you ever think of a transfer?"

'And one of the captains, I don't remember his name, spoke up and said, "The lootin's a lot better up here."

'And Colonel Randolph says, "I wouldn't say that."

'I gave him the lantern and went back upstairs and went to bed. The next morning the sergeant woke me up and says, "The colonel wants you down there."

'So I went down and he says, '"Do you like fried chicken?"'

'"Yeah, I like fried chicken."'

'"You got a mess kit?"'

'"We've got dishes."'

'"Go get one."'

'So he piled it up with fried chicken as the companies were having fried chicken and they take care of the colonel. And I took the chicken upstairs and the sergeant says, "You better tell him you don't want a transfer." But I was already transferred. That was when the Battle of the Bulge started. They pulled us back and then every night would take tanks out and drive them all around in an attempt to make the Germans believe there were a lot of tanks in the area. And then we got orders to move up into the Bulge. At the time, I went with the maintenance tank. Before we got into Luxembourg, we were going up some mountain, got pretty close to the top, and that tank turned completely around. We had to go clear to the bottom again. There was a blizzard the day we moved up. In fact, when we got into Belgium, there were two of us walking in front of the tank trying to find the edge of the road for him to follow us. But we were only up there about two days when they put me in Sam MacFarland's tank. His driver got hit. MacFarland said, "He'll only be gone a day or two. He got up and walked over and got on the jeep himself going back." He died the next day. So I was the permanent driver for MacFarland until he made lieutenant and went in the lieutenant's tank.'

When I wrote to Ray Griffin, the editor of the battalion association newsletter in 1987, he called Sam MacFarland who lived in Pittsburgh. Sam wrote to me suggesting I attend a reunion. It was Sam who took me around and helped find the three men who remembered my father: Jule Braatz, Ellsworth Howard and Charlie Vinson. However, I never got to interview Sam as he died of cancer before I attended my next reunion in 1989. At the time, I did not even know what a battlefield commission was, but Sam was one of the fourteen sergeants in the battalion who received one. When Charles Vorhees was assigned as his driver, MacFarland was the platoon sergeant in the second platoon of A Company. Phil Eckhart was a loader in the second platoon. I never met Phil, but after he passed away, his widow sent me a journal he had kept during the war. He was assigned as a replacement in November, just days before the first Moselle crossing.

'Tuesday (2 January 1945): our driver found a nice heifer and we butchered it,' Eckhart wrote in his journal. 'That night we had fried heart and liver for supper. The house we were staying in was pretty nice, had a good stove and was really nice and warm when you would come in off of guard. On Wednesday, we had steak for supper and it really was good. Went out and got some milk from a cow that was running around and one of the fellows made a kind of a pudding. It was really good and he made several before we left.

'Thursday: it was really snowing and we stayed in about all day except for going and hunting eggs in the evening. We were really surprised to see the captain coming up and he brought us some mail and ice cream. We had found several helmets and had them wrapped for mailing, so he took them along with him. It was on the 6th of January, on Saturday, that General Patton gave orders for the 90th to make their secret move up into Belgium and help in the Bulge.' Interestingly, at that first reunion I attended, one of the veterans told me that as the 90th Division headed north, the badly battered 28th Infantry Division was being relieved. As the troops passed, they would exchange patches so that when the 90th entered combat, the enemy was not expecting to face a fresh division.

'The roads were really icy and the snow was really coming down,' Eckhart wrote. 'On one hill just before getting into Luxembourg, we had to go down in five-minute intervals. Several tanks went off the road, but no one was hurt. On one hill, our tank slid into a tree and I hit my nose on the .30-calibre machine gun. We backed up and before we got by we hit that tree three times. A little farther down the road we went off the side and our track nearly came all the way off. When the driver backed up and pulled on the right lever, I was very much relieved to see it going back on. It was pretty late when we caught up to the rest. They had already reached the town and were getting ready for bed. It was three in the morning and we slept in a cafe on the floor. There were about fifteen of us in there and it was pretty warm. The woman made us coffee and we had a nice drink before going to sleep. The next day was Sunday the 7th of January and we had steak for dinner.'

The captain who visited the platoon was George Cozzens of Lansing, Michigan, who at that time was the A Company commander. Dess Tibbitts was the driver who found the heifer. 'Most of the German people liked us,' Tibbitts said when I visited him in Orland, California, in 1995. 'We learned to get the eggs going across Germany. In France, we had lots to eat, but you had to be careful when you stole off the French people. They didn't like it. I remember Cozzens one time. I was in a house and every house had a chimney. There was a smokehouse that went right up through the chimney and all their hams, bacons and sausage hung in there on little racks.

'I found this one up in the attic and we had field jackets. I had that thing loaded with sausage and bacon. And by god, one of the sausages fell out. One of the women got up and gave Old Cozzens hell for me stealing and boy, he was chewing me out. And he said, "You sonofabitch, now go back and get me some." So I had to go back and steal some more. He made a big show to her and then soon as she was gone we lived off it. Boy, they had good sausage and bacon and hams.

'That time I killed that beef, boy, I had a lot of friends. And everybody was around getting some meat and that Koschen (John Koschen of Brighton, Massachusetts), he found a grinder somewhere. He ground pretty near all the front quarters up and we had frozen hamburger. We'd be cooking 'em and all you had to cook on was those little stoves. You'd no more than get one fried up than somebody'd come along and beg you for it. And we got a lot of good bread off the Germans.'

'The next day, Monday the 8th, we prepared to move out,' Eckhart wrote. 'It was about three in the afternoon when they said to turn them over and not very long after we moved out. We reached the other town about 6.30 in the afternoon and slept in the kitchen. The snow was about a foot and a half deep there, and it was still coming down. Next day, Tuesday the 9th of January, I got my Pfc, wrote several letters and had hot chow twice. That night we moved out about eleven and pulled into position in a wooded area. We slept on the tarp in back of our tank the rest of the night, except the two hours we were on guard. Thursday the 11th of Jan. we had hamburgers and ice cream for chow. We stayed in the same place all that day and the next night. During the night it snowed and when we got up it was about two feet deep. That night I had slept in the tank as the night before I had just about froze out under the tarp. When I went to put my shoes on for guard they were frozen stiff and I had a hard time getting my overshoes over them. Well, as I was saying before, I had slept in the tank that night and kept pretty warm.

'When the other fellows woke up, they had to dig their way out through the snow. It was Friday, the 12th of January. We ate chow and pulled out for the next town. As we were going through a field, we met about two thousand prisoners coming back. We stopped there for a while and got out of the tanks. All of a sudden the Germans started to throw in the artillery and we made a dash for our tanks. One of the shells hit just as I was going in and I heard the assistant driver call out. The concussion had knocked him down. His hatch was open and when they had quit he made a dash for it. Not very far from there had been a mare and her colt walking around a haystack. When we came out they were both laying there dead.

'About three tanks behind us the driver and an infantry lieutenant were hit. The tank driver was Roy Sharpton and he died later on. We asked the captain how he was and they said that he was improving. Next thing we knew he was dead. I have a ten dollar bill out of my first Army pay and one of the names I have on it is his. Well, that night about nine we pulled into a woods and waited for orders to move into town. I was on guard from twelve to one and I had just got off, and was ready to get in my sleeping bag when they called for us. We moved into town and I did not get very much sleep that night.

'The next morning, which was on Sat. the 13th of Jan., we were to go and get some prisoners in a barn. We started down through the field and there were three Germans running towards the woods. My .30-calibre had jammed and the gunner asked me if the 76 was loaded. He fired a high-explosive at them and hit one of them square. Well, you can imagine what happened to him. We went on down to the barn and found there was nothing there, so we started back to where we had been. When we went back, we were in the rear and could see that the Germans were firing at the tanks ahead. They hit two ahead of us but not bad enough to stop them. We were just about behind a building when they hit us in the rear on the right side and knocked out our motor. I was sitting in the turret with an H.E. in my hands, but it did not take long to get rid of it and get out. They kept throwing armor-piercing at us and I was glad it was not H.E. Later on, the driver went back to pull the fire extinguishers and to shut off the master switch. While he was leaning in to shut off the switch, the Germans took a piece of the gun off right over his head with an A.P. Later on, he was put in for the Bronze Star. That gave him one cluster.

'Next day, which was on Sunday, the 14th of January, the crew all but the Lieutenant went back to get a new tank. Our gunner got the projectile that knocked us out. I don't know if he took it home with him or not. When we were on our way back to the company in the ammo truck, our own planes started to bomb and strafe us. We got out and ran in an old building. The fellows were firing at them with the rifles on their peeps and some were firing at them with M-1 rifles. Later on, we found out that they thought the Germans were still in the town as there was a lot of German vehicles knocked out.'

On 13 January, Charles Vorhees said, 'We had just three tanks, MacFarland's tank, Lieutenant (Wallace) Lippincott's tank and there was another tank that was in the second section. MacFarland was in charge of the second section. We were in a farmhouse and we got orders that the infantry wanted us out over the top of a hill and around it. From where we were at, we saw a German tank about every day come down, but they couldn't see us because of the building. We'd try to get the tank out there to shoot at him, but by the time you turned that motor over, 52 revolutions, I mean, to get all the oil pumped out, he'd be gone. So we started out. The lieutenant was in the lead, MacFarland in the middle and this other tank behind us. We get over the crest of the hill, there's a big woods over there and MacFarland says, "I can see the sun shining on faces over in the woods."

'And Lippincott says, "Put a round over their heads and see if you draw fire."

'We put a round over their heads. Nothing happened. So we went on out to this farmhouse where the infantry was and they said they didn't order any tanks. So he starts back again. Now Lippincott's in the rear tank, we're in the middle and the third tank is the front one.'

Lieutenant Wallace Lippincott of Swarthmore, Pennsylvania, had taken over the second platoon about two weeks before when Lt George Cozzens took over as company commander. Pine Valley Bynum was Lippincott's driver. His gunner was Roy R. LaPish of Pottstown, Pennsylvania. The assistant driver was Hilton Chiasson of Thibodeaux, Louisiana, and the loader was Frank Shagonabe, an American Indian from northern Michigan. 'We had to go back over this hill,' Vorhees said. 'Those old Wright radial engines, you had to go in low gear on a hill. As we were coming along there, they put a round in and hit the tank in front of us. All it did was bust his track on one side; he was still able to navigate with it. We went up over the hill. The next round dug up snow between our tank and his tank. And that's when MacFarland said, "Get out of here, Charlie!" So I started up over the hill too. That leaves the lieutenant's tank behind us.

'I was pulling on the levers, going in a zigzag so as not to make a target that's running in a straight line. We get to the top of the hill and the lieutenant and his crew come by us on foot. Their tank took a hit. We get down behind this building again and here's his tank up there with smoke coming out of it, and all the guns are pointing right at us. So the gunner went back up and he's going to pull the fire extinguisher. There's one right behind the driver and he got up on the side of the tank away from where the Germans were and leaned down in there to try to pull it. As he leaned in, another round came in and took the top off the 76-mm tube right above his head. So he got down off the tank, went around to the rear, pulled the extinguisher there and the fire went out. And what it was, there was an AP that went into the oil pan on the motor, the phosphorous had set the oil on fire, and nothing else was burning yet. And he put the fire out.

'That put the lieutenant's tank out of commission. He got another one and I think it was the next day as the infantry liked to wait until almost dark to pull an attack. The lieutenant had a new tank with a

76 on it, too. And we'd just come over the top of the hill when they opened up and started firing at us. MacFarland's tank was one of the old M4A1s with the cast iron hull and the gun had been used so much that it was worn out. When you tried to put a round in the chamber, it would wobble. So we got a pulled round. That is, the projectile came out in the tube and here's this shell in there. It's loaded with powder and a cap, and we had to back up where they can't hit us so the gunner could get out and run a ramrod through and clean the gun. And when we backed up, we could see Lippincott's tank. They were firing APs at it and they weren't hitting the tank, they were going over the top of it, but we could see the tracers. So Mac called Lippincott on the radio and said, "They're firing AP at you." That's the reason he gave the order to abandon tank when they took a hit.'

I did not interview Charles Vorhees until 2001. When I interviewed Big Andy in 1993, he said that although he was in a different platoon, he was listening on the radio when Pine Valley's tank was hit. 'They had a new lieutenant. I heard it all over the intercom. They were in this forest and the Germans were laying artillery, and the shrapnel was coming down and hitting the tank. And this Lippincott said "Abandon tank!" And Bynum said, "No, Lieutenant, that's just shrapnel. Just sit still."

'"I said abandon tank!"

'And they all abandoned tank but one man and he stayed in the tank. He's the only live boy out of that crew. I don't know why Bynum obeyed, but this Lippincott, if he would have listened to an older man, they all might have been alive today. As it was, about two or three days later they asked me if I'd go back and identify Bynum. I would just say you could recognise him. He was full of shrapnel and laying in the snow. Of course, he had his clothes on. A few years ago I went down and saw some of his folks. I don't know why I didn't go down there when we first came out.'

'They hadn't been hit with armor piercing,' said Charles Vorhees, 'but they'd been hit with a high-explosive shell. That's when he told them to abandon tank. Four guys got out, three on one side and one guy on the other. And just as they got out, they took another high-explosive hit and it killed three of them. The other guy, we don't know what happened to him, but after a while the Germans quit firing, I suppose when we quit shooting at them. He came over and knocked on the tank and talked to MacFarland. He said that the three of them are dead but he didn't know where the other guy was. So we went back to the infantry headquarters and Mac was going back to find out what to do about it. And I told the assistant driver and everyone in the tank, "Now, when MacFarland comes back, we'll go up and get that tank and bring it back." In the meantime, the crew from the other tank went up and got it, and they got medals for it. And I went up the next morning and the lieutenant and the other two guys were laying there. But the one guy that didn't show up that night, I don't know what his name was, he's from Louisiana, but they called him Frenchy. He wound up back at headquarters and they never did put him in a tank again.

'I couldn't tell you their names now. Of course, I knew Lippincott and several years ago I was over at Luxembourg at the cemetery and took a picture of his stone and sent it to the 712th. They sent a picture to his wife, or widow I should say, and she wrote me a nice letter thanking me for that. She'd often wondered where he was at. I don't know if he had children, but she had remarried and had a different name at the time she wrote me the letter.'

On 14 January, Phil Eckhart wrote in his journal, 'We got back to the company and slept in a barn that night. Next morning, we got the sad news that our Lieutenant and two other men had been killed that night. When our tank was knocked out, the Lieutenant took No. 4 in the lead and they had orders to take a woods in the night. Well, you know that a tank is not very good for night fighting and when they pulled out the Germans were waiting for them with six anti-tank guns. They hit the lead tank and killed the driver, loader and tank commander. If I had not been knocked out before I would have been the loader in that tank. The driver was Quentin Bynum, the loader was Shagonabe and the tank commander was Lt Lippincott. The gunner was Roy R. LaPish and the assistant driver was Chiasson. That was the fifth tank he had been knocked out of. Him and Roy stayed back for quite some time. Then they sent Roy back up later on but Chiasson never went up again. They kept him back and he worked in the kitchen. On Monday, the 15th of January, we took a tank way to the rear to have ordnance work on it. Tuesday they came and got the driver, Dess Tibbitts, and told him he was going to Paris on pass. That evening they brought another man in and took the rest of us back to the company. We moved to another town and it was really snowing. They got us to paint our tank white. On Monday the 22nd of January, our platoon moved out to relieve the second platoon. The next night they pulled us all back in reserve, and we slept in houses.'

The battalion roster had a listing for Hilton Chiasson in Thibodeaux, Louisiana. I called to see if he were still alive, but he had passed away. I spoke briefly with his widow who said with a thick Cajun accent that her husband never talked about the war. Perhaps, after having five tanks knocked out, he was no longer going to risk an encounter with that shell with his name on it. Roy R. LaPish remained in the Army after the war and was killed in Vietnam. His name is on the Wall in Washington.

One day, someone forwarded me an article published on 6 December 2009 from the *Muskegon Chronicle* about Harlin Shagonabe who was Frank Shagonabe's brother. At the time Frank was killed, according to the article, his father, who adopted him as a toddler, was in prison for alcohol-related crimes and his mother had long since left home. Frank's effects were sent to his employer whom he listed as his next of kin.

Mabel Claire Murphy Bynum died in 1951 at the age of sixty-three. 'We all feel that she finally died if not right away from a broken heart,' James Bynum said. 'She had a big cedar chest in which she kept her memories. And she had Quentin's flag, medals and pictures of him in there. And we would go by once in a while and surprise her sitting in her bedroom on the floor with that flag on her lap crying. I had two appointments to West Point when I was in the service and I had alternate appointments and both times the principal appointment passed all his exams. So I came home on furlough. My captain called me in and said, "I have some bad news for you." And that can only mean one thing in a situation like that. I said, '"What is it?"

'"Your brother was killed in action in Europe. Do you need to go home?"

'"I don't have any money."

'"We'll take care of the money for you. We'll get it from the Red Cross and you can pay them back as you can."

'When I went in the service, I made out an allotment to my mother. I think I was getting $29 a month and the allotment was $21, and whatever I put in the Army matched. So I never had any money. And I loved to play blackjack. I would almost immediately lose whatever pittance I had. But I did go home and we were all there. We were trying to comfort our mother and ignoring our father entirely. He'd been an old cavalryman himself. So he took me back to catch the train and we were standing on the platform. We could hear the train way down in the distance, so I knew it was time to start saying goodbye.

'I said, "Dad, take care of Mom. She's taking this very hard. And it's going to be rough on her." And I looked over at him. And my father never cried. He never patted us. Now I'm a crier. And I'm a hugger. I get the hugging from my mother because she was always touching or laying a hand on. And I looked over at him and I thought to myself, "My god, how stupid can you be? Quentin was his son and he's hurting." And I opened my arms and he walked into them, and we stood there and cried. That's the only time I ever saw my father cry.'

33

At All Costs:
Oberwampach

A photo taken in Amberg, Germany, where the battalion was stationed following VE Day shows six A Company officers, five of whom received battlefield commissions. The six are Bob Hagerty, Morse Johnson, Jule Braatz, Howard Olsen, Sam MacFarland and Ellsworth Howard. I found the picture to be special because my father, having been a replacement lieutenant in A Company, might have been in it if he had not been wounded at Dillingen. Ellsworth Howard was a captain and, when the picture was taken, had only recently returned after recovering from the stomach wound he sustained at the Falaise Gap. MacFarland's platoon lost its lieutenant, Wallace Lippincott, on the night of 14 January and his platoon was in reserve on 17 January. But Hagerty, who was the third platoon's leader; Braatz, who led the first platoon; and Johnson and Olsen, who were still sergeants in Hagerty's platoon, were all involved in the battle for Oberwampach, which lasted from 17-19 January.

Arnold Brown, the 90th Infantry Division rifle company commander, recalled that he was told to hold Oberwampach. According to Dr William McConahey, whose book *Battalion Surgeon* was written shortly after the war, '...the Krauts were ordered to retake Oberwampach at all costs.' The reason for this, according to *Battle of the Bulge: Hitler's Ardennes Offensive* by Danny Parker, was that 'General Van Fleet's infantry took Doncols and Bras east of Bastogne (it was in Bras that Lieutenant Lippincott, Pine Valley and Frank Shagonabe were killed) and close the net on a pocket containing a thousand German (soldiers) from the 5th Fallschirmjager (Parachute) Division.'

Before entering Oberwampach, however, the 712th had to capture Niederwampach, about a mile and a half away on the other side of a valley. 'Niederwampach, this is when I had a couple of tanks,' recalled Howard 'Oley' Olsen when I interviewed him at his home in South Bend, Indiana, in 1993. 'We lined up a company of infantry. We had to go down a hill and there was a wall, so we took off. And a rabbit ran in front of the infantry. Everybody was shooting at it and nobody hit it. We went in that town and took 385 prisoners and never fired a shot.'

'The orders came down to take the infantry battalion I was with,' Jule Braatz said when I interviewed him at his home in Beaver Dam, Wisconsin, in 1994. 'I think it was the 2nd Battalion of the 358. And we're gonna attack this town of Niederwampach, which was below some hills, and it's a long way down with open fields before you get into the town. So they're gonna put a coordinated artillery barrage, what they called time on target, 15 battalions of artillery on the town. The only problem is they missed the town and it came on the other side. So we're attacking down, we were going right into the town and they never fired a shell. There were five anti-tank guns there looking right at us. We took around 300 prisoners. That's Niederwampach. So the next day we go to Oberwampach, which is maybe a mile and a half down this little road and along the river, and we pull in there unmolested. And part of the town is on each side of a little creek. So I disperse my tanks on this side of the town along the ridge. I had Oley and I think it was (Morse) Johnson over here, and I was in the middle. And then there were two other tanks or did we have only one? I don't remember.'

'Oberwampach was just a crossroads with some farm buildings and a few homes,' Bob Hagerty said when I interviewed him at his home in Cincinnati in 1993. 'We needed an outpost and I went up on a side road and pulled off to the right. There was a little culvert where the farmer had cut a path through to move the wagons and horses. We could see up ahead. There were some buildings on fire. Sometimes things like that are set on fire by the infantry. Perhaps they create a kind of super searchlight and then the Germans aren't going to come through and expose themselves while they're highlighted like that. The fires were up the road. The road was a gentle rise and an infantry guy came running toward us. He said there's a halftrack coming. So we thought, "Halftrack, boy oh boy! Where is she?" Big Andy was my driver. He eased the tank back off of the road.

'Ted Duskin was my gunner. He swings the gun out and lays it up the road. And through this smoky haze that the fire is making, here comes this German, but it ain't no halftrack. It's one of the big tanks. And I just remember thinking, "God, this is gonna hurt." Ted shot immediately as that bulk came through the haze and he must have hit the turret; there was a big shower of sparks. They were heavily armored in the front and they were only really vulnerable in the rear.

'About a second after we fired, he fired. A big lick of flame came out of the muzzle of the gun and it hit our tank. It seemed to hit it down low in the carriage and made a hell of a sound. And suddenly, the German began to move backwards into the smoke. How lucky can you be? We quickly took a look at our tank and one of the bogey wheels appeared to be almost severed. He hit us down low. It glanced off fortunately for us. And with the track still intact, Andy could ease her back. We eased her back down the slope and that German didn't come after us. But talk about being scared. Before he made that first shot... They had the firepower. They could penetrate us. We couldn't penetrate them until we got a larger gun.

'After we backed down around a curve in the road, there was a rock wall and there was enough room for us to get in there. Ahead of us, against the same rock wall, was a tank destroyer. They had light armor, but they had a bigger gun than we had so they could knock out a German tank which we couldn't. So as soon as we got behind the destroyer, I ran out and told the destroyer's commander what was probably going to be coming down the road, so he could get a good shot at it. The German doesn't know the tank destroyer is here.

'First thing you know, we could hear little *click-clicks*. That's about all the noise their tracks made: *click-click*. They were real quiet. We would make lots of noise and we'd give ourselves away. He's coming down here and he had a dismounted soldier leading him. Imagine having that as your job because this guy's dead the first time he's seen. But he's going to take the fire and spare the tank. So this foot soldier comes down here with a rifle and as the tank creeps up behind him, the guy in the tank destroyer fired too soon. It went right across the front of him, and with that, the German threw it in reverse and went back up the hill.'

Time and memory filter out many of the sights and sounds of battle. When a veteran describes a bullet snapping a branch above his head, at the same time there may be a thousand bullets whizzing through the air. There could be a hundred snapped branches, noises, screams, rivulets of blood trickling through the snow and mud. Yet as time goes by, there seems to be a disconnect between the memory of battle and its sheer bloody intensity. Dr William McConahey in *Battalion Surgeon* described Oberwampach thus: 'For 24 hours the battle flamed and swirled in the cold and snow in and around the town. Wave after wave of screaming, fanatical enemy soldiers accompanied by tanks and tank destroyers smashed at our men. Point blank tank duels, street fighting, bayonet encounters and heavy artillery made Oberwampach a village of horror and sudden death; but our boys held firm and the Germans could not crack our line... During this 24 hour period, the 344th Field Artillery Battalion fired nearly 3,500 rounds of ammunition, the most it ever fired in a 24-hour period.'

And in a letter to his mother and sister, Morse Johnson, a sergeant in A Company's first platoon who would later receive a battlefield commission, wrote, 'We are not in contact with the enemy all the time, but when we are, dramatic incidents occur which, since I was involved and remained unscathed, probably would interest you. Let me relate one of them that occurred in the Bulge. The town of Oberwampach is in a valley between two hills, on each of which is a road. Oley's (Howard Olsen) and my tanks were located on one of those roads near the crest of the hill and adjacent to two houses in which a squad of infantry was quartered. We had pulled into this position late at night and throughout the night we could hear German tanks on the other hill across the valley. When dawn came we could see no Heine vehicles, but could spot some men in foxholes. These were quickly put out of action by our artillery.

Things quieted down and we assumed the enemy had "parteed" – an oft-used word stemming from the French word partir – when a forward observer spotted some Heinies trying to set up a mortar in a woods on the right of us in the valley. Artillery laid down on them and so did Oley.

'Suddenly Oley yelled, "Tanks, Johnny! Heinie tanks! Get the artillery!" One of the houses blocked my view but I shouted to the telephone man in the house. As I did, I saw Oley's tank belching out armor-piercing shells. I was about to try to manoeuvre my tank into a position so that I could help in the action when I spied a number of German infantrymen in white camouflage uniforms surging through the valley. They were clay pigeons for my tank's coaxial .30 calibre machine gun and I could even see their bewilderment as Tom, my gunner (this was probably Tom Wood of Louisville, Kentucky), fired into them. Naturally, I was focusing all my attention on the Germans and helping Tom guide into them. It was pure luck that caused me, for some reason, to look back up to my left toward the crest of our hill.

'Tom claims that I first yelled, "Oh, my God!" At any rate, I did shout H.E. – high-explosive – and grabbed the power traverse switch to turn my turret and the gun barrel around to the left. For bearing down on us – and at the time I saw him not 40 yards away – was a Heine halftrack with a German officer crouched on its hood, hand grenade in hand. The power traverse worked, my loader was quick in getting the H.E. shell in and Tom was accurate both with our cannon and machine gun. In not more than 15 seconds, the halftrack had been put out of commission. The Ober-Lieutenant had only suffered relatively minor shell-fragment wounds and the Heines' hands were up in the air. In no time at all I was out of my tank and, carbine in hand, waved the German crew into the house where the infantry was. That was the most intense moment we had, but for the next two days we had to deal with more counterattacks. My memories of that time are fitful sleeping, constantly disturbed by one of my crew shaking me and whispering, "Here they are again," and then long periods of listening and watching and occasionally seeing and shooting.'

'I was sitting up on a hill looking down, the town was all on a hill,' Howard Olsen said in 1993. 'I was looking at kind of a ravine going downhill and we were all in the tank. And pretty soon here comes a German tank. *Bang!* We nailed it. Here comes another German tank. James Pack hit him. Stopped them both right there. And we backed up. And just as we backed up, a command car came over the hill firing. We traversed and hit him. The guy in the turret jumped out and the infantry went and caught him. It was a colonel. He was leading it. And one guy on his command car was hurt, the other guy wasn't because we fired an armor-piercing shot right through it. And the way I understand, Hagerty was somewhere behind me and he knocked out a halftrack.

'After the Germans pulled back, I walked over the hill and there was a tank just over on the side of the hill. It had a big hole in the turret. How it got hit I don't know. It might have been an artillery shell. In the meantime, over on our right there was a big Tiger tank coming down. There was a guy leading it, a civilian, and he was pointing to the houses where the soldiers were in. And the tank was shooting in there. And all of a sudden, a bazooka team came out and they ran right in front of that tank and fired that bazooka. And the colonel from the infantry was standing by us. He said, "Get those men's names." Because they deserved something. That takes a lot of guts to get in front of a tank and shoot at it. They would have been better off if they went around behind it. But they had to stop it or they'd have lost a lot of men.'

It was at Oberwampach that Big Andy earned his second of three Bronze Stars. 'Captain Cozzens told us that we had to move out to a certain place at night, and I said, "No, I'm not going to go. I'm not taking my tank out after dark." And him and I went round and round and he assured me that there was nothing down this road. I can't think who else was in on it. I know Hagerty was there. We got down this road and the first tank got hit with a bazooka, and the last tank got hit with a bazooka. And then the three in between, I got a bazooka in the gas tank of my tank. We went to evacuate our tank and got out, and this Owen (John Owen of Montgomery, Alabama) was hit by shrapnel. And I picked him up on my shoulder and I must have carried him a half or three-quarters of a mile. And all he could say is, "I'm hit in my head, I'm hit in the head," and his ass was so full of shrapnel that you've never seen anything like it. But I carried him back to the first aid station.

'He wasn't hit in the head, it's just that he was in such pain. That's where I got my second Bronze Star. Like a fool, I went back and grabbed a fire extinguisher and went down and tried to put out the fire in my tank, that's just how stupid I was. I saw the Germans standing right there, just like they were from about here to that shed up there away from me. Why they didn't shoot me I don't know. Now why did I grab that fire extinguisher? That's just how I felt. This is a true story, this ain't no bull. Why did I take that and go down there and try to put a fire out with a little fire extinguisher in a 33-ton tank?'

The 712th withstood nine counterattacks in Oberwampach. It was during one of these that Ted Davis of Santa Barbara, California, became the only enlisted man in the battalion to earn a Distinguished Service Cross. I never met Davis, but his citation is online at HomeofHeroes. com. It reads in part:

> The President of the United States takes pleasure in presenting the Distinguished Service Cross to Ted R. Davis, Private First Class, U.S. Army, for extraordinary heroism in connection with military operations against an armed enemy while serving with Company A, 712th Tank Battalion, attached to the 90th Infantry Division, in action against enemy forces on 17 January 1945 in Luxembourg. During a determined enemy attack near Oberwampach, Luxembourg, the tank in which Private First Class Davis served as a cannoneer and loader, was set on fire by two direct artillery hits, forcing the crew to take cover. When the tank ceased to burn, Private First Class Davis voluntarily made his way through withering fire to the vehicle, mounted it and repaired the damaged guns. When the enemy advanced to within machine gun range he opened fire, decimating their ranks and forcing them to withdraw. Later, he assembled a crew and drove the tank into action which resulted in the destruction of an enemy tank.

The official unit history of the 712th Tank Battalion sometimes reads like a National Geographic travelogue. Its principal writer was Morse Johnson, a Harvard educated lawyer with a unique prose voice who became a sergeant in the horse cavalry and later received a battlefield commission. The unit history's passage on Oberwampach is one of the instances where, without naming names, he is writing about himself and Howard Olsen.

The 26th Inf. began to pinch off the battered B Co. tankers and on 12 Jan., after outposting at BOULAIDE and HARLANGE, A Co., with 358, moved up through C Co. The 6th Armd., striking east with exposed flanks, was pointing toward BRAS. If juncture could be effected there, a large enemy force would be entrapped. A Co., moving through SONLEZ, was chosen to effect this mission and soon was locked with the strongly resisting Heine in a two-day slugfest. Finally, two tanks, braving devastating anti-tank fire, grasped the other side of the important railroad tracks and joined with the 6th Armd. in BRAS, thus sealing off large Heine forces. From BRAS A Co. battered forward, ploughing across open fields to take NEIDERWAMPACH and, after skirting thick mine fields, reached OBERWAMPACH which they set about to do with desperate resolution and a never-mind-the-cost recklessness. For 3 days and nights the 712th, 773rd TDs and 90th doughs stood firm against 9 major counterattacks, inflicting huge casualties in men and equipment. Fighting became so intense that 1 tank, dealing with the Boche on its right, had just enough time to traverse left and knock out at a 15-yard range the lead half-track of another armored column. Massive artillery barrages assisted each side – the Heine threw 1500 rounds in a 24 hour period; the 344th FA BN. unleashed 6000 rounds in 36 hours. Speaking of this action, 90th Operational Reports state: "German losses were enormous and mounted as heavy snow storms blanketed enemy dead and wounded alike. No exact count was possible but an estimated several hundred Germans were buried from sight for long after the Division had left the area.

During the battle for Oberwampach, Howard Olsen mentioned an encounter with a young Jewish infantryman who enjoyed entertaining his squad mates. 'He could make up a song like nothing,' Olsen said. 'You'd give him a name and he'd make up a song. He was funny. A real nice kid. He was in Oberwampach. After I backed up, the tank shuddered and somebody hollered "We've been hit! Bail out!" Of course, we all bail out. We went in this house and this Jewish boy was there. He was singing. And the people in the house are clapping. A little while later, I looked out and said, "That tank hasn't been hit!" We had backed into a tree and it jarred the tank. It felt just like it had been hit. Then we went back out and got in the tank.'

Morse Johnson, in a letter home, also remembered the infantryman. 'I don't believe I ever told you about "Brooklyn,"' Johnson wrote. 'At one of our tight spots, we shared a room with an infantry squad, all of the members of which we got to know quite well. One was "Brooklyn," obviously from Brooklyn. One night he mentioned having written a song for his C.O. and with little urging sang it for us with a song-plugger's voice and style – like Irving Berlin or even Eddie Cantor.

'I applauded and it really was. "Let's hear some more of your stuff." Here was an extrovert of the first order and for a half-hour he stood in the middle of a Heine kitchen singing his songs and telling the story behind each with a smart vaudevillian patter. I began to doubt whether all these songs were his and told him so. At once he asked me the name of my girl – which I faked – and my home town. Not five seconds later, he was singing a catchy ditty about me, the girl, Cincinnati, etc. I told him to do the same for Mac, my driver, and he had just started when the guard rushed in and we had to rush out to repel the umpteenth counterattack. We worked a lot with those boys and Oley's and my crew were always happy to see them.

'The other day, "Brooklyn" rode on my tank and I coaxed him to write a song for us. At once, he burst out with a really dandy tune, the first words of which were: "There will be no more falling arches, there's no more walking Yank; going to hitch a ride, going to hop inside, going to Berlin on a tank." The tank stopped and "Brooklyn" was just about to write it all down for me when his squad was called to clean out a slight pocket. We tanks were in close support, but the terrain did not permit us to be right with them. I guess I heard the shots – there were a lot of them – but I didn't see him get it. I did see him, however, and fortunately he had died instantly.'

34

The Gypsy's Prophecy

The one name I remembered from my father's stories was that of Ed
Forrest. He said he got the impression Ed either did not want or did not
expect to come home from the war. It was a bit of a mystery, so when
I would ask the A Company veterans who remembered Ed, I would
relay my father's impression. My father said Ed's father may have been
a minister who did not approve of him going off to war. I thought if
his father was a minister in Stockbridge, Massachusetts, there must
be people there who remembered him. So I called information. The
operator said there was no one in Stockbridge by the name of Forrest,
but there were three in the neighbouring town of Lee. I made my first call
to Elmer Forrest. I asked if he were related to Ed Forrest, a lieutenant in
the Second World War and Elmer said, 'He was my brother.'

'Was your father a minister?'

'No,' Elmer said. 'My father was an alcoholic.' I do not have it
on tape, but he really said that. The minister, he explained, was the
Revd Edmund Randolph Laine of St Paul's Episcopal Church in
Stockbridge. Ed did odd jobs for the priest after school and when their
mother died, Ed blamed her death on their father's drinking. They had
a fight and Ed moved into the parish house. Ed and Elmer's maternal
grandmother, Hannah Climena Pixley Ariail, lived with a spinster
daughter in a remote house on Beartown Mountain in the Berkshires.
After the daughter's death, among her possessions was a notebook
in which her mother wrote her life story. She did not exactly write
it. She dictated the story, which the daughter wrote in the notebook
with no punctuation. The notebook ends on a cliff-hanger note and
no one was ever able to find a second notebook. Ed and Elmer's niece

211

– Flora Brantley, the daughter of their sister Vera – took the notebook and transcribed its contents, adding punctuation along the way. The story was so moving that the New Jersey Superior Court judge who bought the house the grandmother lived in until her death made some photocopies and the *Monterey News*, a local newspaper, published it.

More important to this story, however, Flora encouraged her mother, Vera Forrest McCarthy Beckley, to write her own story, which she began doing at age seventy-six. I quoted from that memoir earlier. Although I would eventually determine that Ed Forrest very much wanted and expected to come home – before leaving, he even proposed to his girlfriend, Dorothy Cooney – Vera's journal provides some insight into his tragic life. Dorothy and I became great friends over the years. She still lived in Stockbridge in the house her father built, about a quarter mile from St Paul's and I would visit her every few months when I could find an excuse to go to the Berkshires. One day, we were talking and she said that she could not tell me for certain, since she did not know Ed until after he was fourteen and moved to Stockbridge, but if I looked into it, I might find that Ed's mother may have committed suicide. I did not know if she knew more than she was telling me or if she had always wondered about it herself.

I remembered Elmer telling me Ed blamed his mother's death on his father's drinking, but I had not pursued it any further. So I called Elmer and arranged another interview. This time I asked how his mother died. Elmer was seven years younger than Ed and would have been seven at the time – he might not have known. 'She committed suicide,' he said. And then he described how, at seven years of age, he sat in the kitchen, frightened and eating ice cream while others were out searching for his mother who had jumped into the Housatonic River in the middle of the night. Later, Flora Brantley sent me a copy of her mother's memoir. Vera wrote that when her mother went into labour with her fourth child, their father was drunk. The doctor sent him to get the midwife, and the midwife, who drank on the weekend, was drunk.

'The doctor sent her home, got Dad upstairs to bed, called Edward at home and sent him across the covered bridge up Tiger Hill for a domestic nurse,' Vera's memoir continued. 'Mother was furious at Dad even as sick as she was and around 9 p.m. she gave birth to another baby boy. When we got up in the morning, Mother told us she was naming the baby after the President of the United States, Warren Harding, so Warren Joseph Forrest it was. Dad had sobered up enough so that he was able to get our breakfast, and afterwards, Elmer and I were told we had to go away for a couple weeks so Mother could rest and the house would be quiet...

'At last my two weeks were up and I came home. Mother was still in bed; complications had set in. (Today I feel she had not been properly taken care of by the doctor. An infection had set in where he had torn her during the birth of the baby. He should of sewn her up.) The pain became so bad that it affected her mind. She never complained and one night she got up and swallowed some poison tablets, Laudanum (Tablets that Dad had when he had smashed a thumb, using them to soak his thumb in.) Dad caught her and she was rushed to the hospital. There they pumped her stomach, plus they sewed up the vagina after cauterising it. She healed there but poor soul, her mind was gone.'

A few weeks went by when one morning Vera wrote, 'Dad went to work. Mother seemed better for a few days, so he left her. We children got up and got ready for school and all Mother did was to stand in the window and look out at the river, which was about 200 yards away from the house. Edward realised she was bad again; he set the clock back two hours, told me to stay there till the kitchen clock said 9 a.m. (really 11 a.m.) and he went off to school. She began to get wise (I think); started the washing of the clothes. At just 9 a.m., I left but Edward was late in returning.

'When I came home at noon, one hour later, a woman was washing the clothes in the back room. Mother's clothes were on the floor and the doctor was there. I went in and never shall I forget the scene I saw. Mother lay on the bed crying so hard and loud. When she saw me she said, "Vera, it's terrible. I was born white, then I went to see a Chinaman and he made me yellow." I started to cry and the woman who was there gently put her arms around me and drew me out of the room. She led me to the kitchen where she placed me in a chair. She sat down next to me and told me that Mother had gone out just as soon as I had left and had thrown herself into the river. Mind you, this was March 23, 1924, and ice was still on the river in places. A man who was getting off the trolley, in front of the house, saw her and ran and dove in, good clothes and all; he saved her.'

After two more failed attempts to poison herself with Laudanum and one attempt to hang herself (the ceiling was too low), her husband made arrangements to have his wife transferred to a sanatorium. 'Mother and Dad went to Lee and the judge there made out papers for poor Mother to be sent away to Northampton. She was quiet all day long. She must of realised what was up, but she never let on. Night came and before we went to bed, she asked Edward to sing for her. He did, then she kissed us all good night. We went to bed; she sat in her usual place, a large rocker in the dining room. She would never have a light on, just sit and rock. The nurse didn't stay nights as Dad always slept with Mother, so he felt he could watch her, being a light sleeper. Around eleven o'clock after they had been in bed a couple of hours, he felt her move and get up. He arose and there she was coming back from the kitchen with a potato knife in her hand. He asked her for it and why she had it. She said she just wanted to go upstairs and show it to her children. He got her back to bed and he fell asleep.

'Poor Dad, he had so little sleep of late that he must of fallen into a sound sleep for Mother arose and quietly left the room, opened the back door and walked barefooted in her nightgown to the river where she threw herself in. Dad awoke; it must of been just minutes as the bed was still warm. He realised immediately what had happened. He rushed out the door but saw or heard nothing. He called Edward and I. Before I could dress, Edward had dressed, lit a lantern and rushed out and awoke all the neighbours. Hunting parties were formed and by 3 a.m. the whole town was out searching. The local and state police came and the Boy Scouts. This was March 29, 1924, and it was cold outside. There had been a light snow but only in spots.

'At 5 a.m. there was no trace of her body, but several footprints were found leading to the river, so the search was at the river, the Housatonic River. Grappling irons were brought in and there were boats afloat. We children sat on our wood pile and watched it all. At 6 a.m., my father was walking down by the dam, a quarter of a mile from our house, when he thought he saw something, then decided it was just foam, laying up near an old log. He passed by. Edward and his scout master were just behind. Edward climbed a limb of a tree that hung out over the water. He screamed, "There she is! There she is!" It was poor Mother and she was dead. Dad rushed back, threw off his coat and made for the river but two state troopers grabbed him. A boat made its way out to the place and two men lifted her into the boat and brought her to shore. Thank God, I didn't witness this scene. We had gone through so much already. I felt so sorry for Edward as he idolised Mother. Never did he forget it all. That night always haunted him and he blamed Dad for her death.

'I had been left at Mrs Everett Charter's home taking care of Elmer... News came that Mother had been found and had not gone over the dam as was feared. Such sorrow; four motherless children. Edward, fourteen; I, eleven; Elmer, five, and Warren, three-months old. It wasn't right that she should be taken. It doesn't seem as if God is just to take someone like her. One who had always been such a worker, good, true and only thirty-five years old; while bums walk the streets, crooks rob and kill and they all live to grow old...

'Mother was kept at the funeral parlour so I never saw her until the burial... And poor Dad, he was trying to drown his sorrow in drink. The day of the funeral came; such a crowd of people at the church. I remember little at the church; only they played Mother's favourite piece, "Flow Gently Sweet Afton." Edward had told the organist that Mother loved that piece. I don't recall going to the cemetery either, but I do remember just before they lowered her into the grave, the funeral director opened the lid so we could see her. God help me. It couldn't be her. Never will I forget how she looked. They had dressed her in black. Oh God, why black? Her long copper hair, instead of being done up pompadour style as she always wore it, hung down her back. And she was black and blue from drowning. Why did we have to see her? Why couldn't we have remembered her as we last saw her? I fainted dead away and was carried to the car and I remember nothing of the ride back. The gypsy's prophecy had come true and it was over.'

35

The Iron Cross and
a Three-Day Pass

'When Lieutenant Gifford was evacuated, we waited for a replacement tank. That's when we got this new tank and Sergeant Holmes (Eldon K. Holmes of Cleveland, Ohio) became our acting platoon leader,' Bob Rossi said during the group conversation in 1992. 'And on 8 February 1945, we were knocked out again at Habscheid, Germany. We were in a wooded area. They called us during the night.'

'In high ground, no?' Tony D'Arpino, the tank driver, asked.

'In high ground. And it seemed like the Germans were just waiting there for us.'

'They had it all zeroed in,' D'Arpino said. 'They had three lines of machine gun fire. Some just grazed the ground. Some came waist high.'

'When light came, it seemed like everything opened up at one time. They knew we were there, in the woods, and they had mortar, artillery, machine gun fire. All of a sudden, Sergeant Holmes collapsed in the turret and I was yelling, "Holmes! Holmes! Are you hit?" And Spahr says to me, "Sure, he's hit." And with that we picked him up and put him behind the gun. Shrapnel had gone through his steel helmet. He was hit in several places. The towel that was around his neck was sopping wet with blood. Later, after this happened, I noticed I had blood all over my left sleeve. And I asked D'Arpino, "Give me the first aid kid." And with that, he can't open it. The darn thing was rusted shut. So with a chisel he opened up the first aid kit and I bandaged Sergeant Holmes as best I could. And as he's laying on the floor, he called up Sergeant Gibson (Maxton C. Gibson of Nashville, Tennessee, another of the battalion's fourteen battlefield commissions). He says, "Gib, I'm hit. I'm getting out of here." And Gibson called back. He says, "We're all getting out of here." With that, Gibson started up the hill and this is when we found out that the Germans had the hill zeroed in. As Gibson stopped, they fired two rounds in front of him and missed. He took off. We came up the hill and *bang!* We got hit. The 88 went through our engine compartment and landed between Jim Sessions' legs.'

'He was a recruit.'

'First time up.'

'I think it was a day before or a day after his 18th or 19th birthday.'

'I was driving and I knew there was another tank behind me to get out,' D'Arpino said, 'so I tried pulling over to the right to give him room to get around me and nothing was working. Sessions, he was new, he grabbed the fire extinguisher and I says "Jump you crazy bastard, jump!" Matter of fact, I didn't even unplug the radio or nothing. I just got out.'

'He never did attempt to get out till I got hold of him. I jumped back up on the tank and I grabbed him.'

'I neglected to say, one tank was already knocked out in the woods. Their bogey wheels were knocked off and we had taken two guys from that crew into our tank, so there were five of us in the turret when there should have been three. When we got hit, I was the last guy to get out. I was on my hands and knees waiting for the others to get out, and I no sooner got out of the turret than the ammo started to go.'

'It's taking a while to tell this story, but it all happened within seconds,' D'Arpino said, 'and when that thing hit and I saw that red projectile land beside Sessions' foot – it came right alongside by the transmission. The transmission was between the driver and the assistant driver – it was laying right down by his left foot.'

'The projectile gets red hot,' Jim Gifford said.

'Cherry red,' Spahr commented.

'I didn't even bother unplugging my helmet radio,' D'Arpino said. 'I just put my hand outside, tried to pry myself up and that tank was as hot as a stove.'

'When they hit us,' Spahr said, 'it just felt like it drove the tank ten feet forward.'

'I automatically turned around when we were hit,' Rossi said. 'I turned around to pull the extinguisher. We had an inside extinguisher. It didn't do any good. The fire was so tremendous with all that gasoline. And right after we got hit, just before I got out of the tank, that's when the other tank, which was just about on our left rear, they got hit. But they weren't as fortunate as us in the sense that La Mar, who was the driver, he got burned pretty bad. I can remember when he took that stocking mask off he took the skin right off his face. And Whiteheart (Gary L. Whiteheart of Winston-Salem, North Carolina) who is now dead, the type of tank they had, they had ammo stacked in back of the assistant driver. It shifted and hit him right in the back. Van Landingham (Sgt Carl Van Landingham of Los Angeles) was the tank commander and part of his heel was torn off from the shrapnel.'

'I remember we got all the way down,' D'Arpino said. 'We crawled all the way down that hill and Van Landingham was missing, right? He's still back up there. So I don't know who the other guy was and myself, we grabbed a stretcher, we went back up – we crawled back up. They were shooting right over our heads. I thought that was my last day. I had three tanks knocked out from under me and out of all of them, I thought that was it. I had it. So we crawled up there with a stretcher to get Van Landingham, right? We finally get to him and he's moaning and groaning. I'm looking for blood. I don't see nothing. He's got them combat boots on. I look and he goes, "Ohhh, ohhh," real sharp. Now he must have been hit someplace, I don't know where. I couldn't see any blood. We're trying to get him on that stretcher and we're trying to crawl on our hands and knees with the stretcher, get him down over the crest where they couldn't see us.

'They had that place zeroed in. We'd go a few feet and then *Shooom!* We'd drop the stretcher. The third time the stretcher hit solid ground with Van Landingham groaning. Anyway, God willing, we got him down to the bottom and I don't know who that man is today. I've thought about this a million times, but somebody saw me and whoever else had that stretcher, it was an officer. He wasn't in our company and he took our names. He thought we should get the Silver Star for what we had done. And then I was told later on that this man was called back to England. He had to be a witness in a court martial. I don't know who the officer was. He wasn't in our outfit.'

'He was a captain in the infantry,' Spahr said. 'You remember, we all got up in that bunker?'

'We were going from pillbox to pillbox.'

'I'll never forget that day. The snipers were watching us. You raised up a little bit and *Ping!*'

'Every time we'd hear *ping*, we'd drop the stretcher and Van Landingham would hit and he'd groan.'

'You know what was ironic? We were running from pillbox to pillbox to get out of the line of fire after all this happened. And the infantry was dug in foxholes. They said, "Don't run on this road, it's mined. Don't run in the gully, it's mined." And we finally got to this one pillbox and I think it was a major or a lieutenant colonel, he wanted American wounded put outside because he complained that they were in the way of him conducting business. And we were PO'd at him. I was so mad at the time. I was only a kid, but I was so mad I felt like shooting the German prisoners who were there because they did this to us.'

'I remember that one infantry boy. This captain pointed to him and said, "Get up there and get that sonofabitch!" And that infantry boy was sitting there, he handed him his M-1 and he said, "Here, you get him."'

'If you remember, that night, it was dark when the infantry moved us up there.'

'It was raining.'

'We argued about it,' D'Arpino said. 'You move the tanks at night. Jesus, they make too much noise. But the infantry officer said, "I'm giving you an order."'

'So Holmes says to me, "Rossi, get out." He handed me his tank commander's watch with the luminous hands. He said, "Lead the tank." Now I'm running in front of the tank in the rain, holding the watch up as I'm running so D'Arpino can see it in the dark. And when we got knocked out the next morning, I said to myself, "Thank God my clothes were soaking wet." I think that's what saved me from burning to death in the tank.'

'We lost four tanks that day.'

'Three out of four.'

'That's right, Gibson's was the only tank that got out.'

'Two tank destroyers were lost and we lost about a company of infantry. I mean, we took a beating.'

'When daybreak came, I looked around and said, "Hooooly shit." You could see for miles. I mean, we were really exposed.'

'You remember later on we were kidding. It was bad, but later on we kidded, "That German gun crew must have all got the Iron Cross and a three-day pass."'

A year after that conversation at the 1993 battalion reunion, I interviewed Grayson La Mar who drove the tank in which Sergeant Van Landingham was injured and who himself was badly burned. 'Holmes was the platoon leader,' La Mar said. 'We were on top of this hill. We were taking orders from a 90th Infantry Division lieutenant and we didn't run into anything. So we were supposed to take up positions the next morning and since we didn't run into anything, he wanted to go on down to the bottom of the hill (in the morning) and stay down there. But by daybreak, all of a sudden all hell broke loose. We had four tanks and a tank destroyer. They threw a shell in the tank destroyer, killed all of them. And one boy, we could see, they broke his leg or something. He just tried to climb out, then they threw another round in there and finished him off.

'Then they got the second tank I believe. So when they got that, that left three tanks. Sergeant Gibson, he didn't know what the rest were going to do, but he's gonna get the hell out of there and he's the only one that got out. When he left, Holmes followed him. I automatically backed up and followed Holmes. When I got to the top of the hill, his tank was sitting in the middle of the road burning. I couldn't get around, so I had to go off into a field, and when I did my backend blew up. The shell came in there and set me on fire. It took three tries to get the hatch open. See, the hatch would hit the gun barrel. The gunner was killed and nobody could operate the gun to get the barrel out of the way. So finally, on the third try, I slipped by. If the gun was over a quarter-inch more I'd never have got out.

'The concussion from the shell blew my helmet off. When I got out, there were blazes all around and I had to keep my eyes shut, so naturally I was in the dark. The tank commander was hanging over the side. He said, "Help me." He got his heel blown off. I dragged him off into the snow and I just fell in, too, about ten inches of snow. I drove my head in the snow. And Holmes, he was laying out there in the field. A jeep came up there and got him and got me, and that other guy. They put some kind of powder on us. Then Holmes got in an ambulance and went to a field hospital and they put stuff on us. It smelled like axle grease. They put that all over our head where we were burnt. And they put him in one ambulance and me in another. I remember them giving me a carton of cigarettes. He says, "Take these. It might be a long time before you get one." So they got me to the hospital. They put me in a chair, kind of like a barber chair, and put more of that stuff over me. I was then wrapped like a mummy, wrapped in gauze all over my head for 18 days. They just cut holes for my nose, mouth and my eyes. Got a shot every four hours. Man, I never had seen so many needles in my life. Stayed in bed and stayed there 18 days. When they took the gauze off, it was like you stuck your head in ice water. A lot of my skin came off. I didn't have a beard, eyelashes or nothing. In fact, I can now wash my face with a rough washrag and roll the skin up on my face, it's just been that way ever since. When I wash I don't bear down, I just rub lightly. It makes my face raw to rub it hard. But I had orders to go by some bivouac area and pick up another tank, and they showed me where to go to find my platoon. I didn't even go back to the company. I went on back out on the line. Right from the hospital...'

36

Pfaffenheck

The headline in the *Northern Virginia Daily* dated 16 March 1945 with all its attendant sub-heads blares: 'Mile of Superhighway Held by Yanks/Reds Slash East Prussian Pocket Into Two Segments/Five American Armies Strike Along Blazing Western Front/Assault Beyond Rhine Captures Four German Towns/Stab Into Five Others.'

Paris, Friday, March 16 (AP) – The U.S. First Army deepened its Rhine bridgehead to 6 miles yesterday, seizing command of more than a mile of the great six-lane highway to the Ruhr, and the Germans said five American armies were striking along 235 miles of the blazing western front.

The drive beyond the Rhine gained more than a mile during the day, swept up four more German towns, and stabbed into five others.

The Germans said the new U.S. 15th Army had sprung into action on the bridgehead where 100,000 American soldiers now were massed.

The U.S. Third Army smashed 6 miles south from its newly won Moselle River bridgehead near Coblenz in an offensive that was cutting in 80 miles or so behind the Siegfried Line facing the Seventh Army front.

The push had sealed off the Rhine transit city of Coblenz, was nearing the Rhine south of the city, was pinching off the enemy's little Ruhr, the Saar Basin, and was challenging the Nazis' last 150-mile grip on the Rhine's west bank. 'The Third Army was by far the deepest into Germany of any Allied army in the west.' On 16 March 1945, the 712th Tank Battalion was with General Patton's 3rd Army and had just crossed the Moselle River for the second time in combat.

Billy Wolfe, who joined the battalion as a replacement in March, wrote in a high school assignment, 'If I were to be blind after today, I would want to go off by myself in the mountain, climb to the highest cliff and look out across the valley at the towns, farms and farmhouses. I would want to picture each native tree in my mind, the rough bark and the shapely green leaves. I would want to see the squirrels running and leaping from one walnut tree to another and the birds flying. I would like to see the deer run and jump swiftly and gracefully and leap across the fences and lie in a tree that leans across the water and watch bass laying under the rocks and dart out after a fly. I would go through the house from one room to the other picturing each piece of furniture, every corner and everything, in my mind. I would like to see all my sisters, brother and parents together as we were, and picture each as they look for future reference. I would want to see all my friends and relatives so I would know what the person looked like when I would talk to them after being blind. I would want to go fishing and hunting and do the things I know I couldn't do after being blind.'

'I am in Company C and in Germany now,' Billy wrote in the letter dated 5 March 1945. The letter arrived at his parents' home in Edinburg in the picturesque Shenandoah Valley on 16 March. That morning, an ocean away, the second platoon of C Company was about to fight its way into the village of Pfaffenheck, Germany, in the picturesque Rhine-Moselle Triangle.

'Pfaffenheck,' Otha Martin repeated when I asked if he remembered it. 'The 16th day of March in '45. I was there. I can tell you every *man* that was there and what happened to each tank.'

'Do you remember Billy Wolfe?' I asked.

'Billy Wolfe was in Number 3 tank and was killed in the tank and burned in the tank.'

'He had just joined the platoon, hadn't he?'

'Ten or twelve days before that.'

'What was he like?'

'Just a youngster. He had come to us. We was just getting out of the Bulge. We hadn't crossed the Rhine yet. We crossed the Rhine just shortly after that.'

'Describe the events.'

'Well, we crossed the Moselle River. It was the first time that we had crossed the Moselle River in combat.'

'Was that when it was at flood stage?'

'I said the first time. It was the second time we had crossed it. No, it wasn't flooded. It was flooded the first time we crossed it near Metz. But then the second time was after the Bulge. But we're not far from the mouth of it where it runs into the Rhine when we crossed it the second time. We crossed it on a treadway bridge under artificial moonlight. Those huge lights bouncing off the clouds, you remember the artificial moonlight? So, our whole company crossed and we went to this little village, Udenhausen, and pulled in before daybreak. There was a bunch of haystacks out there and Germans was in 'em, and there's one runnin' toward Number 3 tank. Are you familiar with Bob Rossi? He was a loader that day. He was on guard and I'm on the cannoneer's seat, kinda dozing. We had a reunion in Orlando several years ago and he tells me, "I'm lucky to be here."

'"How come?"'

'"I thought you was gonna kill me."'

'I said, "We never had no problem."'

'"You jerked me out of that hatch up there and slammed me against that tank wall. I thought you were gonna kill me."'

'That tank is solid steel. Here's what he was doing. He hadn't been with us so long, but he was saying, "Heinies! Heinies!" He saw 'em, but he wasn't doing anything. Well, if they're out there, I want to know. So I jerked him out of that hatch so I could get up there and I had a Thompson sub laying on the radio. I slammed him over here and I got up in there, and that German was running towards the tank. He had a long coat on, an overcoat, and it was flopping. I started to work on him with that Thompson sub. They'd always said if you could shoot a man anywhere, even in the hand with a .45, it'd knock him down. That's not true. I like to cut that one in two with .45 slugs and he finally did fall behind the tank. Hayward hollered at me, "You got the sonofabitch!" I buggered him up real bad and he was dead. He was going to our tank. I don't know if he intended to throw a grenade in there or what.

'So we stayed there. We moved up and had a little firefight. It wasn't real bad and got that under control. We stayed there that day and night. And sometime before daylight the next morning, on the 16th of March, somebody came after us. The infantry had tried to take Pfaffenheck and got treated bad. There was a crossroads there and the Germans were holding it. It was an SS mountain division. When it began to break day, we moved across and it wasn't far to Pfaffenheck from this little village. I don't know how many kilometres, three, four, maybe five. We moved across country abreast and the third tank was hit in an orchard. We went through the little town, but they'd dug up the road and had their guns camouflaged. And they cut Hayward's leg off below the knee. I remember him holding and dragging it with him. He got out on the ground and they cut him down. They machine gunned him on the ground.

'The shell hit Billy Wolfe in the midsection and he burned. I never did get to examine him, but he was dead. Hayward is on the ground dead. Wes Harrell who was from Stonewall, Oklahoma, and lives in Hobbs, New Mexico, was the driver. He got out. And the bow gunner was a little Chinese boy named Moy. Koon L. Moy. We called him Chop Chop. He got out. And the gunner was John Clingerman and he got out without a scratch. But then he got on Snuffy's tank. He got on it and when it was hit he lost an eye. Didn't kill him, but he lost an eye. And it killed Jack Mantell. He was the cannoneer in the No. 1 tank, Snuffy's tank.'

Mantell joined the battalion as a replacement at the same time as Billy Wolfe. He was married and had a son whom he had probably never seen. The day before in Udenhausen, a shingle came loose from a roof and struck Mantell on the forehead drawing blood. Russell Loop, the gunner in Lieutenant Fuller's tank, urged him to go to an aid station, but Mantell insisted on staying with the platoon.

'In that crew Carl Grey was the driver,' continued Otha. 'A Mexican boy named Guadalupe Valdivia was the bow gunner and he wasn't hurt. The gunner was Russell Loop. He lives in Indianola, Illinois. He's a farmer. And Jack Mantell was the cannoneer and he was killed. It came through the gun shield. Snuffy was the tank commander and lieutenant, the platoon leader. So that's 1 and 3. As for my tank, they put a man in there fresh from Fort Knox named Russell Harris. He was one of these gung-ho type fellows. He told me the first time I saw him, "I'm not afraid of the damn Germans. They'll not make me pull my head in."

'I told him, "Harris, you're a fool. These people here, they're not necessarily afraid of the Germans, but they respect them. They're good soldiers. They'll kill you. If they shoot your head off, you're done. But as long as you can stick your head back out and fight again, you're worth something." That's just what he done. He never pulled his head in and they shot him in the head with a 40-mm gun.'

'Sheesh!' Paul Wannemacher, who was listening to the conversation, exclaimed.

'That'll get you every time,' Otha said. 'And the tank looked like you'd been up on it with a chopping axe. But it was just four men in that tank. John Zimmer was supposed to be the cannoneer, but he wasn't there. He had gone to the medics back across the river. So they're short of one man. The driver was Leroy Campbell from Meridien, Mississippi. The bow gunner was Lloyd Seal, but he was the cannoneer in the turret in John's place. And the gunner was Clarence Rosen. He was from Ogilvie, Minnesota, and a top-notch gunner, too. So it was knocked out. That's three tanks gone. That just left 4 and 5. I was in 5. Byrl Rudd was the platoon sergeant and he was in the No. 4 tank. Rudd's tank was hemmed in behind a building.'

Martin said, 'That just left No. 5 tank and we were the only one that could move. The Germans tried the whole day to come back across the highway, but they never did get back. But I burned the barrel out of a .30-calibre air-cooled machine gun. We changed barrels. I never counted them, but we stacked up a whole bunch of SS troops.'

Maxine Wolfe Zirkle and Madeline Wolfe Litten, Billy Wolfe's twin sisters, were at the first reunion I attended at Niagara Falls in 1987. John Zimmer of upstate Macedon, New York, had tried several times with no success to get my father to attend a reunion. Several times he asked me why my father never responded to his letters and newsletters. I could not give him an answer other than that he worked seven days a week and that his health was poor when he retired. But I know he would have loved exchanging stories had he gone to a reunion. In 1983, Zimmer, then the C Company secretary, wrote to the Office of Vital Statistics in Edinburg, Virginia, inquiring about the next of kin or any friends of Billy Wolfe. The Wolfe sisters and their husbands lived just 10 miles down Route 11 in Mount Jackson.

'Doris Stover, the secretary at the town Chamber of Commerce, called me one afternoon and said she had talked to someone and they told her that they thought that our brother was Billy Wolfe,' Maxine said when I interviewed her and her sister in October of 1993. '"We have a letter here from New York, someone inquiring." Right away I thought, after all these years, nobody's interested. It's a gimmick that they wanted to present us with a plaque.' (The battalion association had a tradition of presenting a plaque with the unit insignia to the family of any battalion veteran who passed away and to the next of kin of the men who were killed in action. I was presented one of the last plaques on behalf of my father before the plaques were replaced by certificates due to the cost.) 'I got to thinking, "What's the purpose? How much is it going to cost?" I checked it with my husband and he said, "It sounds authentic to me." So we sat down and wrote a letter. And it took off from there,' she said, displaying two volumes of correspondence and documents.

John Zimmer and his wife, Sylvia, brought the plaque to the Wolfe sisters on 5 August 1983. 'We began to ask him questions and he couldn't answer too many,' Madeline Wolfe Litten said. 'So he put us in touch with Ray Griffin.'

The Wolfes were friends with John Marsh who grew up in Winchester, Virginia, and became the secretary of the Army under President Ronald Reagan. They wrote to Marsh and he sent them copies of Billy's war records, which included statements from Otha Martin and two of the crew members of Billy's tank.

'8 June, 1945,' one of the statements begins. 'I, Corporal Otha Martin, was a member of the Second platoon of Company C, 712th Tank Battalion, when the platoon entered the town of Pfaffenheck, Germany, on the morning of 16 March, 1945. During the engagement in the town, I saw the No. 2 tank of our platoon receive a hit by an anti-tank gun and saw the tank burst into flames. This tank was commanded by Sergeant Hayward with Corporal Clingerman as gunner, Private Billy Wolfe as cannoneer, Private Moy as assistant driver and T-4 Harrell as driver.

'The tank continued to burn all that day and during the burning all the ammunition exploded. The next morning, 17 March, 1945, I went over to look into the tank. The interior of the tank was completely burned and the exploding ammunition had turned the interior into a shambles. The only remains that I could see of Private Wolfe were what looked to be three rib bones and these were burned so completely that upon touching them they turned to ashes. Staff Sgt. Otha A. Martin.'

'I, T-4 William W. Harrell, was driver of the No. 2 tank, second platoon, Company C, 712th Tank Battalion,' Wes Harrell's statement begins, 'when we entered the town of Pfaffenheck, Germany, on the morning of 16 March, 1945. Another platoon of tanks from the company was pinned down by anti-tank fire from the edge of the woods to the right of town, so we attempted to circle around to the left of the town to get positioned to knock out the gun. As we passed an opening between two buildings, the tank was hit in the right sponson by an anti-tank gun and immediately burst into flames. I managed to get out safely and took cover behind a pile of dirt when machine guns opened up on us. I saw Pfc Moy and Corporal Clingerman get out safely, and Sergeant Hayward got out and crawled a short ways away even though he was badly wounded in both legs. I didn't see Private Billy Wolfe get out of the tank. The ammunition started to explode, so at the first opportunity I ran to cover in the nearest building. Later, I borrowed a rifle from another tank and worked my way to the aid point where I was joined by Pfc Moy. During all this time I did not see Private Billy Wolfe.'

'I, Pfc Koon L. Moy, was a member of the crew of the No. 2 tank,' Koon Leong Moy's statement begins, 'second platoon, of Company C, 712th Tank Battalion, when we entered the town of Pfaffenheck, Germany, on the morning of 16 March, 1945. There was an anti-tank gun in the woods to the right of the town and we were trying to work around through the town to get into position to knock it out. As we pulled out from behind a building to cross an open place, the gun hit us in the right sponson and the tank started to burn all at once. Before I could get the hatch open and get out, I got burned on the hand and face. When I got out they began shooting at me with machine guns, so I jumped down and took cover behind a pile of dirt. I saw Corporal Clingerman and T-4 Harrell get out, and I saw Sergeant Hayward crawl away on the ground, but he was hurt in the legs. The ammunition began to explode as soon as I got out of the tank, so I crawled away as fast as I could. I didn't see Private Billy Wolfe get out of the tank. I was at the aid station and then taken to the hospital, so I never saw him again.'

I interviewed Russell Loop, the gunner in Lieutenant Fuller's tank, at his home in Indianola, Illinois, in October of 1993. 'We moved into town and we pulled around buildings and got on the road where this 75 mm was just across the road and down, he said of Pfaffenheck, 'and I could never get that thing in my sight. It was too low down. I couldn't get my gun down that far. I could have knocked that silly thing out and saved a lot of trouble if I could have got my gun down. But I couldn't do it. Then they started firing a lot of "footballs" (panzerfausts), so we had to back out of there. We thought we could pull around behind these buildings and then come in facing them. That was a mistake. They'd already knocked two tanks out and we pulled around and we were the third one. But ours would still move, so we backed around behind a building. Then Snuffy and I went out to pick up one of the boys that had both of his feet shot off, one of the other tank commanders. He had managed to crawl down over the back of the tank. We got out there and got him up between us, but they hit him about half a dozen times right between us. So we let him back down and took off pretty quick. There wasn't any use to try to carry him back. It sounded like a bumblebee's nest, but we didn't get hit.'

'Sergeant Loop and I went out and tried to get Hayward,' Francis Fuller said when I interviewed him in 1994. 'He was out of the tank when we got to him and laying on the ground, and both his legs were off, halfway from the knee up to the groin. There was nothing we could do for him. We gave him some morphine and took a belt and put a tourniquet on one of his legs. We couldn't get the medics. In fact, I went and got a medic's brassard and put it on, hoping they wouldn't shoot at me. They still shot at us.'

'Did he say anything?' I asked.

'No. In fact, none of them said anything, except the little Chinaman. We sent him back to the medics. He was burned pretty bad. It might have been more than his hands, but in the moment, you know. I wonder whatever happened to him. Griffin tried to look him up and couldn't find him. We called him Chop Chop. Just a pleasant little guy, didn't bother anybody. He was an assistant driver.'

'Hubert was wounded the day before Billy was killed,' one of the Wolfe sisters said. 'He was two years older than Billy. We tried to keep it away from him, but our sister Peg wrote him a letter and she thought that he already knew and she said, "Wasn't that terrible about Billy?" He didn't know what was terrible about Billy, but he always had a feeling that something had happened to him because he never heard from him. I think it was about May that he got a letter from Peg and he wrote to Fuller to confirm it, and Fuller wrote back.'

Hubert Wolfe, Billy's brother, received a letter from Lieutenant Fuller describing in detail the battle at Pfaffenheck, but the letter was written 'soldier to soldier' and the officer said it was up to Hubert how much he should share with his family. Hubert became an accountant after the war and never mentioned the letter until he was on his deathbed in the final stages of cancer. His parents had passed away, but he told Maxine and Madeline that in his desk there were some letters he wanted them to have. He died the next day. The sisters, not wanting to pile one tragedy on another, did not retrieve the letters and they passed into the possession of Hubert's widow. Hubert Wolfe died in 1980. After the visit from John Zimmer, the sisters decided to read the letter. Only by then Hubert's widow had passed away and the letter passed on to the widow's sister. So they contacted her and finally read Lieutenant Fuller's letter to Hubert Wolfe.

'To PFC Hubert L. Wolfe Jr, Company M, 310 Infantry, APO 78, 14 July, 1945,' Fuller's letter to Billy's brother who was still with the 78th

Infantry Division begins. 'I hardly know how to start this letter as you don't even know who I am. Anyway, Lieutenant Seeley, the adjutant of our battalion, received a letter from you asking the facts about your brother, Billy Wolfe. As I was his platoon leader and was there when he was killed, he has asked me to try to give you the information you requested. Captain Sheppard has already written to your mother, but perhaps he has not told her exactly how he died. But I am trusting that since you are a soldier, I can tell you the true facts and then perhaps you can tell your folks what you think they ought to know.

'To start off, our battalion has been attached to the 90th Infantry Division since July 3, 1944, which as you probably know is in the 3rd Army. My platoon, the second platoon of C Company, 712th Tank Battalion, was attached to the 2nd Battalion of the 357th Infantry Regiment. Your brother joined my platoon on the 4th of March while we were driving to the Rhine River, following up the 11th Armored Division. We drove to a town called Mayen and then changed direction and started driving to the Moselle for the second time. On the evening of March 14, we crossed the Moselle and found that the infantry that had preceded us had gotten into a jam and lost over half of their men and gotten cut off, so we were called upon to rescue them. We succeeded in reaching the town where they were, and cleared it okay, and stayed there the rest of the day, and stayed there the night of the 15th. Then, on the morning of the 16th, we were told to attack the town of Pfaffenheck, which was about 2,000 yards north of where we were. The TDs (tank destroyers) started into the town first, but as they rolled over the crest of a hill, the lead tank destroyer was knocked out by an anti-tank gun. They withdrew and succeeded in knocking out the gun and another.

'We were then ordered to try to enter the town and by going down a draw, I managed to get into the east side of the town. Your brother was in No. 2 tank, which was commanded by Sergeant Hayward with Johnny Clingerman as gunner, William Harrell as driver, Koon Moy as bow gunner and your brother as loader. As I said, all of the tanks got into the town okay except No. 3, which encountered a 40-mm AA (anti-aircraft) gun, which killed the tank commander. We took all but three houses when the infantry got stopped by firing from the woods east of the town. I sent the second section along the backs of the houses while I took the first section into an orchard. My tank was in the lead and the tank your brother was in was on my left flank, slightly behind. Just after we had passed an opening between two houses, my loader told me No. 2 tank had been hit. I looked over and the men were piling out, and the tank was blazing. The shot had went through the right sponson, puncturing the gas tank.

'I didn't know then how many men had gotten out, so I tried to get my tank into position to rescue the men, but as I moved into position, my tank received a direct hit through the gun shield, killing my loader. Fortunately for the rest of us, my driver was able to move the tank before the Heinies could fire again. After giving Clingerman first aid and getting the rest of the boys calmed down, I took my gunner with me and we crawled out to where Sergeant Hayward lay wounded. I found that he would have to have a stretcher to be moved. I went back to get the medics and then I learned from the rest of the crew that your brother never got out of the tank. As the tank was burning all this time, we could not get near it. I don't know if you have ever seen one of our tanks burn, but when 180 gallons of gas start burning and ammunition starts to explode, the best thing to do is keep away.

'When I got the medics back out to Sergeant Hayward, I found he had been killed by a sniper. The other section of tanks finally took care of the Heinies and we secured the town. Your brother's tank continued to burn all that night, but in the morning we were able to go out to investigate. We determined that your brother had been killed instantly as the shell had hit right above his seat. There was nothing visible but a few remnants of bones that were so badly burned that if they had been touched they would have turned to ashes.

'As for personal effects, you could not recognise anything because the intense heat and the exploding ammunition had fused most of the metal parts together. The incident was reported to the GRO of the 357th and as we moved on to the Rhine the next day, I didn't think anything more about it until two weeks ago when I received a letter from the 3rd Army asking for information. I sincerely trust that by this time they have everything straightened out. If you ever get into the neighbourhood of that town, the tank may still be there. The town of Pfaffenheck is about 13 miles south of Coblenz on the main autobahn that runs straight down that peninsula formed by the Rhine and the upper Moselle.

'Maybe I have told you more than I ought to, but I really would like to help you in any way that I can. Your brother was very well liked by all the rest of the crew, but he was so doggone quiet that we hardly ever knew he was around. Of the other members of his crew, William Harrell is still with me as is Koon Moy. Clingerman lost his eye and had his legs filled with shrapnel and is now back in the States. That was the worst day I had in combat. I lost three tanks, had four men killed and three wounded. But that is the way things went. It might be interesting to you that in the town there were seven anti-tank guns, one 40-mm anti-aircraft gun, plus plenty of determined SS troops. We counted ninety-two dead Germans and had twenty-three prisoners.

'I am enclosing a snap one of the boys took which has your brother on it. I will also try to draw a sketch of the town, so if you ever get there you can find the place. Incidentally, you will have to use your judgement as to how much of this story you want to pass on to your mother. Don't forget, if I can be of any further help to you, I will be more than glad to hear from you at any time. There is no use in trying to tell you how sorry I feel, because you have been through the same things yourself, so I'll just say so long and good luck. Francis A. Fuller, First Lieutenant.'

27 March 1945 'was the most beautiful day' in the Shenandoah Valley, Maxine Wolfe recalled. 'It was downright what you'd consider summertime. And we had gone to school. I remember what I had on.' The twins, who always dressed the same, were wearing brown and white saddle oxfords and white anklets. They wore yellow broomstick skirts with rag dolls around the bottom, white blouses and blue sleeveless sweaters. Their brunette hair was long with curls. 'Very stylish at the time,' Madeline Wolfe said. 'We had gone to school, it was about noontime, and somebody knocked on the door. One of the classmates went and answered the door and they wanted the Wolfe

twins,' Madeline said. 'We didn't know what in the world because nobody ever called for us.'

'Mr Ritz, the principal, and our two sisters, Peg and Mary, were there and told us and we were just numb. We came back in and just began to gather up our books. Mr Ritz was teaching our class, civics, that day and he knew something was wrong. He went out and when he came back in, he walked us out the door and told us to stay home as long as we needed. He was crying. And after we left, we learned that he had called all the classes into the auditorium, had a prayer and dismissed school.'

Some two months earlier on 14 January 1945, '...there was a widow lady,' Maxine said, 'and her only son was killed. Ours was the last house in the lane and hers was the first. The road was a mile long and the very first house, the lady there lost her only son in January and then in March, our house was the first one on the road. It seemed like quotation marks. And when we heard about the first son being killed, Mom went to visit her and Mom told her, "You've had your problems. Mine are coming." She felt like something was going to happen to one of the boys.' After the telegram arrived, Mrs Wolfe continued to write to her son and the twins would find the notes hidden under her pillow.

'Dear Billy,' one of the notes written 14 April 1945, begins, 'I just have to write a few lines to you tonight. Although I haven't heard from you for a long time I'm still hoping and praying to hear from you soon, so please, Billy, take care of yourself and write to me. Until I hear from you I will always be waiting and hoping.' And that Christmas she wrote, 'While others' hearts will sing with joy, mine will mourn for my dear boy. He died for his country, his life he gave, his dear body is sleeping in a lonely grave. Dear God up in heaven, send your angels I pray to watch over his grave on Christmas day. God bless our dear boys who are still in lands far away who cannot be with us on this Christmas day. Speak peace to their dear hearts and remove all their pain and bring them home safely before Christmas again.'

At the time the telegram arrived, Billy's father was away working in the Norfolk Navy Yard. He began to write a letter the twins said, but he never sent it. 'Monday the 9th of April,' the letter began. '1.25 o'clock. Just got through my wash and will try to write you a few lines. I worked last night. Gigi and Phil are working today. We came to Richmond Friday, got there about 5 o'clock, stayed there until Saturday night's p.m. o'clock, got home about 11 o'clock p.m., stopped at the post office, got the mail, got three letters from Hubert written March the 20th and 23rd and 27th of March. Poor child said he'd just written William. He never had but one letter from him since he has been in Germany. He wanted to know when we heard from him. Poor child, I just cannot hardly read the letters. I just think they will break my heart to hear him wondering about his brother Billy. But God knows it is not my fault for the Democrats bring sorrow every time they get in, then they all try to creep back or hide behind a petticoat or get where they never have to get into battle. But thank God I never helped to put him there. Well, I must close and get my supper and pack my lunch.'

'Oh, Daddy hated Roosevelt with a passion,' Maxine said.

Instead of accepting Billy's $10,000 life insurance policy in a lump sum, his mother chose to receive a monthly payment. 'I think it was $42.80,' Madeline said. 'She was very secretive about receiving them and she would just put it in the bank. She wouldn't cash it because she said she just couldn't spend the money. That's the way she was.' After Billy's mother's death in 1977, there was $36,000 in the account. 'Mom just kept everything,' Madeline said. 'This is the almanac for the year he was born, May 1, 1926. And here's his death certificate. There's the Purple Heart. And here's what he wrote, another high school assignment: "Why I don't want to choose an occupation now. I don't want to choose an occupation now because I am not sure what type of work I want. I will soon be of draft age and may be put in the service. After serving my time my views may be vastly changed. I may, if the war don't last too long, want to take a little more schooling. Or I may get specialised training from Uncle Sam which might be my life's work..."

'It was his life's work,' Madeline Wolfe said.

37

Thirteen Days in April

Edmund Randolph Laine, the portly, middle-aged, charismatic pastor of St Paul's Episcopal Church on Main Street in Stockbridge, Massachusetts, slept late on 3 April 1945. He wrote in his journal that he woke at 10.55 a.m. and that the weather was 'cool and grey.' He listened to the news on the radio. In the afternoon, he read the *New York Times* and the *Berkshire Eagle*. He took the flowers that Mrs Merwin brought to his monthly Shakespeare discussion group over to Virginia Fields, a socialite who lived around the corner from the church. He noted that fifty-five people attended the discussion. Mrs Merwin was the socialite who helped pay for Ed Forrest's last year at Clark University when Ed's money ran out. Laine wrote an air mail letter to Ed and enclosed some newspaper clippings. In the afternoon, an air mail letter dated 20 March arrived from Ed. He read it in the kitchen while eating sunshine cake that his housekeeper, Jessica French, who was known as Aunt Jess, made. He answered Ed's letter with a V-mail letter. In the evening, he spoke at the Rotary Club in Lenox. At 11 p.m., back in the rectory, he listened to the news and finished reading *When the French Were Here*, a book about the role of the French in the American Revolution.

In Europe, the 712th Tank Battalion, in which Lieutenant Edward L. Forrest was now the executive officer of A Company, was on the outskirts of Heimboldshausen, a village on the west bank of the Werra River. After the town was secure, Ed was tasked with setting up headquarters and choosing houses in which to billet the service and maintenance personnel. In Stockbridge, 4 April was 'cold and very dark' in the morning. Laine wrote both an airmail and a V-mail letter to Ed whom he called 'E' in his journal to conserve space. The journal was a large, leather-bound day book with 365 pages and a few pages at the end for notes. Each page was partitioned into five sections with eight lines apiece for the years 1941 through 1945. Laine meticulously recorded the time he woke, the weather (sometimes twice a day), what he listened to on the radio, where he went and what he was reading. He was an expert on Shakespeare and regularly read both *The Times* and the *Eagle*. Sometimes, the entries were so crammed, especially later in the Second World War, that he squeezed two lines of writing into one line of space or three lines into two. In the evening on 4 April, he listened on the radio to Raymond Graham Swing. As I flicked through the journal and often saw the same name, I assumed Raymond Swing was a musical group until I was informed that he was a news commentator.

Sometimes it seemed like the 712th Tank Battalion had been through a thousand Heimboldshausens. From La Haye du Puits, Beaucoudray, St Jores, Le Bourg St Leonard, Avranches, Le Mans, Mairy, Maizieres, Hyange, Thionville, Distroff, Gross Hemmersdorf, Pachten, Dillingen, Kirschnaumen, Bavigne, Nothum, Sonlez, Niederwampach, Oberwampach, Habscheid, Binscheid and many others. After the fighting on the outskirts of Heimboldshausen, a village in Phillipsthal province, the troops moved on in pursuit of the Germans and the rear echelon personnel began setting up for the night. It was 3 April.

On 7 April, Laine began writing an airmail letter to Ed when he noted in the journal he '...was interrupted by phone from New York from Gertrude Robinson Smith saying that her mother had died.' Dorothy Cooney, who was Ed's girlfriend before he went overseas, had poor eyesight. So after I photocopied Laine's journal, I read passages from it to her, which was helpful as she knew who many of the people mentioned were. She asked if I knew who Gertrude Robinson Smith was.

I said I didn't.

Dorothy said one word: 'Tanglewood.'

On Sunday, Laine rose at 7.40. The day was sunny and warm. He went to South Lee to perform a baptism. In the afternoon, he wrote a

V-mail letter to Ed and noted in parentheses that it was the 1,106th letter he'd written since Ed went into the service in 1942. He did not say it in so many words. Rather, he wrote 'Wrote V-mail letter to E. (No. 1106).' At 3 p.m., a handyman came to repair Laine's radio and after working on it for a while said he had to take it home. Laine wrote that he went 'over to E's Study in Par. House to get E's radio ... 1st time in E's Study in one and a half years.' On 9 April, he wrote a V-mail letter to Ed and prepared a press note for VE Day. 10 April brought two V-mail letters from Ed 'written March 26 and 29.' In the afternoon, he presided over the funeral for Mrs Robinson Smith. On 11 April, he noted 'Holy Communion (for peace)' and spoke with a parishioner about her son's upcoming marriage. He wrote an airmail and a V-mail letter to Ed, and in the evening he read *The Captain from Castile*. On 12 April, he wrote a V-mail letter to Ed '(No. 1111)' and at 5.50 p.m. noon, he 'turned on Radio (WABC) - heard news of death of Pres. Roosevelt.'

13 April was 'very hot – rose to 84 degrees.' He listened on the radio to the news and the memorial services for President Roosevelt. On 14 April, he wrote, 'Heard the terrible news of the death of Tommy Burt on the Western Front.' He phoned Mrs Merwin and wrote both an airmail and a V-mail letter to Ed. At 4 p.m., he conducted a memorial service for President Roosevelt. He noted that the choir sang and the congregation was large. After it was over, he put newspaper clippings in an airmail letter to Ed and mailed it on the way to call on June Burt, Tommy's mother. There was 'great sorrow,' he wrote in the journal. (James Burt, Tommy's brother, would be awarded a Medal of Honor as a captain in the 2nd Armored Division for his actions during the battle for Aachen, Germany, in October 1944.) In the evening, he went to the church for the 'rehearsal of Te Deum for VE Day' and made out the programme for Tommy Burt's memorial service.

On 15 April, the reverend heard on the news that the '90th Infantry Div. (E's) was near Czecho-Slovakia – 13 miles).' He spoke of Tommy Burt during his sermon in St Paul's and wrote a V-mail letter to Ed. In the afternoon, he dozed in the Morris chair in his study. The repairman came and set up his radio, and put Ed's back in his study. Aunt Jess brought him a V-mail letter from Ed 'written April 1.' He read some more of *The Captain from Castile* and listened to music on WQXR.

On 16 April 1945 at 1 p.m., he listened on the radio to President Truman's speech to Congress. At 2.30, he noted that it was fifty-four degrees. He spoke with a parishioner about the baptism of her daughter and went to the church with her to get a prayer book. While he was eating a filling came out of his tooth. He phoned a dentist in Lenox to make an appointment. At 7 p.m., he listened on the radio to Fulton Lewis, Jr. He wrote 'a note of thanks to Miss Robinson Smith' for what was no doubt a generous contribution to the church. At 7.15, he listened to Raymond Swing. At 7.45, he listened to H. V. Kaltenborn. At 8.20 p.m. while reading the *New York Times*, he received a phone call from the Great Barrington Telegraph Office informing him of a message 'that E. was killed – April 3.' The wire arrived at 9 p.m.

In Heimboldshausen on 3 April, two tanks that needed repairs were parked near the house in whose basement Ed Forrest set up the A Company headquarters. A truck stacked with 300 five-gallon cans of fuel was parked outside the house. The truck was only supposed to carry 250 cans, but Joe Fetsch, who had been driving fuel and ammunition to the tanks on the front for ten months, figured out a way to stack them so the truck could carry an extra fifty cans. Dick Bengoechea, the nineteen-year-old assistant tank driver from Boise, Idaho, was up on the fuel truck oiling the .50-calibre ring-mounted anti-aircraft gun. When Fred Hostler shouted 'Plane!,' he swung the gun around. 'Everybody wants to get a shot at a plane,' Bengoechea said at the battalion's 1995 reunion in Louisville, Kentucky. 'And then I turn around and look right up this valley and it's just like in the movies. This plane was coming in, I could see the bullets coming down. And I don't remember from this point. I woke up pinned under all kinds of stuff and I couldn't get out.'

'When A Company's headquarters got blown up, my truck got demolished,' Joe Fetsch said at one of the battalion's reunions. 'It didn't burn or blow, but a building fell on it. And a building fell on us. A plane had been following us all day. There was a little railroad depot and two empty tank cars – we didn't know they were empty at the time – and a boxcar with black ammunition powder in it that we didn't know about. And this airplane that had been following all day came back at us and started strafing. And when it started, somebody hollered, "Here comes a plane!" I was in the truck and had to get the gun. I knew it wouldn't hit him, but before I could get out I looked around the building. It seemed as if the plane was sitting on the crosswire and he hit the ammunition car and the empty tank cars. He blew everything, the whole town. I think there were 32 of us in that area and out of 32, there were only four guys able to move. It buried them under the house.

'One of the guys that got killed was Lieutenant Forrest. But the rest of them were really beat up, including myself. That was the third time as he had been injured twice before and he finally got it the third time. (According to battalion records, Ed Forrest was wounded once before. Also, four other battalion members including a cook, Ervin Ulrich, were killed in the explosion.) I was injured all over the face and head. And a steel girder came in behind my legs and held me up or I'd have been under that rubble also. I didn't have a steel helmet on. I had a knit cap, backwards. One of these damn ole' Army knit caps and everything came down on my head. I always wore the knit cap because you couldn't sling gas cans with a steel helmet on. It would be in the way. I never wore it. I always left it on the seat of the truck. I don't know how true it is when they came and found me. They dug me out and I was saying my legs are broken. And about 17 hours later, I woke up in the hospital. You see, they gave me a break that day. We'd been running and running. Damn, we'd been up to the front taking gas and ammunition day in and day out. Harry Moody came up and they said, "You stay back, take a break. Let Moody run." They said that nobody shot the plane down. It came in and its own explosion caught it.'

Charles Vorhees only attended two reunions. At one of them, he was speaking with Sam MacFarland whose tank he was driving the day Lieutenant Lippincott, Pine Valley Bynum and Frank Shagonabe were killed. Vorhees said MacFarland asked him why he was not there when the explosion took place at the A Company headquarters. He said, 'You were the lieutenant then. I wasn't in your tank anymore.

240

That's the reason I got blown up. He was in combat and I was back there. We got a new tank and there were metal fragments in the transmission. They'd get in the gears and you couldn't move it. You'd be going forward and then you'd have to back up... You'd throw it out again. Usually, when the transmission got hot it wasn't bothering us, but when you started it up cold in the morning that would happen. So the first sergeant said, "Vorhees, get your bedroll. You're gonna take the tank back to ordnance." And I went and got my bedroll. I come walking along and Lieutenant Forrest was standing there.

'"Vorhees, where are you going?"

'"I'm taking the tank back to ordnance."

'"Oh no you're not. You're the only spare driver we've got. You're staying right here."

'And he took the loader out of our tank. I can't think of his name. He was Polish, a nice young Polish boy. He took us over to clean the Germans out of the buildings that they were going to take over for the company. And it was a big three-storey building. It had running water and everything. The first thing we did when we got there, we'd go scouting around to see if we could find anything. And I found a camera. I told this Polish boy where it was at and he went and got the camera. Because he helped me, he got me a pistol in one place we were at. I took a bath. And I'd won money playing poker the night before and I had a money belt on. I laid it on the radiator and took a bath. I got out of there, went downstairs and I thought, "Oh, I forgot my money belt." I went back upstairs and it was gone. So all I had when I went to England was a 10-shilling note. And when we got over there, you had to buy your toothbrush and cigarettes.

'There were steps that came up, a big concrete block and steps, and at the time they dug me out I was sitting on that bottom step. The house was destroyed entirely. And Lieutenant Forrest, I could have reached out and touched him at the time it happened, but when I got out of there, I never thought of Forrest or anything else. All I was thinking about was getting out of there. It was probably a half-hour after I took the bath. It was an overcast day, the clouds were real low. This German Bf 109 came down strafing, so we got behind the building.

241

And there was one guy in a halftrack parked outside, he was firing at the plane with a machine gun. It had a skate mount on top.

'I saw the explosion and that was the last thing I remembered. When I came to, I had my hands on my ears, I was doubled over and could hardly breathe. The dirt was right up against my face and I took my tongue and scraped the dirt away because I couldn't move anything else. I tried to yell. I wasn't getting much air, so I shut up and then I heard someone talking and I yelled. And they said, "We'll get you, buddy!" After a while they said, "Sound off again, we can't find you." They finally did find me and uncovered me down to my waist. They took off my pistol belt and they tried to pull me out. And I said, "It feels like you're pulling my leg apart." So they dug down some more and there was a timber laying across one of my legs. I had one leg down laying on the concrete and the other was under a four-by-four timber. And they went and got a bar and pried it up and then pulled me out.

'In the meantime they'd given me a shot of morphine. So they loaded me in an ambulance and took me over to an aid station. They got this sulpha powder and put us in another ambulance and started back for Frankfurt. It was about dark and they took us in and were working on us. They cut our clothes off. And the doctor, he was working on my leg, and on the next table I could hear them sawing somebody's leg off. I couldn't see it, they had things up between them. Then he left and came back and had another doctor with him, and they're standing there talking. He reached down and pulled my eyelid and said, "Oh, you've got an eye there."

'"Yeah, I've got an eye there."

'"I didn't know. It was closed."

'A couple of days later, a sergeant was going through there and he had a mirror. I said, "Hey, Sergeant, come over here. I'd like to see that mirror." And my face was red, yellow and black. I'd been hit in the face with stones and stuff in that explosion. It blew my helmet off.'

'My right eye took about six weeks to heal,' Joe Fetsch said, 'and Christ, I had cuts in my hair. And when I came to, the doctor said, "What else hurts you, son?" I looked up and saw him and passed out again. About 17 hours later, I was in an evac hospital and all I could see was streamers hanging down, and I thought, "Where am I?" And finally the next day I was all right after I got straightened out and they gave me some medication.'

When Dick Bengoechea came to he was buried under rubble and could not get loose. His hollering caught the attention of Fred Hostler who crawled over. 'He couldn't see. He rubbed the stuff off of me and got me out of there,' Bengoechea said. 'Somebody said the aid station was a little way away, so I guided him and he dragged me to the aid station. They gave me morphine and I don't know a thing until the next morning. An American nurse in a field hospital said, "Wake up. We're sending you to Darmstadt and then you're going to fly to Paris in a C-47." And there was a Purple Heart on my pillow. Then they gave me another shot and I woke up the next day in a Paris hospital. A day or so after that I ran into Hostler and the first remark he said was, "That little girl blew up." He said there was a little girl standing in the window. He was going to dive into the building from the side of the truck...'

A couple of days later, Bengoechea said he and Hostler were both in wheelchairs going towards each other. 'We knew goddamn well we weren't going to be back on the front for a while, so we greeted each other with a "Heil Hitler in case we lose." A major saw us and said, "You assholes." He was really shook up. We made a big joke out of it.'

When Bengoechea recalled Fred Hostler's remark about the little girl, he said that Hostler might still be 'a little rummy' from the explosion. At one of the 90th Division reunions, Ted Hofmeister, who had been in Headquarters Company of the 358th Infantry Regiment, bought a copy of my book *Tanks for the Memories* and the next day talked about Heimboldshausen. 'I was about 200 yards away and I saw the German plane go out of control,' he said. 'He hit a house about 4 or 5 miles up the road. And we left town because it was mashed. The whole town was mashed. And as we were leaving, we saw the German 109 up against the side of a building, smashed. I saw the explosion. Half of the sky was red. The railroad station was flattened. There wasn't anything left of it. The buildings across the road from it were occupied by Germans. I don't know how many of them were killed. And a whole bunch of us went up there and started rescuing these people. They were buried under rubble. And when we got up there, we saw an old man – I say old man, he was probably younger than I am now – and he was trying to lever up a staircase that had fallen on his wife's legs. He had a timber that was eight or nine feet long, but he wasn't strong enough. So about four big guys took hold of the timber and they pried it up. When they did, another fellow and I reached in and grabbed her under the armpits and pulled her out. And while we were doing this, she was praying in German and telling us what good soldiers we were and she kept patting me on the arm. It wasn't until later I found out the whole sleeve of my field jacket was bloody as she had cuts all over. We rescued her, they got her on a litter and took her away. We went on to the next building and it was occupied by about three families. And the first thing we discovered when we went in there was a landing and there was an old lady, maybe eighty years old. She was about half buried in the rubble and all that was sticking up was her arm and one side of her face. And her arm was having spasms. We dug her out and put her on a litter. I have an idea she died.

'We went up to the next door and a woman came running up to us and she started talking in German. I can understand a little German and she said something about her baby that had been blown out of her arms. We looked all over for that child and couldn't find it. We figured it had been blown out the window and been buried under the rubble. And we rescued about ten kids. I particularly remember one boy about twelve years old. He had his nose pushed way over to one side of his face and he had a broken arm all cut up. All the people were cut up. We went on to another building to see what we could do. About that time, one of the men from our company ran up and said we were evacuating the town because it was so shattered. So we loaded up and that was the last I saw of it. About five minutes after the explosion, one of our fellows, a big Swede, took his helmet off to wipe his forehead. When he did so, tiles fell from a roof and hit him on the head and knocked him out. As a matter of fact, one fellow, even after the war was over, while we were on occupation duty, was still picking glass out of his face.'

In Baltimore, Joe Fetsch explained a story that was told to him by his sister. 'There was a kid next door to me, Buddy Rogers. He got drafted after me. He was about a year or so younger than me and he went over just before the Bulge. He was in the infantry. And there was a little old guy that delivered the telegrams in the neighbourhood. My mother and sister were going out and it was getting dark, and here comes that little guy with the flashlight. They knew who he was and he stopped at my house. My sister said my mother almost dropped. And then he went to the next house and put the flashlight on, knocked and went in there. The first telegram was to state that he was missing in action. A couple of days later, he came back with a telegram saying he was killed in action. Mom went over and nursed the lady. It took a couple of weeks to get her back together. He got killed at the end of January, and sure enough, a month or two later, here comes that little old man. It was April and my mother's sitting in the sun parlour and sees this. Here he comes up our steps and my sister said she thought my mother was gonna die. But she made it.'

In 1929, Reverend Laine gave Ed Forrest a hardbound book titled *England to America*. It was reprinted from a story that first appeared in the *Atlantic Monthly* and later won the first Ohenry Prize for short stories. It was a story of the First World War in which Laine served as a chaplain and still suffered from the after-effects of having been gassed. In *England to America* by Margaret Prescott Montague, a young American lieutenant, Skipworth Cary, gets a two-week leave from the front where he is flying with the Royal Air Force. He spends his first week in London and then, at the urging of his captain, Chev Sherwood, he spends a few days with Sherwood's family in the countryside. He is baffled, however, by the odd customs of the family, which he attributes to the cultural differences between the English and Americans. For instance, when he says to his commanding officer's father that he would follow his son 'into hell and out the other side,' the father turns and walks away. After a week of one similarly odd occurrence after another, a girl who had been engaged to the commanding officer, takes

Skipworth aside and tells him that shortly after he went on leave Chev Sherwood was killed in a dogfight. She says the family, knowing how precious a soldier's leave was, did everything possible to shield him from learning of his captain's death.

Laine gave Ed's copy of the book to Ed's best friend, Dave Braman, who had been a fighter pilot in the First World War. On the inside cover is a sticker that states 'From the library of Edward L. Forrest.' On the first inside page, Laine wrote:

To David E. Braman,

Dear Dave,

This classic little story of the First War of 1917-1918 was a great favourite with Eddie. I gave it to him in 1929 and he read it many times. You and I can appreciate the truth, the grace and the poignancy of this narrative, since Like Chev Sherwood, Eddie passed over, fighting gallantly for his country. Little did he think as he read it, that the years to come would call him to the same manly sacrifice. You were his beloved friend, keep this cherished book of his, in proud remembrance.

From, Edmund Randolph Laine, June 21, 1946.
Stockbridge, Massachusetts.

38

Nazi Gold

On 4 April 1945, only a day after the explosion at Heimboldshausen, the 357th Infantry Regiment entered the town of Merkers on the east bank of the Werra River. Two days later, MPs stopped two women on a road outside the town. According to *The U.S. Army in the Occupation of Germany 1944-46* by Earl Ziemke, published by the Center for Military History in 1990, 'Since both were French displaced persons and one was pregnant, the MPs decided rather than arrest them to escort them back into the town. On the way, as they passed the entrance to the Kaiseroda salt mine, the women talked about gold that the Germans had stored in the mine – so much gold, they said, that unloading it had taken local civilians and displaced persons who were used as labour 72 hours.' When it was learned that 'the mine had 30 miles of galleries and five entrances,' the book continues, 'the division, which had already detailed the 712th Tank Battalion to guard the Merkers entrance, had to divert the whole 357th Infantry Regiment to guard the other four.'

There is one discrepancy. According to *The U.S. Army in the Occupation of Germany 1944-46*, the two women were stopped on the morning of 6 April. According to John Busterud, a 90th Division veteran whose memoir, *Beneath the Salt*, describes the Merkers salt mine, the two women were out at night after curfew. Both accounts agree that one of the women was pregnant and that they were stopped by a pair of MPs. 'Somebody in the *Detroit News*, they have a column in there: "Ask us a question, we'll answer,'" Forrest Dixon said. We were seated at a table in the hospitality room at the 1995 mini-reunion in Bradenton along with Jack Reiff, one of the battalion's two medical officers. 'And somebody wrote in to the *Detroit News* and said, "Which was the largest robbery? The great railway robbery in Britain, the Brinks at Boston or the…"'

Dr Reiff interrupted him: 'Or the 357th Infantry at Merkers…?'

'…and the fellow came back and said which was the largest, but the largest of all time was the five tons of gold that was robbed or removed from the Merkers salt mine.'

After losing himself in thought for a moment, Dixon turned to Dr Reiff and said, 'Let me ask you a question. When you went down in the Merkers salt mine, was the door of the first vault blown open?'

'Here we go again! I was just telling Aaron, I wish we had started this thirty years ago because I think I just subconsciously blotted a lot of that stuff out of my mind. You know, I was there when we picked up these prisoners, the guys that had been starved.'

'You were with the group when we caught up to the inmates that left the concentration camp, Flossenburg?'

'I was with the 357th at the time. I had been transferred to Company A in the 315th Medical Battalion, which was with the 357th. I wasn't with you, but I saw them. That's when I got my picture in the *Stars & Stripes*.'

'All night there were little fires burning and they were roasting chickens, and about half a dozen of them died from overeating.'

'Somebody in our outfit said that I bawled him out for giving them candy. But as I was telling Aaron, I guess I subconsciously blotted it out.'

'Well, you know, on that Merkers salt mine, it came out a couple of years later that there was five tons of gold missing.'

'Every time we went in the elevator, when we took the trailer, we had to sign for every bar. We had little jeep trailers and we had to account for every dang one, sign for each one separately. After talking about it, as I remember, that was a little scary six hundred metres down in the mine.'

'How far down?'

'Six hundred metres, wasn't it?'

'I don't know, I thought it was close to 2,000 feet.'

'Six times three is eighteen, 1,800 feet. We can't start an argument.'

'One article about the Merkers salt mine said there were 30 miles of tunnels and I'm sure that whoever hit the computer hit the damn decimal point in the wrong place. I think it was maybe more like 3 miles of tunnels. Did you see a lot of tunnels when you were down there?'

'Yes. My family are miners. I mean, it wasn't completely strange to me. (Dr Reiff was born in Muskogee, Oklahoma.) Those things are not miles long.'

'I remember the one big drill on the very end where the gold was and they couldn't get that door open. There were vault doors on the other side tunnels and there was art and paintings. The second one had money in it. The third one had paintings. The fourth one had sculptures. And there were others. And two million books. You see, the area was only lit where we were (Dixon was one of the first officers to go down into the mine). Apparently, that steam turbine that we got going during the night operated the ventilation, elevator and everything. So the whole thing wasn't lit up, just where we were, so I had no idea. Later, they said there was five million missing.'

According to the book *Documentary: Gen. George Patton, Jr., 2nd Lt. Peter Bonano and A Vanishing Cache of Nazi Gold* by Joseph Sprouse, the contents of the Merkers salt mine were recorded as: '3,682 bags of German currency; 80 bags of foreign currency; 8,307 gold bars; 55 boxes of gold bullion, 3,326 bags of gold coins; 63 bags of silver; 1 bag of platinum bars; 8 bags of gold rings; 207 bags and containers of SS loot; and 400 tons of artwork.'

Whew. The gold rings came from victims of the Holocaust as did the mountain of spectacles and row after row of suitcases that Forrest Dixon witnessed.

39

Joe the Englishman

'This was at Merkers,' Lex Obrient, a lieutenant in D Company, said when I interviewed him at his home in Albuquerque in 1999. 'We went into the town and it was a beautiful, lazy day. It seemed like the sun was shining and the weather was just perfect. As we went into the town, everything was quiet and we saw very few if any people. And as we went on down, all of a sudden we ran into some British POWs. There must have been four or five. They had escaped. And one of the sergeants said, "Hey, you know what's in this town back here?"

'It looked like there was nothing there of any interest. I said, "No, I sure don't."

'"Do you want to know?"

'"Sure, what is it?"

'"Well, we've been used to haul gold and art treasures, and you name it."

'"Really?"

'"Yes. There's a guy out there that's got a key that can open the door to let you in."

'So we looked for that guy and we couldn't find him. So I said, "Okay, I'll just believe you." And I called Captain (Alton) Wagnon and told him. "Listen, I've run onto the tail end of a POW column and I want to get down there and see if I can't get the rest of those guys freed. Can somebody come down here and take a look? I've been told there's a lot of gold and so forth in there. So I had somebody to wait and then I took off. I was trying to catch the end of this column. I had the sergeant come with me and ride my tank, and sure enough, we caught the tail end of them. What we did, we didn't hurt anybody, we just started firing. The column stopped and everybody went in every direction. So we went right on past that and then we went down the road, I would say no further than a mile. We then ran into their kitchen and they were getting ready to eat. So we fired a few more rounds. We hit one of the trucks that they were trying to get out. We stopped him, but the rest of them got away. But we did liberate quite a few British prisoners who had also been used to work back there in the salt mines to put this stuff down in there. But by the time all of that caught up, I heard that there was more brass in that town than you could imagine.'

One of the former British POWs asked to stay on with the tankers according to Dale Albee who by now had received a battlefield commission and was in charge of another platoon. 'We liberated 200 Englishmen and brought them back,' Albee said, 'and Joe Green, he had been captured at Dieppe, and he said he didn't want to go back. He had a score to settle. So with no place to put him, I said, "You'll have to ride the back deck of the tank." Which he did for a while and then one of the men was wounded, so we put him in his position and he rode there. He later became a gunner and Joe became one of us.

'And back at headquarters, nobody knew that I had an Englishman in my platoon as we dressed him in American gear and it was so seldom that we spent a lot of time near the headquarters. Even when we went back and turned track, Joe was right in there and nobody ever paid any attention to him. And it was kind of surprising to them that all of a sudden I came up with a British prisoner up in Czechoslovakia. But I had to let Joe go because I could have been court-martialed for not sending him back. And if the old man (Captain Wagnon) had found out, he'd have been more than willing to court-martial me. Anything to get rid of me. He had me on orders to go to Japan.'

40

Flossenburg

'Do you remember Flossenburg, the concentration camp?' Paul Wannemacher asked as we were sitting at a table in the hospitality room during the 1993 battalion mini-reunion with Forrest Dixon and a couple of other veterans. 'And do you remember how we liberated it on the 23rd of April, something like that? Lindy Brigano was telling his kids about this and one of his sons decided he was going to see what he could find out about Flossenburg because Lindy didn't know a heck of a lot about it.

'Therefore, he sent photocopies of some information to me. The following is from the *Encyclopaedia of the Third Reich* that was published by McMillan in 1991. It tells of Flossenburg, when it was built and where the people came from. However, the interesting part is that the majority of Nazi concentration camps were base units which also controlled surrounding satellite stations. For example, what follows is a inventory of Flossenburg and the satellite camps that it controlled.

'...Then he gets a map and if you'll notice, here they have Flossenburg. See the symbol above it, the circle with a vertical line through it? With the double circle, this means it is a headquarters. Now, all the other cities that work in conjunction with this camp have the single symbol. Look how far this ranged. They had up to 90 of these satellites.'

'The camp was occupied by an average of five to six thousand prisoners,' Dixon said, reading from the material Wannemacher brought, 'the number increasing to fifteen to eighteen thousand in the closing months of the war. In March 1945, some 900 female prisoners arrived at Flossenburg from another concentration camp, but in the same month they were transported to Bergen-Belsen. As time went on, more and more satellite and annex camps were established near the main Flossenburg camp, their number growing to ninety and more.

'The prisoners in these satellite camps worked in such areas as armament production, aircraft industry and mineral oil extraction. Flossenburg's prisoners came from various European nations, the majority from the Eastern territories, Poland, Russia and so on. In each year, German political prisoners in protective custody and later criminals, too, in preventive custody were brought in. The prisoners worked in the quarry, 200 metres from the camp and in a variety of construction projects. Sick and disabled prisoners were sorted out by the camp physician and killed. The housing conditions were bad. Three or four prisoners slept in a single bunk, sparsely covered with one blanket. Mistreatment of prisoners resulting in death was not uncommon.'

'They had evacuated Flossenburg three days before our arrival,' Dixon said, no longer reading. 'Then we took out after them and we caught up with them after dark. The fighting units took all the Germans prisoners and then there were about 1,600 inmates that went amok. Where we took the Germans was at a poultry farm and I'll never forget all night you could see these little fires. And they kept sending people around, "You're going to kill yourself eating." We lost several that night from overeating. And the next morning they found a dairy farm. They killed all the cattle and ate them. The furnaces were still burning when we went in.'

'I remember when we went in,' Wannemacher said. 'I was with C Company at the time. As we drove in, we came up to this little block building and we stopped the jeep. We walked into the building and there was Lieutenant Gifford from C Company. He was standing in front of an open oven door and I got a picture of him standing there. We heard water running and we didn't know where, so we followed the sound. And there was a room right next to the entrance where there was a guy standing with a hose and it looked like he was spraying the room. So we went over and looked closer, and what he was spraying there was a bunch of dead bodies. They were just stacked up in the room. There must have been twenty-five or thirty of them. I guess they were getting ready to cremate them and they were trying to keep some semblance of sanitation. Then we saw the two big buildings where they gassed them. At the foot of one, they had a huge pile of shoes and at another one there was a big pile of eyeglasses, just laying there, a huge pile. We got pictures of all that. There were maybe a thousand left in the camp and they were so emaciated.'

'Colonel Kedrovsky was the battalion commander at the time,' Lex Obrient said during the 1999 interview, 'and I think he did the right thing. He had the townspeople come and get those people out of that makeshift grave and line them up. He then he made everybody in that town come and walk past there.'

'I want to show you something,' Lindy Brigano said when Paul Wannemacher and I visited him at his home in Utica, New York, in 1995. 'This is one of the towns where I was telling you about. It's Flossenburg.'

'Why don't you summarise that?' Wannemacher asked.

'This article here is about this gentleman who was in Flossenburg. He came to the Utica area. So when I saw this in the *Observer-Dispatch*, it brought to my mind about this fellow named Mike. We liberated Flossenburg. And I saw this young fellow no older than us. He was holding his arm. And I was doing something, bringing a message someplace. So I stopped and I says to him, "Can I help you?"

'Well, he was frightened of us. He didn't know what to expect and he said, "No, no, no, no, no." So I let it go, but it bothered me. So I took care of what I had to do and when I came back you could see that he was in such pain holding his wrist. So I asked him, "Can I help you?"

'"No, no, no, no, no."

'"Would you like a cigarette?"

'"Okay." So I gave him a cigarette and I lit it for him. And that was the end of it. So the war had ended and I was in business with my brothers. We had a grocery store. And maybe five or six years later there was an influx of Hungarians and Eastern Europeans coming into this area. And I saw this fellow cleaning the windows. He stopped and he looked at me. And I looked at him. And he just stared. I said, "Geez, that fellow looks awful familiar." So he put the squeegee down and he came in and said to me, "Aren't you the fellow that tried to help me at Flossenburg?"

'"Yes, and you didn't want any help."

'"That's right." He grabbed hold of me and he hugged me. And it was really something. So I never forgot it. We were friends for an awful long time. Thirty years or more.'

'Did he say why he didn't want any help?' I asked.

'He was frightened. He didn't know what to expect. So one day, he was quite active in the Russian Orthodox church and they had bingo going on there. And we had a tremendous downpour. So he told the priest, "I've got to go home and close the windows of the house." He got in his van and as he drove out onto the North-South arterial, a tractor-trailer hit and killed him. And all these years, I only knew his name as Mike. Then one day, I went to the Russian Orthodox church and started to inquire about Mike. The priest that knew him had passed away. But there was a lady, a secretary. She said, "I know who you're talking about." And this is what they published in the *Observer-Dispatch*. He never did have his arm fixed. His arm was still bent out of shape and this was his name: M-Y-K-O-L-O-R-C-Z-U-K. Michael Mykolorczuk. Ukrainian. Born 1921, died 1965. I never knew his last name and if I did know it, I couldn't pronounce it anyway.'

41

'Boys, This is It'

Jake Driskill – the motor sergeant who in the first week of combat lifted the turret hatch on a knocked-out American tank and said to a dead German soldier, 'Don't be looking like that at me, I didn't kill you,' – was in a recovery vehicle on 8 May 1945 shortly after the battalion crossed into Czechoslovakia. 'We came to this tank that had rolled over. So we went to work, straightened it up and got it running and brought it back up,' he said when I visited him in 1993. 'We were still working on it and old Colonel Kedrovsky came by – he was our company commander back in Fort Benning and he knew everybody by name – and he saw us and said, "Boys, this is it. We've had orders to cease firing." That was a real happy, a happy time. Old Colonel Kaye or Kedrovsky, he was telling me one time that the 712th Tank Battalion had the best so and so maintenance in the whole such and such army. He didn't say so and so and such and such. He could really cuss. He said we had the best maintenance in the whole US Army. It made us feel good anyway, whether we did or not.'